ARTS & CRAFTS DESIGN

A Selected Reprint
of
Industrial Arts Design

written by
William H. Varnum

foreword by
Timothy L. Hansen

GIBBS·SMITH
PUBLISHER

SALT LAKE CITY

First reprint edition
97 96 95   3 2 1

This is a Peregrine Smith Book, published by
Gibbs Smith, Publisher
P.O. Box 667
Layton, UT 84041

Cover design by Traci O'Very Covey and Marty Lee
Printed and bound in Canada

ISBN 0-87905-699-1

SALT LAKE CITY

FOREWORD
ARTS & CRAFTS DESIGN

Originally published as *"Industrial Arts Design, A Textbook of Practical Methods for Students, Teachers, and Craftsmen,"* this book makes explicit in the form of rules what was intuitively known by many of the best craftspersons during the Arts & Crafts Period. Since the rules were intuitively known, no arguments for their correctness are given. Proof is in looking at a large number of examples and seeing that the rules apply. The examples given draw on work from manual arts classes as well as what appears to be the work of Gustav Stickley, Stickley Brothers, Rookwood, Teco, Newcomb, and many others.

While original copies of the book are scarce, it has already had an impact on the current Arts & Crafts revival. Michael Adams, master coppersmith of Aurora Studios, uses it as the basis of his design work. Bruce Bradbury of Bradbury & Bradbury Art Wallpaper referred to it while developing a palette for an Arts & Crafts line of wallpapers. Dianne Ayres, Arts & Crafts Period Textiles, interprets the information to determine such things as proportions for window treatments and how far down table runners should hang on sideboards and tables. Collectors familiar with the work use it to evaluate the merits of original and modern Arts & Crafts pieces. Still others use it simply to gain a deeper understanding of why they love the period so much.

William Varnum believed that his design rules applied to the best work from all periods. Few people today would make such a sweeping claim. Still, many designers and craftspeople feel there is something fundamentally correct about the work as applied to design. The rules are not used to *define* Arts & Crafts design, they are used to understand it.

The rules regarding color are not so sweeping. Varnum first introduces basic color terminology then surveys current–1915–home interior coloring practice and offers some generalizations. Based on these generalizations, he gives specific rules for coloring small surfaces. The applicability of these rules in today's predominately high-contrast, white interiors is debatable. However, the generalizations regarding interior coloring are invaluable to the colorist or homeowner trying to create the cheerful, comfortable, friendly atmosphere which is the hallmark of the

Arts & Crafts period style. The craftsperson working on pieces for those decorating in the style will also find the information on color useful.

This is a practical book in that the rules apply to specific design problems. A more theoretical approach can be found in Arthur Wesley Dow's book *Composition: a Series of Exercises in Art Structure for the Use of Students and Teachers* (1899), Ernest A. Batchelder's books *The Principles of Design* (1904) or *Design in Theory and Practice* (1910), and Denman W. Ross's book, *A Theory of Pure Design: Harmony, Balance, Rhythm* (1907). While all of these books are currently out of print, they do occasionally turn up in rare books shops. Many public and private libraries also carry them.

It is hoped that with the reprinting of this book, other craftspeople and collectors who weren't as fortunate in acquiring it in its original form will also reap the many rewards the work has to offer.

TIMOTHY L. HANSEN.

Arts & Crafts Collector and Designer
Berkeley, California
April, 1995

PREFACE

Place for the Book. As a textbook, INDUSTRIAL ARTS DESIGN is a practical guide for designing in wood, clay, and base and precious metals. It is intended for individual student use in the High Schools, Normal Schools, and Colleges and as a reference book for elementary school teachers. Its more complex problems are intended as definite helps to the industrial arts designer or craftsman. The wood problems are treated with special reference to their adaptability to bench and cabinet work.

Need of the Book. It has been written to fill a decided demand for a textbook that shall, without loss of time, directly apply well-recognized principles of general design to specific materials and problems encountered in the Industrial Arts. A brief description of the decorative processes adapted to the materials under discussion with the design principles directly applying to these processes, insures designs that may be worked out in the studio or shop. It is hoped that this provision will eliminate the large number of impractical designs that are frequently entirely unfitted to the technic of the craft. This lack of mutual technical understanding between the teacher of design and the shop work instructor is the cause of friction that it is hoped will be removed by the methods advocated in these pages.

The Author's Motive. It has been the intention to reduce unrelated and abstract theories to a minimum and reach directly rules and conclusions that shall be applicable to typical materials in common use in the schools and industries. The original conception materialized in the publication of a series of articles upon Design in the *Industrial Arts Magazine*, in 1915. These articles were favorably received and their results in the schools proved highly satisfactory. Through this encouragement, the articles have been reprinted in book form, enriched by the addition of illustrations, review questions, and three chapters on color with its applications.

INDUSTRIAL ARTS DESIGN develops the principles of industrial design in a new and logical form which, it is believed, will simplify the teaching of craft design. Chapters I to V deal with the elementary problems confronting the designer as he begins the first steps on his working drawing; Chapters VI to VIII show the methods by which he may express his individuality through contour or outline enrichment, while Chapters IX to XVII explain the treatment of the most difficult form of decoration, that of surface enrichment.

The Appendix. The appendix is added to show the manner in

which the rules may be directly applied to a course of study in either pottery or art metal. The present work is not intended to include the chemistry of glaze mixing or other technical requirements to which reference is made in the appendix; consequently the reader is referred to "The Potter's Craft" by C. F. Binns and "Pottery" by George J. Cox for fuller explanations of the formulae and technicalities of the craft.

Source of Principles. The principles herein advocated are directly related to architectural design which is to be regarded as the standard authority for the industrial arts designer. It was necessary to state these principles in the form of sufficiently flexible rules which would allow the student to use his own judgment, but at the same time, restrict him to the essential principles of good design.

Rules. This presentation of the principles of design by means of flexible rules in concrete form, serves to vitalize design by virtue of their immediate application to the material. The rules likewise save time for both pupil and instructor. This is regarded as an important factor, inasmuch as the amount of time usually allotted to classroom teaching of design is limited.

While these rules are applied to the specific materials, the designer may readily adjust them to other materials and find them equally applicable. Direct copying of designs from the illustrations is a dangerous expedient and is to be discouraged as a form of plagiarism which will eventually destroy the student's initiative, originality, and reputation for creative work.

Results. From the tests so far observed, it has been seen that under design guidance, the projects become more noticeably individual in character, lighter and better in construction, and more fully adjusted to their environment. The student's interest and initiative in his work are strengthened, and he completes the truly valuable cycle of the educative process of evolving his own idea and crystallizing it in the completed work. It is hoped that this book will tend to develop higher standards of good design in schools, industrial establishments, and the home.

In conclusion, the author expresses his thanks to the following for their valuable suggestions and assistance in contributed illustrations: Miss D. F. Wilson, Miss Edna Howard, Miss Elizabeth Upham, Miss A. M. Anderson, Mr. J. M. Dorrans, Mr. J. B. Robinson, author of "Architectural Composition," and others to whom reference is made in the text.

Madison, Wisconsin. WILLIAM HARRISON VARNUM.
April, 1916.

CONTENTS

INDUSTRIAL ARTS DESIGN

Chapter I

DIVISIONS OF INDUSTRIAL ARTS DESIGN

This book has been written with the view of presenting design from the standpoint of the industrial arts. An instructor generally experiences difficulty in finding the exact word to use when criticizing a student's drawing. The student has equal difficulty in understanding the criticism. There is little wonder that he is confused, when the rather ambiguous terms "good-looking," "ugly," "squatty," and "stiff" are used to express qualities that can be expressed only in terms of design.

Non-technical Criticism

The lack of understanding between the pupil and the teacher may be compared to the attitude of the average individual "who knows what he likes." He is on an equally insecure footing regarding industrial design. His reason for liking or disliking a certain thing may depend upon some whim or fancy, the popular fashion of the times, or a desire to possess a duplicate of something he has seen. As a consumer with purchasing power, he should have the ability to *analyze intelligently* the contents of catalogs and store windows with the thought of securing the best in industrial art — something that may be accepted as standard one hundred years from now.

Intelligent Analysis

It is, therefore, the intention to present design of industrial character in its simplest form, freed from technicalities or ambiguous statements. It is intended to give the average individual not particularly interested in drawing or design a knowledge of the subject, based upon principles that have survived for hundreds of years in architectural monuments and history.

It is possible that the presentation of these principles may enable the instructor in the public schools to guide his pupil away from the heavy and expensive stereotyped designs, and by clear and simple criticism, lead him to better forms of construction. He may also be

Results of Clear Criticism

THE FIRST MAJOR DIVISION OF INDUSTRIAL ARTS DESIGN····

A GROUP OF OBJECTS WITH THE EMPHASIS PLACED MAINLY UPON STRUCTURAL OR CONSTRUCTIVE DESIGN PRINCIPLES·

·CLASS ROOM PRACTICE OF CONSTRUCTIVE DESIGN·

PLATE 1

helped to lead the pupil to design problems in harmony with his home surroundings and thus avoid the introduction of an inharmonious element into what may possibly be a harmonious setting. The teacher, pupil, or layman should use his knowledge of the subject as a basis for criticism or appreciation of the field of the industrial arts.

In order to start successfully upon a design, it is necessary to know what qualities a good industrial article should possess. Whether one is designing a bird-house, a chocolate set, or a gold pendant, the article must meet three needs: (1) It must be of service to the community or to the individual; (2) It must be made of some durable material; (3) It must possess beauty of proportion, outline, and color. **Requirements of an Industrial Problem**

Ruskin said that a line of beauty must also be a line of service. The "stream line body" in automobile construction is the result of the automobile maker's attempt to combine beauty with service. This is the attitude that should govern the union of beauty and service in all of the industrial arts.

There are three divisions or phases in the designing of a structure and its enrichment. These are: (1) Structural Design; (2) Contour Enrichment; (3) Surface Enrichment. Some objects are carried through only one of these divisions, while others are developed through all three of them. **Divisions in Design Evolution and Enrichment**

Plate 1, illustrative of the first division, deals naturally enough with the planning of the constructive or utilitarian lines of an object and its parts. It may be termed Structural or Constructive Design. Questions of how high or how long an object should be, to harmonize with its width, the proper placing of rails, shelves, and brackets, the determination of the greatest and least diameter of vase forms have to be decided in this period of Proportions and Space Relations. **First Major Division**

The knowledge of tools and materials, and of the manner in which they may be used for constructive purposes, influences the solution of these questions and others which we shall shortly discuss. Strictly utilitarian objects are seldom carried past this stage of development.

Plate 2 indicates the next logical division — Contour Enrichment — or the period of the enrichment of the structural outline or contour. The bounding lines, or contours, of the structure may be **Second Major Division**

THE SECOND MAJOR DIVISION IN INDUSTRIAL ARTS DESIGN

A GROUP OF OBJECTS SHOWING THE INTEREST ADDED TO A PROBLEM BY THE INTRODUCTION OF STRUCTURAL CONTOUR ENRICHMENT

FIG·A·

BLACK OUTLINE SHOWS VERTICAL PRIMARY MASS OF FIG·A— WHITE OUTLINES INDICATE THE STRUCTURE

FIG · B ·

'C' SHOWS PLAIN POST ENRICHED AT 'D'

Plate 2

enriched in many ways, as, for example, curving certain portions to soften the severity of the plain structure. The garden urn and small stool have contours treated in this manner. Chippendale, Sheraton, and Hepplewhite furniture, simplified to the accepted range of shop technic, vary the straight lines of mission furniture and come within the possible developments of this division. **Effects of Second Division**

The cement fence post at *C*, Plate 2, is a strict utilitarian problem without interest. The post at *D*, enriched by a bevel, has equal utilitarian and increased aesthetic interest and value.

Plate 3 illustrates the last division of evolution and concerns itself with the application of design to the surface of the otherwise complete structure. This division is commonly called applied surface design or decorative design. It is readily seen that this division should be considered after the structure has been carefully planned. To separate this division from the period of structural or contour enrichment we will call it Surface Enrichment. **Third Major Division**

It may be seen from the foregoing discussion that a design may be carried through the following steps: (1) Blocking in the enclosing lines of the design, as at Figure B, Plate 2, adding to this whatever may be needed for structural purposes, keeping the lines as nearly vertical and horizontal as possible; (2) Enriching and varying the outline or contour. It is well for elementary wood workers to use this step with extreme caution, while less reserve is necessary in clay and metal; (3) After careful consideration in determining the need of additional decoration, the last step, surface enrichment, should be used. The following chapters will take up these steps in the order stated above. **Steps in Design Evolution**

The ideal method of developing the principles set forth in this chapter includes correlated activity in the shop by working out the project in the required material. As the technic of the individual improves, the larger range of design principles will be found to accompany and parallel his increasing skill. **Ideal Correlation**

REVIEW QUESTIONS

1. What three requirements should be met in a well designed industrial article?
2. State three major divisions in industrial arts design.
3. State briefly the problems to be considered in each division.
4. What is the last and ideal step for the designer?

·THE THIRD MAJOR DIVISION IN INDUSTRIAL ARTS DESIGN·

A GROUP OF OBJECTS SHOWING THE INTEREST ADDED TO THE STRUCTURE BY THE INTRODUCTION OF ·SURFACE ENRICHMENT·

SURFACE ENRICHMENT (RAFFIA)

SURFACE ENRICHMENT APPLIED

PLATE 3

CHAPTER II

THE PRIMARY MASS AND ITS PROPORTIONS

Upon first observing a building, one seldom notices details of structure. He sees the large mass as it is silhouetted against the sky. Nearer approach discloses mouldings, cornices, and doorways; while careful analytical study shows the technical points of construction. The architect, in his original planning, thinks in terms of masses, widths, and heights, disregarding at first the details and color. As architecture stands for parent design principles and represents some of the world's best examples of composition and design, industrial design should be based upon the best examples of architectural design. To a certain degree, also, the methods of the industrial arts designer should be those of the architect. *The Architectural Method*

It is necessary to think at first of our problem as a single mass or solid, bounded by enclosing dimensions of width, height, and thickness. Details like a mirror, handles, brackets, or knobs may project outside of this mass, but for the time being, they may be disregarded. Figure B, Plate 2, shows this manner of thinking, and will enable us to regard the problem as a big, simple mass so that the entire object, unobstructed by small details, may be seen. *The Industrial Arts Method*

This is the method of *thinking* about the problem which should precede the drawing. To further describe this mass, which will be called the single or Primary Mass, it is necessary to think of the intended service of the project. A rather hazy idea of making a vase or a stool to be put to no particular use, may have been the original motive. Now the exact service should be defined as it will have a marked effect upon the shape of this primary mass. *The Primary Mass*

Rule 1a. *A primary mass must be either vertical or horizontal according to the intended service, unless prohibited by technical requirements.* Service is an important factor inasmuch as it limits the intended use of the mass. A mass is horizontal when its largest dimension is horizontal. When the horizontal dimension of this *Service*

[13]

· ANALYSIS · OF · THE · PRIMARY · MASS ·

· A HORIZONTAL PRIMARY MASS ·
FIG · 1 ·

· A VERTICAL PRIMARY MASS ·
FIG · 2 ·

· A VERTICAL PRIMARY MASS ·
FIG · 3 ·

· A HORIZONTAL PRIMARY MASS ·
FIG · 4 ·

THE MAIN STRUCTURAL
LINES DETERMINE THE
CHARACTER OF THE PRIM-
ARY MASS · THESE LINES
ARE INDICATED BY DARK
BANDS OR DIMENSION LINES
IN THE ILLUSTRATIONS ·
THREE DIVISIONS OR
CLASSES OF MATERIAL
HAVE BEEN EMPHASIZED ·

PLATE 4

mass is reduced until the main vertical dimension is longer than the main horizontal one, it becomes a vertical mass. As an example, a davenport is generally a horizontal mass intended to hold a number of people. When the mass is narrowed to the point where the vertical dimension exceeds the horizontal, it becomes a chair for one person. A low bowl may be intended for pansies, but as soon as the service changes and we design it for goldenrod, it becomes a vertical mass. The fable of the fox who, upon being invited to dine with the stork, found the tall vases unfitted for his use illustrates the change of mass with the change of service.

Horizontal and Vertical Primary Masses

Figures 1 and 4, Plate 4, are examples of horizontal masses with the dark lines indicating the dominance of the horizontal lines and planes. The shelter house contains a long bench, making necessary the long horizontal lines of the building. The calendar holder has to be a horizontal mass because of the restrictions imposed by the shape of the calendar pad.

Figures 2 and 3 are vertical masses. The vase is intended for tall flowers, while the chair, as has already been mentioned, must meet the needs of a single person. Utility and service then have been found to give the primary mass a given direction or dominance.

The designer now represents this mass by drawing a rectangle similar to the block outline of Figure B, Plate 2. It is now necessary to see if the foundation stones of this rectangle have been laid correctly; in other words, to test the proportions of the primary vertical or horizontal mass.

Drawing the Primary Mass

Rule 1b. *A primary mass should have the ratio of one to three, three to four, three to five, five to eight, seven to ten, or some similar proportion difficult for the eye to detect readily and analyze.* Proportions are generally expressed in terms of ratios. A surface of five by eight inches would give a ratio of five to eight; ten by sixteen feet is reducible to the same ratio. Certain ratios are monotonous and offend the eye by their lack of variety. Ratios such as one to one or one to two are of this class and should be avoided. If these ratios could speak they would resemble people talking in a low monotonous tone of voice.

Proportions of the Primary Masses

Certain other ratios are weak and indeterminate, showing a lack of clear thinking. They are like people with no definite or clean-

· PROPORTIONATE · RATIOS ·
· PROCESS · OF · DESIGNING ·

FIG · 5 ·

EXAMPLE OF UNSATISFACTORY PRO-
PORTIONATE RATIOS ··· 1:$\frac{1}{16}$ - 1:1$\frac{1}{3}$
AND 1:2 HAVE BEEN USED AS THE
BASIS OF THE PRIMARY MASS ·

FIG · 6 ·

EXAMPLE OF SATISFACTORY PRO-
PORTION ··· 1:3$\frac{1}{4}$ - 1:3 AND 3:5
SHOW DEFINITE THINKING IN THE
TERMS OF DESIGN ·

FIG · 7 ·

DEFINITE THOUGHT IN DESIGN REQUIRES A
KNOWLEDGE OF THE LAWS OF DESIGN; A KNOWLEDGE
OF THE TECHNICAL LIMITATIONS OF TOOLS AND MATER-
IALS AND THE APPLICATION OF THESE FACTS TO
A CONCRETE MODEL OR WORKING DRAWING
OF THE PROJECT ···

PLATE 5

cut ideas upon a subject they discuss. Examples in this class show ratios of two to two and one-eighth, or three to three and one-fourth, neither positively square nor frankly rectangular. They hide around the corner, as it were, waiting to be anything. Figure 5, Plate 5, is an example of unsatisfactory proportionate ratios of the primary mass. The blotting tablet is nearly square, while the candlestick and sconce, which should have been designed with strongly vertical masses, lack the type of definite thinking that results in a decided vertical dimension.

Disregarding the improvement in technic, Figure 6 shows problems designed with a definite knowledge of proportion. The metal objects are refined in their dimensions, and pleasing to the eye. Tests have been made with the idea of determining what the eye considers perfectly natural and agreeable proportion. This has been found to be the ratio of two to three. Consequently, it is clear why Figure 6 shows objects more pleasing than those in Figure 5.

It may be felt that too much space is being given to this subject of proportion. It should be remembered, however, that the industrial arts are intimately associated with daily life and that unless proportions are pleasing to our aesthetic sense, many articles of common use shortly become intolerable.

This preliminary portion of the designer's task has been given to thinking out the problem and drawing one rectangle. There is a tendency to start the design by pushing the pencil over the paper with a forlorn hope that a design may be evolved with little mental effort. This should be regarded as illogical and unworthy of the desired end. A rectangle of the most prominent surface of the problem, based upon the desired service of the project, and the best proportions which our knowledge of design and understanding of the limitations of construction will permit, should be the final result of the first study. From now on through the succeeding steps, the details of the problem will become more and more clear, as the technical limitations of the tools and materials governing the designer's ideas and controlling and shaping the work are better understood, until all governing factors become crystallized in the form of a working drawing or model. This is a strictly professional practice as illustrated in Figure 7, which shows the skilled Rookwood potter developing a vase form, the definite embodiment of correct thinking in terms of the material which is constantly before him.

SUMMARY OF RULES

Rule 1a. *A primary mass must be either vertical or horizontal according to the intended service, unless prohibited by technical requirements.*

Rule 1b. *A primary mass should have the ratio of one to three, three to four, three to five, five to eight, seven to ten, or some similar proportion difficult for the eye to readily detect and analyze.*

REVIEW QUESTIONS

1. How does the architect first plan his elevations?
2. How should the designer first think of his problem?
3. Define a horizontal primary mass.
4. Define a vertical primary mass.
5. State some desirable ratios to be used in designing the proportions of the primary mass. Explain.

CHAPTER III

HORIZONTAL MAJOR DIVISIONS OF
THE PRIMARY MASS

In the second chapter we discussed the nature of the primary mass in its relation to the intended service or duty it has to perform. It was found that the demands of service usually cause the primary mass to be designed with either a strong vertical or horizontal tendency.

It now becomes imperative to carry the designing processes still further and divide the vertical or horizontal primary mass into parts or divisions, demanded either by structural requirements or because the appearance of the object would be materially improved by their presence. This latter point is sometimes referred to as the aesthetic requirement of the problem. There are two simple types of divisions, those crossing the primary mass horizontally and those crossing the primary mass in a vertical direction. This chapter will be limited to the subject of horizontal divisions.

Divisions of the Primary Mass

If a city purchases a piece of land for park purposes, presumably a landscape architect is assigned the task of laying out the paths and drives. He does this by crossing his plan at intervals with lines to represent paths connecting important points. Under favorable conditions the architect is free to curve his path to suit his ideas. He has considerable freedom in selecting his design but the paths or roads must dip and curve in sympathy with the contour of the land and in accord with the aesthetic requirements.

Nature and Need of Horizontal Space Divisions

While the landscape designer has a broad latitude in his treatment of land divisions, the industrial designer or architect is restricted, on the other hand, by the structural requirements of the object and by his materials. He must cross his spaces or areas by horizontal shelves, or rails, or bands of metal that hold the structure together. As architecture is of fundamental importance in industrial design, let us see what the architect has in mind in designing a structure.

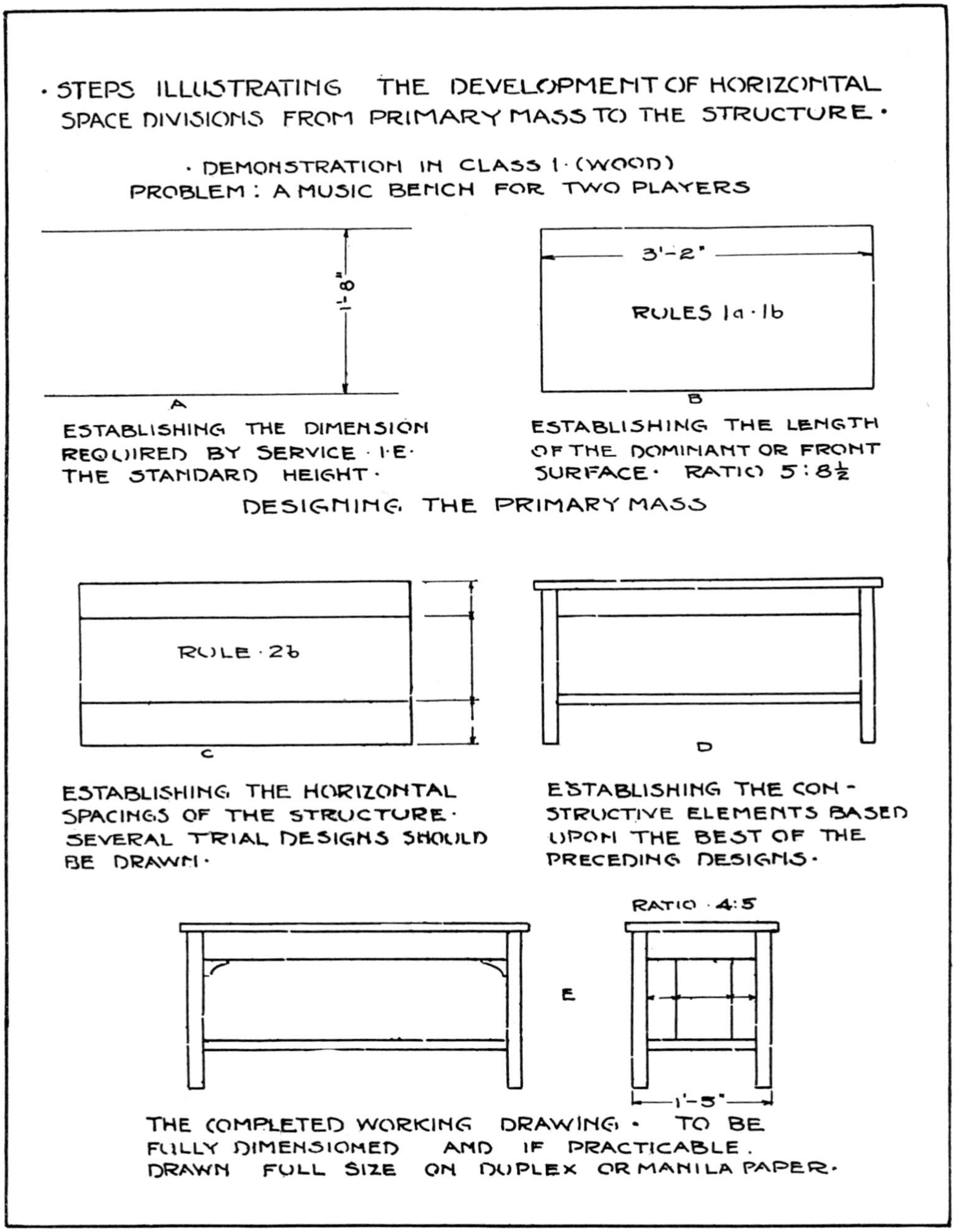
· STEPS ILLUSTRATING THE DEVELOPMENT OF HORIZONTAL SPACE DIVISIONS FROM PRIMARY MASS TO THE STRUCTURE ·
· DEMONSTRATION IN CLASS 1 · (WOOD)
PROBLEM : A MUSIC BENCH FOR TWO PLAYERS
1'-8"
A
ESTABLISHING THE DIMENSION REQUIRED BY SERVICE · I·E· THE STANDARD HEIGHT ·
3'-2"
RULES 1a · 1b
B
ESTABLISHING THE LENGTH OF THE DOMINANT OR FRONT SURFACE · RATIO 5 : 8½
DESIGNING THE PRIMARY MASS
RULE · 2b
C
ESTABLISHING THE HORIZONTAL SPACINGS OF THE STRUCTURE · SEVERAL TRIAL DESIGNS SHOULD BE DRAWN ·
D
ESTABLISHING THE CON-STRUCTIVE ELEMENTS BASED UPON THE BEST OF THE PRECEDING DESIGNS ·
RATIO · 4:5
E
1'-5"
THE COMPLETED WORKING DRAWING · TO BE FULLY DIMENSIONED AND IF PRACTICABLE . DRAWN FULL SIZE ON DUPLEX OR MANILA PAPER ·

Plate 6

The architect has the surface of the ground with which to start. This gives him a horizontal line as the base of his building. He considers it of major importance in his design. We find him crossing the front of his building with horizontal moulding or long bands of colored brick, paralleling the base line and otherwise interestingly dividing the vertical face of the front and sides. His guide is the bottom line of his primary mass or the line of the ground which binds the different parts of the building into a single unit. It can be readily seen that if he shifted the position of his mouldings up or down with the freedom of the landscape architect in locating his roads, he would not be planning his horizontal divisions in sympathy with the structural requirements of his primary mass. Architectural Horizontal Divisions

These horizontal divisions or lines have a tendency to give apparent added length to an object. Thus by their judicious use a designer may make a building or room look longer than it really is.

Let us now turn to the simpler objects with which we may be more directly concerned. The piano bench has horizontal lines crossing it, giving an effect quite similar to that of horizontal mouldings crossing a building. There may also be ornamental inlaid lines crossing the bench and intended to beautify the design, but it is to be remembered that at present we are considering the *structural divisions* only.

Plate 6 represents a concrete example of the methods to be used in designing the horizontal divisions of a piano bench. The steps may be divided as follows: Designing Objects with Horizontal Divisions

(*a*) The height of a piano bench may be determined either from measurement of a similar bench or from one of the books on furniture design now on the market. The scale of one inch or one and one-half inches to the foot may be adopted. Two horizontal lines should be drawn, one for the bottom and one for the top of the bench. The distance between these lines we will arbitrarily fix at twenty inches.

(*b*) Many objects are designed within rectangles which enclose their main or over-all proportions. With this in view, and keeping in mind the width of the bench necessary to the accommodation of two players and the requirements of a well proportioned primary mass (Rule 1b), the lines are now drawn completing the rectangular

· APPLIED AND CONSTRUCTIVE DESIGN ·

PRINCIPLE 1 : A · PROPORTIONS OF THE SINGLE PRIMARY MASS WITH
DOMINANCE OF THE HORIZONTAL DIVISION ·
PRINCIPLE 2 : A · RELATION OF HORIZONTAL SUB-DIVISIONS ·
PROBLEM: HORIZONTAL SPACE DIVISIONS · CLASSES 1 · 2 · 3 ·

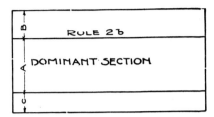

RULE 2a

· DOMINANT SECTION
IN EITHER UPPER OR
LOWER PORTION ·

RULE 2b

DOMINANT SECTION

TWO HORIZONTAL DIVISIONS   THREE HORIZONTAL DIVISIONS
PRIMARY MASSES   2:3 · 3:5 · 5:8 ETC·

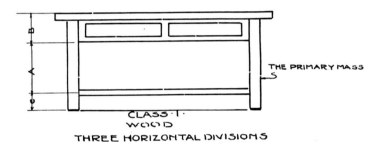

THE PRIMARY MASS

CLASS · 1 ·
WOOD
THREE HORIZONTAL DIVISIONS

X   A HORIZONTAL DIVISION

THE PRIMARY MASS

CLASS 2 · CLAY: CLASS 3 · METAL
TWO HORIZONTAL DIVISIONS

DRAW THREE DESIGNS IN A SELECTED CLASS · DESIGNS OF REC-
TILINEAR SOLIDS SHOULD INCLUDE FRONT AND SIDE VIEWS ·
COMPASS CURVES ARE TO BE AVOIDED IN PROFILES OF CUR-
VILINEAR FORMS IN CLASSES 2 · 3
DESIGNS SHOULD HAVE A DOMINANCE OF THE HORIZONTAL PROPORTION

PLATE 7

boundaries of the primary mass. The limitations of service and the restrictions of good designing give the width of the primary mass so designed as three feet and two inches, with a ratio of height to length of five to eight and one-half. It is simpler to design first the most prominent face of the object to be followed by other views later in the designing process.

Designing Objects with Horizontal Divisions— (*Continued*)

(*c*) By observing benches similar to the one being designed it will be seen that the horizontal divisions will take the form of a rail and a shelf, making two crossings of the primary mass dividing it into three horizontal spaces. Several trial arrangements of these structural elements are now made with the thought of making them conform to the rule governing three horizontal spaces. Rule 2b. We shall later discuss this rule and its applications fully.

(*d*) By selecting the best sketch of many which the designer will make he has the basis for the application of Rule 2b for the structural elements. The project now begins to take on concrete form. The top board may project slightly beyond the primary mass without materially affecting the value of the designed proportions.

(*e*) The last step is the designing of the side view in relation to the front view. This enables the designer to comprehend the project as a whole. It is strongly urged that the final or shop drawing be of full size. In more elaborate designs the finer proportions are lost in the process of enlargement from a small sketch, often hurriedly executed in the shop. Again much time is lost by necessary enlargement, whereas a full size curved detail may be quickly transferred to wood by carbon paper or by holes pricked in the paper. It is not expensive or difficult to execute full size drawings; it is in accord with shop practice and the custom should be encouraged and followed on all possible occasions. See Figure 102a.

Value of a Full Size Drawing

The process of designing round objects is identical to that just described as illustrated by the low round bowl in Plate 7. It should be designed in a rectangle of accepted proportions. Rule 1b. The primary mass may have excellent proportions and yet the vase or bowl may remain devoid of interest. It may be commonplace.

As will shortly be shown, the rules governing horizontal divisions serve as a check on the commonplace. A horizontal division generally marks the point where the outward swell of the vase contour

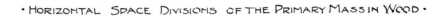

· HORIZONTAL SPACE DIVISIONS OF THE PRIMARY MASS IN WOOD ·

· FIG · 8 ·

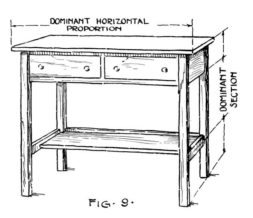

· FIG · 9 ·

· A VERTICAL MASS WITH TWO HORIZONTAL SPACE DIVISIONS ·

· A HORIZONTAL MASS WITH THREE HORIZONTAL SPACE DIVISIONS ·

· STRUCTURAL NEEDS SUPPLY THE HORIZONTAL LINES FOR THIS TYPE OF SPACING ·

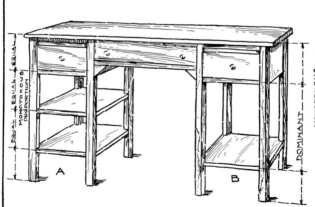

FIG · 10 ·

THE HORIZONTAL PRIMARY MASS AT "A" HAS BEEN DIVIDED INTO THREE EQUAL AND ONE UN-EQUAL DIVISIONS · BY OMITTING THE CENTRAL DIVISION, GREATER UNITY IS SECURED AT "B."

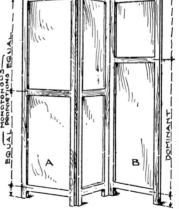

FIG · 11 ·

A VERTICAL MASS WITH THREE POORLY SPACED DIVIS-IONS AT "A" CORRECTED BY PRINCIPLE 2a AT "B."

PLATE 8

reaches its maximum width. If this widest point in the primary mass (X-Plate 7) is pleasingly located between the top and bottom of a vase form the contour will be found satisfactory.

It is possible to continue *ad infinitum* with these illustrations but horizontal space divisions are nearly always present in some form, due to structural necessity or aesthetic requirements. It is an easy matter to say that these lines must divide the primary mass into "interesting" spaces, well related to each other, or "pleasingly located," but the designer must have some definite yet flexible rule to govern his work. From the analysis of many famous historic buildings and well designed industrial projects it has been found that all horizontal masses may be analyzed as dividing the primary mass into either *two* or *three* divisions or spaces, regardless of the complexity of the project.

Architectural Precedent for Horizontal Divisions

ANALYSIS OF HORIZONTAL SPACE DIVISIONS

Rule 2a. *If the primary mass is divided into two horizontal divisions, the dominance should be either in the upper or the lower section.* Plate 7 shows this division of the primary mass — the simplest division of the space. A space divided just half way from top to bottom would be monotonous and expressive of the ratio of one to one. This arrangement as we have already discovered in the second chapter is not conducive to good design.

Two Horizontal Space Divisions

By the stated rule, 2a, the varied adjustment of this double horizontal division affords all possible latitude for constructive purposes. It is better to place the division in such a manner that the upper division (or lower) will not appear pinched or dwarfed by comparison with the remaining area. Thus a ratio of one to three, or three to five, or five to eight is better than a ratio of one to one or one to eighteen, but there is no exact or arbitrary ruling on this point.

Figure 8 illustrates two horizontal divisions in wood construction and also the freedom of choice as to exact proportions. The eye will be found a good judge of the proper spacings subject to the limitations already mentioned.

Two Horizontal Divisions in Wood

It is best to keep the design within the limits of two horizontal

HORIZONTAL SPACE DIVISIONS OF THE PRIMARY MASS IN CLAY

FIG · 12 ·

A WALL SURFACE DIVIDED INTO TWO HORIZONTAL DIVISIONS · THE HOOD OF THE FIRE PLACE AND THE DOOR ECHO BY SIMILAR PROPORTIONS THIS DIVISION · UNITY THUS SECURED IS VARIED BY THE THREE DIVISION SPACING OF THE PANELLING ·

POTTERY FORMS SHOULD AT FIRST BE LIMITED TO TWO HORIZONTAL DIVISIONS

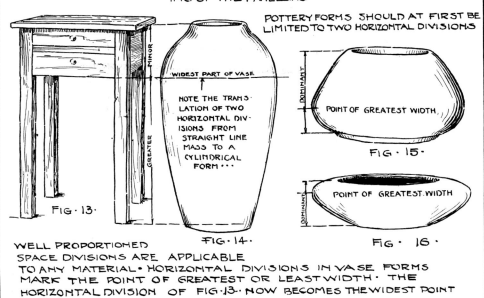

WIDEST PART OF VASE

NOTE THE TRANS-
LATION OF TWO
HORIZONTAL DIV-
ISIONS FROM
STRAIGHT LINE
MASS TO A
CYLINDRICAL
FORM · · ·

POINT OF GREATEST WIDTH

FIG · 15 ·

POINT OF GREATEST WIDTH

FIG · 16 ·

FIG · 13 ·

FIG · 14 ·

WELL PROPORTIONED
SPACE DIVISIONS ARE APPLICABLE
TO ANY MATERIAL · HORIZONTAL DIVISIONS IN VASE FORMS
MARK THE POINT OF GREATEST OR LEAST WIDTH · THE
HORIZONTAL DIVISION OF FIG · 13 · NOW BECOMES THE WIDEST POINT
OF FIG · 14 ·

PLATE 9

space divisions in designing cylindrical clay forms, particularly in the elementary exercises. Enough variety will be found to make pleasing arrangements, and the technical results obtained by two divisions are much better than those obtained from a greater number of divisions.

Figures 14, 15, and 16, Plate 9, are clay forms with the dominance placed in either the upper or lower portion of the primary mass. Figure 13 has been used to illustrate the fact that horizontal space division principles are applicable to any material. The horizontal divisions in Figure 13 are due to structural needs. A horizontal line carries this division across to Figure 14, a clay vase. The horizontal division line now becomes the one which marks the widest part of the vase. It gives the same relation between the top and bottom horizontal spaces as in Figure 13. It marks an aesthetic point in the design of the vase, or a variation of the contour, introduced by reason of its effect upon the beauty of the vase, not called for by the needs of actual service. Two Horizontal Divisions in Clay

A musical composition is often played in an orchestra first by the wood instruments, taken up and repeated by the brasses, then by the strings, and finally played as an harmonious whole by the entire orchestra. There is a close parallel in Figure 12, an adaptation of one of Gustav Stickley's designs. The two-division rule is used in the relations of the plaster and wainscoting; again in the plaster over, and the cement or tile around the fireplace. It is repeated in the arrangement of the copper and cement of the fireplace facing and hood and in the door panels. By repeating again and again similar space divisions the wall space becomes a unified and harmonious whole. Variety is secured by the introduction of three horizontal divisions in the details of the wainscoting. This method of repeating similar space divisions is called "echoing" and is one of the most effective means known for securing the effect of *unity*.

The horizontal subdivisions in metal are usually made for service. Figures 17, 18, and 19, Plate 10, are examples of such divisions. The location of the clock face in Figure 18 calls for the placing of its horizontal axis in accordance with Rule 2a. The lamp in Figure 19 shows an instance where the entire design once divided by Rule 2a, may be again subdivided into a similar series of divisions. This Two Horizontal Divisions in Metal

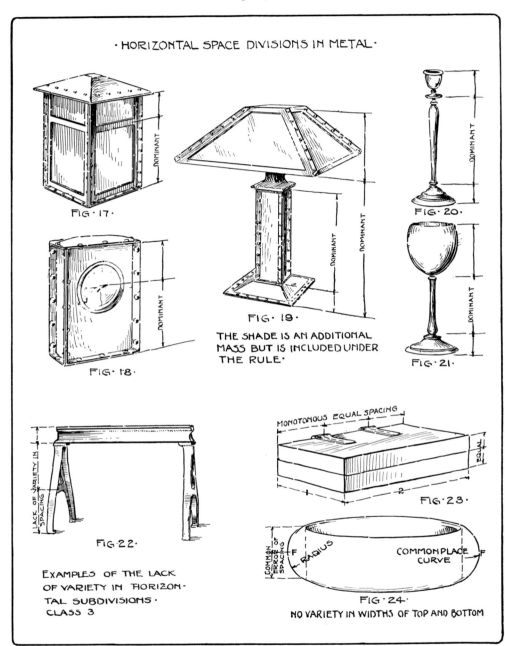

· HORIZONTAL SPACE DIVISIONS IN METAL ·

FIG · 17 ·

FIG · 18 ·

FIG · 19 ·

THE SHADE IS AN ADDITIONAL MASS BUT IS INCLUDED UNDER THE RULE ·

FIG · 20 ·

FIG · 21 ·

FIG · 22 ·

EXAMPLES OF THE LACK OF VARIETY IN HORIZONTAL SUBDIVISIONS · CLASS 3

MONOTONOUS EQUAL SPACING

FIG · 23 ·

COMMONPLACE CURVE

FIG · 24 ·

NO VARIETY IN WIDTHS OF TOP AND BOTTOM

PLATE 10

arrangement is quite similar to the system of repetitions seen in Figure 12 and termed "echoing" the original divisions.

Rule 2b. *If the primary mass is divided into three horizontal divisions or sections, the dominance should be placed in the center section with varying widths in the upper and lower thirds.*

When it becomes necessary to divide the primary mass into more than two sections the designer's problem becomes more difficult. With the addition of a greater number of horizontal divisions there is a manifest tendency for the design to become cut up into so many small sections that the simplicity of the whole mass is lost. Here, as elsewhere, that principle which we call *unity* or the quality of "holding together" is necessary and should be the constant test of the design. The instant any part of the design seems to fly apart from the main mass it becomes the designer's duty to simplify the design or pull the parts together and thus restore the lost unity.

As a restriction against loss of unity it is necessary to group all of the minor horizontal divisions into a system of two or three large horizontal divisions. Referring to Rule 2b, it is seen that when three divisions are used, it becomes the practice to accentuate the center section by making it larger. This arrangement is designed to give weight to the center portion and by this big stable division to hold the other subdivisions together and in unity.

Two horizontal masses and one vertical mass shown in Figures 9, 10, and 11, Plate 8, illustrate the application of this three-division rule to wood construction. It is seen that the construction of rails, doors, and shelves is responsible for the fixing of all of these divisions. It may also be seen that three divisions are applicable to either the vertical or the horizontal primary mass. Figure 10 illustrates the violation of this type of spacing at the point *A*, where the shelves are no more pleasingly arranged than the rounds of a ladder. Later on we shall be able to rearrange these shelves in a pleasing manner but at present it is better to relieve the monotony by omitting the center shelf. This applies the three division rule to the satisfactory appearance of the desk at *B*.

Similar monotony in spacing is seen in the screen, Figure 11. The correction in *B* appeals at once as a far more satisfactory arrangement than that secured by placing the cross bar half way up as in *A*.

There are no infallible rules for this readjustment beyond those already stated. The eye must in part be depended upon to guide the artistic sense aright.

It is suggested that it is desirable to keep clay forms within the limitations of two divisions. Rectangular posts, pedestals, and other vertical forms in cement may be developed by the application of Rule 2a or 2b, if care is taken to group all minor divisions well within the limitations of these rules.

Three Horizontal Divisions in Clay

The statement just made in reference to simplified groupings is illustrated in the candlestick and cup in Figures 20 and 21, Plate 10. The construction based upon the three functions performed by the cup, the handle, and the base, suggests the use of these horizontal divisions. The minor curves have been subordinated to, and kept within, these three divisions. The final result gives a distinct feeling of unity impossible under a more complex grouping. The Greek column will afford an architectural illustration of a similar grouping system.

Three Horizontal Divisions in Metal

The lathe bed of Figure 22 shows one of innumerable examples of space violations in the industrial arts. A slight lowering of the cross brace would add materially to the appearance and strength of the casting. Figure 23 is a copper box with the following more or less common faults of design: commonplace ratio of length and width (2 : 1) partially counteracted, however, by a more pleasing ratio of the vertical dimension, equal spacing in the width of cover of box and box body, and equal spacing of the hinges of the box from the ends of the box and from each other. By applying the two and three horizontal division rules these errors may be avoided.

Freehand Curves

Figure 24 shows a low bowl with a compass curve used in designing the contour. This has brought the widest part of the design in the exact center of the bowl which makes it commonplace. In addition to this the top and bottom are of the same width, lacking variety in this respect. Correction is readily made by applying a freehand curve to the contour, raising or lowering the widest point (F), at the same time designing the bottom either larger or smaller than the top.

INSTRUCTION SHEET

Plate 7 is a sheet suggestive of the application of Rules 1a, 1b, 2a, and 2b, with an indication of the type of problem to be required. The steps of the designing processes in either wood (class 1), clay (class 2), or metal (class 3), are summarized as follows:

SUMMARY OF DESIGN STEPS

(a) Construction of the rectangle representing the vertical or horizontal character of the primary mass with desirable proportions. It is better to select a typical view (Plate 6, *D*), preferably a front elevation.

(b) Subdivide this rectangle into two or three structural sections; horizontal in character. Make two or three trial freehand sketches for varied proportions and select the most pleasing one in accordance with Rules 1a, 1b, 2a, and 2b.

(c) Translate the selected sketch to a full size mechanical drawing or at least to a reasonably large scale drawing. The structural elements: *i.e.*, legs, rails, posts, etc., should be added and other additional views made.

(d) Dimension and otherwise prepare the drawing for shop purposes.

(e) Construct the project.

SUGGESTED PROBLEMS

Design a nasturtium bowl, applying Rules 1a, 1b, 2a.

Design a writing table 2 feet 6 inches high with three horizontal divisions.

SUMMARY OF RULES

Rule 2a. *If the primary mass is divided into two horizontal divisions, the dominance should be either in the upper or the lower section.*

Rule 2b. *If the primary mass is divided into three horizontal divisions or sections, the dominance should be placed in the center section with varying widths in the upper and lower thirds.*

REVIEW QUESTIONS

1. State two methods of subdividing the primary mass.
2. Define the nature and need of horizontal space divisions.
3. Give five steps to be used in designing a foot stool or piano bench.
4. What point constitutes a horizontal division in the contour of a simple clay bowl?
5. State the rule governing two horizontal space divisions and furnish illustrations in wood, clay, and metal.
6. Give the rule governing three horizontal space divisions and supply illustrations in wood, clay, and metal.
7. State five steps in the designing of a project in the industrial arts involving the use of horizontal structural divisions.

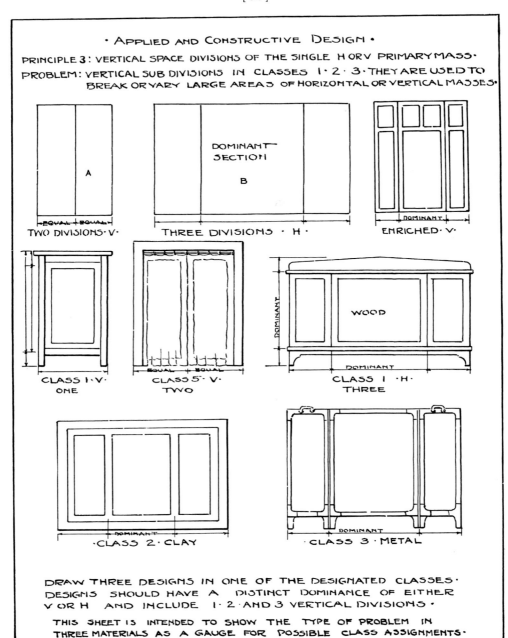

· APPLIED AND CONSTRUCTIVE DESIGN ·

PRINCIPLE 3 : VERTICAL SPACE DIVISIONS OF THE SINGLE H OR V PRIMARY MASS.

PROBLEM : VERTICAL SUB DIVISIONS IN CLASSES 1 · 2 · 3 · THEY ARE USED TO BREAK OR VARY LARGE AREAS OF HORIZONTAL OR VERTICAL MASSES ·

A

TWO DIVISIONS · V ·

DOMINANT SECTION

B

THREE DIVISIONS · H ·

ENRICHED · V ·

CLASS 1 · V ·
ONE

CLASS 5 · V ·
TWO

WOOD

CLASS 1 · H ·
THREE

· CLASS 2 · CLAY

CLASS 3 · METAL

DRAW THREE DESIGNS IN ONE OF THE DESIGNATED CLASSES ·
DESIGNS SHOULD HAVE A DISTINCT DOMINANCE OF EITHER
V OR H AND INCLUDE 1 · 2 AND 3 VERTICAL DIVISIONS ·

THIS SHEET IS INTENDED TO SHOW THE TYPE OF PROBLEM IN
THREE MATERIALS AS A GAUGE FOR POSSIBLE CLASS ASSIGNMENTS ·

PLATE 11

CHAPTER **IV**

VERTICAL MAJOR DIVISIONS OF
THE PRIMARY MASS

The design of the primary mass has now been considered under Rules 1a and 1b, and its horizontal divisions under Rules 2a and 2b. The next logical step is the consideration of the nature of the lines that cross the primary mass in a vertical direction. In the original planning of the primary mass it was found that the horizontal bounding lines and the horizontal divisions were parallel to the base line of an object and that the base line was necessary to ensure stability. Vertical lines are necessary and equally important to give the needed vertical support to an object.

So accustomed is the eye to vertical lines in tree trunks, tall buildings, and thousands of other examples that the upward eye movement in viewing an object, having a predominance of vertical elements, seemingly adds to its height.

The designer thus has a most useful device with which to increase the apparent height of an object that, for structural or other reasons, must in reality not have great height. Chapter III drew attention to the influence of horizontal lines on a project. Vertical lines on an object are found to produce an analogous effect vertically.

Gothic cathedral builders used the vertical line, repeated again and again in buttresses, pinnacles, and spires to give great apparent height to a building and to make it a unified vertical mass of great beauty. The modern church spire, together with the long, vertical interior columns, similarly affects our present day church edifices.

This idea of repeating the vertical bounding lines of the primary mass by cutting the mass into vertical spaces is also useful in breaking up or destroying the monotony of large unbroken surfaces. Pilasters may cut the front of a building into interesting spaces; piers may break up the regularity of a long fence; legs and panels may, each

[33]

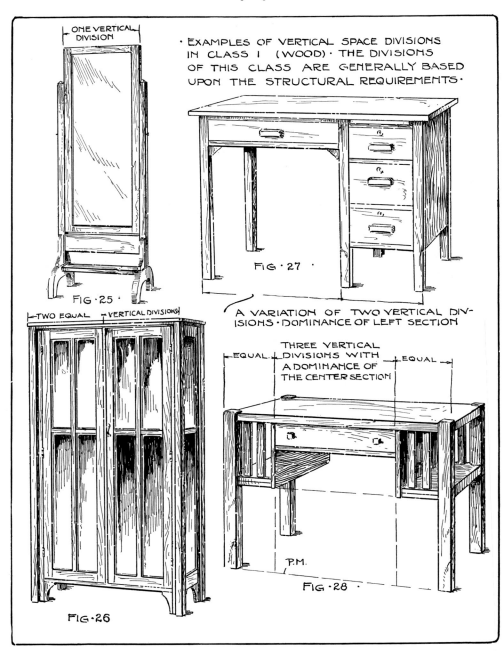

ONE VERTICAL DIVISION

FIG · 25 ·

· EXAMPLES OF VERTICAL SPACE DIVISIONS
IN CLASS I (WOOD) · THE DIVISIONS
OF THIS CLASS ARE GENERALLY BASED
UPON THE STRUCTURAL REQUIREMENTS ·

FIG · 27 ·

A VARIATION OF TWO VERTICAL DIV-
ISIONS · DOMINANCE OF LEFT SECTION

TWO EQUAL VERTICAL DIVISIONS

FIG · 26

THREE VERTICAL
DIVISIONS WITH
A DOMINANCE OF
THE CENTER SECTION

EQUAL EQUAL

P.M.

FIG · 28 ·

PLATE 12

for the same purpose, cross a cabinet. While some of these may be structurally necessary and some not, they are all witnesses to the desire to produce beauty in design. As these examples are so numerous in the industrial arts, it is well to study in detail their proper adaptation to our needs.

Upon analyzing one vertical space division, it will be found to be a primary mass, vertical in character and governed by Rule 1a. Figure 25, Plate 12, illustrates one vertical division. The foot is an appendage to be considered in Chapter V.

One Vertical Space Division

Rule 3a. *If the primary mass is divided into two vertical divisions, the divisions should be equal in area and similar in form.* Exception may be made in case of structural requirements. By imagining two adjacent doors of equal size, the design effect of two vertical divisions may be made clear. Plate 11 illustrates a rectangle (*A*) divided in this manner, preliminary to the development of a problem. Figure 27, Plate 12, represents the type of object to which the exception to the rule may be applied. In the design of this desk, the structure practically prohibits two equal vertical divisions, necessitating an unequal division in the section occupied by the drawers.

Two Vertical Space Divisions

In Plate 12, Figure 26, the designer had his vertical spacings dictated by service in the form of two doors. As service demands a tall vertical primary mass, it is but natural to design the doors to conform with the primary mass. This gives a monotonously long space for the glass panels and suggests structural weakness. To relieve this the designer applied Rule 2a and crossed the vertical panels by horizontal subdivisions, relieving the monotony and still retaining the unity of the primary mass.

In Figure 27 his problem was a variation of that presented in Figure 26. Structural limitations called for unequal divisions of the vertical space arrangement. The left portion of the desk becomes dominant as demanded by service. The drawer or brace is necessary in this design as it acts as a sort of link, binding the two vertical legs together. The omission of the drawer would destroy the unity of the mass.

Two Vertical Divisions in Wood

As vertical space divisions are principally applicable to rectilinear or flat objects and moreover as it is in such forms only that they

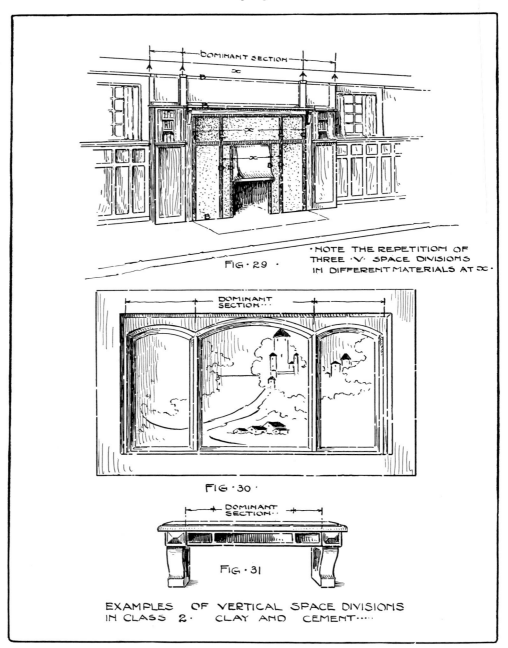

· NOTE THE REPETITION OF
THREE · V · SPACE DIVISIONS
IN DIFFERENT MATERIALS AT ∝ ·

FIG · 29 ·

FIG · 30 ·

FIG · 31

EXAMPLES OF VERTICAL SPACE DIVISIONS
IN CLASS 2 · CLAY AND CEMENT ·····

PLATE 13

have structural value, they are not commonly met in cylindrical pottery ware. Vertical divisions are, however, occasionally used in architectural tiles and other flat wall objects. As three divisions are much more commonly used in clay and cement, this material will now be left for later consideration in this chapter.

Vertical spacings in metal are quite similar to space divisions in wood. Wrought iron fences are, by reason of structural limitations composed of vertical and horizontal lines, varied by the introduction of piers and curved members. As they are typical of a certain branch of iron construction, two designs of the Anchor Post Iron Company have been introduced. Figure 32, Plate 14, represents two equal vertical divisions made so because of structural and aesthetic demands. The piers in this instance form a part of the general design of the entire gate and must be considered accordingly.

The vertical subdivision in Figure 32, Plate 14, has been repeated or echoed by the long vertical bars, alternating with the shorter ones and producing pleasing variety. The horizontal divisions are designed according to Rule 2b. In designing the newel lantern in Figure 34 the designer was required to form a vertical primary mass to conform with the similar mass of the post. This he determined to subdivide vertically in practically the same manner as the cabinet in Figure 26. Threatened with the same monotony he met the situation by subdividing the vertical sections into three horizontal divisions in accordance with Rule 2b. The structural supports, however, rising up in the center of this mass, destroy its unity. They would have carried out the lines of the structure of the newel post and continued the lines of the lantern better, if they had been attached to the corners rather than to the sides of the newel post.

Rule 3b. *If the primary mass is divided into three vertical divisions, the center division should be the larger, with the remaining divisions of equal size.* A large building with a wing on either side will give an idea of this form of spacing. The size of the main building holds the wings to it, thus preserving the unity of the structure, while equal divisions on either side give balance. Plate 11 (*B*) gives an example of a rectangle divided in this manner. This three-division motive is a very old one. In the middle ages painters and designers used

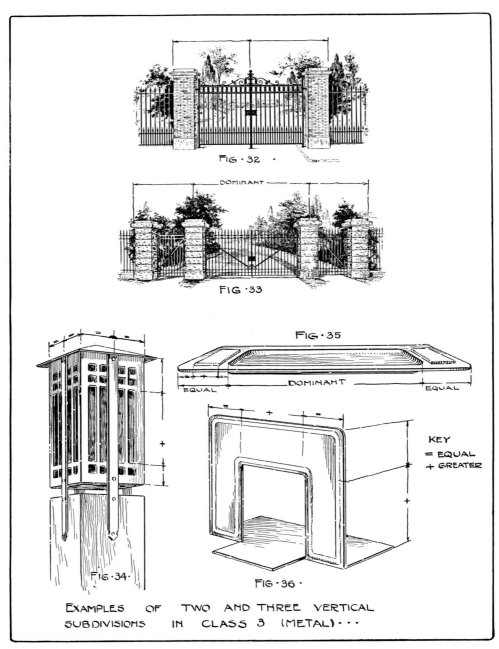

FIG · 32 ·

FIG · 33

DOMINANT

FIG · 35

DOMINANT

EQUAL

EQUAL

KEY
= EQUAL
+ GREATER

FIG · 34 ·

FIG · 36 ·

EXAMPLES OF TWO AND THREE VERTICAL
SUBDIVISIONS IN CLASS 3 (METAL) · · ·

PLATE 14

three divisions or a triptych, as it is called, in their altar decorations. A painting of the Virgin was usually placed in the center division with a saint in each of the remaining panels to the right and left. Designers and mural decorators have been using the triptych ever since that period.

The desk in Figure 28, Plate 12, is a good example of the three-vertical space rule. The drawer in the center forms the mid or dominant section and by its greater length holds the two smaller sections together. This design is better than Figure 27, which has a similar mass. The prominent vertical lines in Figure 27 counteract and destroy the effect of the long horizontal dominant lines of the table top, whereas in Figure 28, the vertical lines in the center of the design are so short that they do not interfere with the horizontal lines of the table top. Figure 28 supports the horizontal tendency of the primary mass while Figure 27 neutralizes or practically destroys its character. *Three Vertical Divisions in Wood*

Figure 30, Plate 13, represents an overmantle by the Rookwood Potteries. It is typical of a class of overmantles which may be developed in tiles or in cement, forming an agreeable contrast with the brick of a large fireplace. The three divisions or triptych should be proportionately related to the opening of the fireplace and to the enclosing mass of brick or wood work. We will consider Figure 29 to show how this may be carried out. *Three Vertical Divisions in Clay and Cement*

Figure 29 bears a strong resemblance to Figure 12, Plate 9, and is an elaboration of a simple three-division theme of spacing. The design seems to be complex until it is analyzed into two rules. The primary mass of the entire fireplace motive (including the surrounding panelling) has first been planned with strong and prominent horizontal lines. This was then divided vertically (A) to conform with Rule 3b, the three-division theme, giving the divisions for the bookcases and mantle. The horizontal divisions (B) were then constructed within the remaining space, affecting the distance from the picture moulding to the mantle and from the mantle to the floor line, in accordance with Rule 2a. That left the space of the width of the cement work (C) to be subdivided again by Rule 3b, while the top of the wainscoting panels re-echoed the previous horizontal divisions of Rule 2a. The fireplace opening merely carries out at D

• THE EVOLUTION OF A DESIGN INVOLVING THE USE OF TWO HORIZONTAL AND THREE VERTICAL SUBDIVISIONS •

• THE COMPLETED PROBLEM •

FIG·A· THE HORIZONTAL AND VERTICAL DIVISIONS ARE BASED UPON STRUCTURAL REQUIREMENTS ·

FIG·B· THE PRIMARY MASS WITH TWO HORIZONTAL DIVISIONS · RULES·1·2·

FIG·C· THE ADDITION OF THREE VERTICAL DIVISIONS · RULE·3·b·

APPENDAGE

PROPORTION OF MASS APPROXIMATELY 9:5

FIG·D· THE ADDITION OF SUB·DIVISIONS AND APPENDAGE · RULES·3· AND·4·

FIG·E· ADDITION OF DETAILS AND ENRICHMENT·

• FOR SHOP WORKING DRAWINGS : ONE·HALF OF FIG·E· SHOULD NOW BE ENLARGED TO A FULL·SIZE PENCIL DRAWING WITH CONSTRUCTION AND PARTIAL END VIEW ADDED·

PLATE 15

the same proportionate relation that dominates all vertical divisions, Rule 3b, while the wainscoting follows the general horizontal divisions of Rule 2a. By this method we have variety in spacing and unity through repetition of similar proportions.

The cement bench, Figure 31, has a three-division arrangement to break up the monotony of the long rail, and at the same time to repeat the characteristics of a horizontal primary mass.

Figure 33, Plate 14, is a common example of three vertical divisions in metal suggested by the needs of service. Figures 35 and 36 are thin metal problems. The familiar pen tray is primarily a horizontal mass, so determined by its required service as a pen holder. The projecting handles form the outer divisions, and the spacing motive, Rule 3b, has been repeated in the raised projection, decorating the handles. The book rack in Figure 36 is an example of the manner in which a nearly square mass, so designed for structural reasons, may, by Rules 3b and 2a, be broken into a fairly pleasing arrangement of divisions.

Three Vertical Divisions in Metal

Rule 3c. *In elementary problems, if more than three vertical divisions are required, they should be so grouped as to analyze into Rules 3a and 3b, or be exactly similar.* The eye becomes confused by a multitude of vertical divisions and it is much better designing to keep them within the number stated in this chapter. There are instances, however, when this is impossible. Under such conditions the following treatment should be adopted:

More Than Three Divisions

Unless, as stated, a large number of vertical divisions may be grouped into two or three vertical divisions it is better to make all of the divisions of the same size. This does not fatigue the eye as much as would the introduction of a number of complex spacings. This solution enables the amateur designer to deal with complex problems with an assurance of securing a degree of unity.

INSTRUCTION SHEET

Plate 15 is practically self-explanatory and shows the order in which the various divisions, so far considered, are to be introduced into the design together with the grouping of details within those divisions. Figure D introduces the additional element termed the appendage to be considered in Chapter V.

SUMMARY OF DESIGN STEPS

(a) Construction of the rectangle representing the vertical or horizontal character of the primary mass with desirable proportions. Select the most prominent surface for this rectangle, preferably the front elevation.

(b) Subdivide this rectangle into two or three structural sections, horizontal and vertical in character. Make two or three trial freehand sketches on cross section paper for varied proportions and select the most pleasing in accordance with rules.

(c) Translate the selected sketch into a scale or full size drawing and add additional views to complete the requirements of a working drawing. Add additional structural elements: legs, rails, etc.

(d) For shop purposes, enlarge a scale drawing to full size, dimension and otherwise prepare it for actual use. See Figure 102a, page 68, for character of this change.

(e) Construct the project.

SUGGESTED PROBLEMS

Design a fire screen with two horizontal and three vertical major subdivisions.

Design a bookcase 4 feet 2 inches high with three horizontal and two vertical major subdivisions.

SUMMARY OF RULES

Rule 3a. *If the primary mass is divided into two vertical divisions, the divisions should be equal in area and similar in form.*

Rule 3b. *If the primary mass is divided into three vertical divisions, the center division should be the larger, with the remaining divisions of equal size.*

Rule 3c. *In elementary problems, if more than three vertical divisions are required, they should be so grouped as to analyze into Rules 3a and 3b, or be exactly similar.*

REVIEW QUESTIONS

1. What is the nature and need of vertical space divisions?
2. State the rule governing the use of two vertical space divisions and give illustrations in wood, clay, and metal.
3. Give the rule relating to the use of three vertical space divisions and furnish illustrations in wood, clay, and metal.
4. What is the treatment of more than three vertical divisions? Why?

CHAPTER V

APPENDAGES AND RULES GOVERNING THEM

An appendage is a member added to the primary mass for utilitarian purposes. In the industrial arts, when an appendage is added merely for the purpose of decoration, it is as useless and functionless as the human appendix and, as a source of discord, should be removed.

An appendage in industrial arts may be, among other things, a plate rail, bracket, spout, cover, or handle, all of which are capable of service either for or with the primary mass. In architecture it may be a wing or ell added to the mass of the building. Simple as its design may seem, it is often so placed in relation to the main or primary mass that it does not seem to "fit" or to be in unity with that mass.

Rule 4a. *The appendage should be designed in unity with, and proportionately related to, the vertical or horizontal character of the primary mass, but subordinated to it.*

Rule 4b. *The appendage should have the appearance of flowing smoothly and, if possible, tangentially from the primary mass.*

Rule 4c. *The appendage should, if possible, echo or repeat some lines similar in character and direction to those of the primary mass.*

All of the foregoing rules are intended to promote the sense of unity between the primary mass and its appendages. If a mirror on a dresser looks top-heavy it is generally due to the fact that it has not been subordinated in size to the primary mass. Rule 4a. If the handle projects from the primary mass of an object similar to the handle on a pump, it has not been designed in accordance with Rules 4b and 4c. Again, if the appendage projects from a primary mass like a tall chimney from a long flat building, it has violated Rule 4a and has not been proportionately related to the character of the vertical or horizontal proportions of the primary mass.

It should be readily seen that if the primary mass has one dominant proportion while the appendage has another, there will be a

[43]

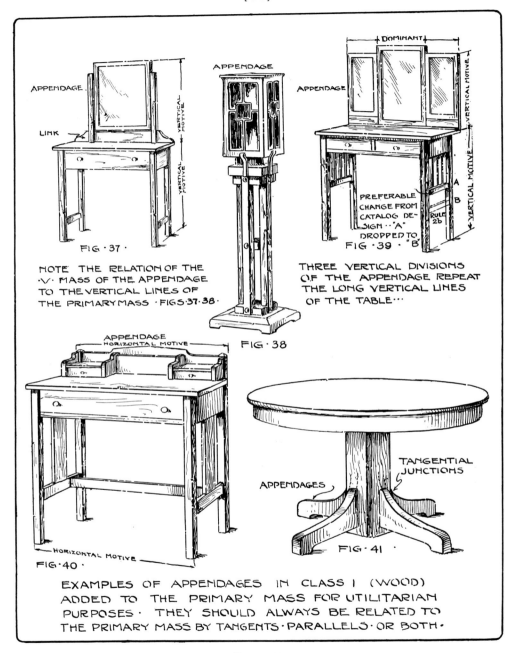

FIG · 37 ·

NOTE THE RELATION OF THE
·V· MASS OF THE APPENDAGE
TO THE VERTICAL LINES OF
THE PRIMARY MASS · FIGS · 37 · 38 ·

FIG · 38

THREE VERTICAL DIVISIONS
OF THE APPENDAGE REPEAT
THE LONG VERTICAL LINES
OF THE TABLE ···

PREFERABLE
CHANGE FROM
CATALOG DE-
SIGN ·"A"·
DROPPED TO
FIG · 39 · "B"

FIG · 40 ·

FIG · 41 ·

EXAMPLES OF APPENDAGES IN CLASS I (WOOD)
ADDED TO THE PRIMARY MASS FOR UTILITARIAN
PURPOSES · THEY SHOULD ALWAYS BE RELATED TO
THE PRIMARY MASS BY TANGENTS · PARALLELS · OR BOTH ·

PLATE 16

serious clash and the final result will be the neutralization of both motives, resulting in either an insipid and characterless design or a downright lack of unity.

The design of the small dressing table, Figure 37, Plate 16, with the mirror classing as an appendage, is an excellent illustration of Rule 4a. The main mass of the table is vertical in character and the mirror carries out or repeats the character of the primary mass by having a similar but subordinate vertical mass. In this instance it is so large that it has nearly the effect of a second primary mass.

Appendages in Wood

As tangential junctions are difficult to arrange in wood construction and particularly in furniture, the break between the table top and the mirror has been softened by the introduction of a bracket or connecting link. The curves of the link cause the eye to move freely from the primary mass to the appendage and thus there is a sense of oneness or unity between the two masses.

The lantern in Figure 38 becomes an appendage and is subordinated to the large pedestal or support. The tangential junction has in this case been fully possible and the eye moves freely from the vertical lines of the base to the similar vertical mass of the lantern without noticeable break.

The service of the dressing table, Figure 39, with its three-division mirror makes the problem of adaptation of the appendage to the mass of the table, in accordance with the rules, much more difficult. Under the circumstances, about the best that can be done, at the same time keeping within the limitations of desired service, is to plan the mirrors in accordance with Rule 3b, with the dominant section in the center. To secure an approach to unity, each section of the mirror should echo the vertical proportion of the primary mass of the table.

Unifying Appendage and Primary Mass

The top of the writing stand, in Figure 40, is an example of a horizontal appendage which repeats the horizontal character of the front or typical face of the primary mass of the table. The small drawers and divisions again take up and repeat the horizontal motive of the table, while the entire appendage may be subdivided under Rule 3b, giving the dominance to the center portion. The short curves in the appendage all tend to lead the eye in a satisfactory and smooth transition from one mass to the other or from the table

FIGURE 41a

top to the appendage. The proportions of the small drawers are similar to the proportions of the table drawers. Rule 4c. All of these points of similarity bring the masses into close unity or oneness of appearance.

The table legs, in Figure 41, are more difficult to adjust satisfactorily. The idea of the designer is, however, apparent. The legs leave the column of the table with a tangential curve and, sweeping out with a strong curve, repeat the horizontal line of the table top in the horizontal lines of their bottom surfaces.

Figure 41a, a modification of Figure 39, shows close unity between the three divisions of the mirror due to the pleasing curve of the center section with its tendency to bind the other sections to it. Again, the echoing of the spacings of the three drawers in the similar spacings of the three mirrors, makes the bond of unity still closer to the ideal arrangement. Rule 4c.

Industrial Applications

Figures 41b and 41c are, in a way, parallel to Figure 41. The eye moves freely from the feet (appendages) along the smooth and graceful curves to the tall shaft or column of the primary mass. The turned fillets, introduced at the junction of the appendage and the primary mass, in Figure 41c, have a tendency to check this smooth passage making the arrangement in Figure 41b preferable. The hardware for the costumers is well chosen and in sympathy with the vertical proportions of the design.

With the word "clay" all difficulties in the treatment of appendages vanish. It is by far the easiest medium for the adaptation of the appendage to the primary mass. Covers, handles, and spouts are a few of the more prominent parts falling under this classification.

Appendages in Clay

The process of the designer is to create the primary rectangle, subdivide it into two horizontal subdivisions in accordance with Rule 2a, and proceed to add the desired number of appendages. The result may be suggested by the following illustrations. In Figure 43, Plate 17, the cover is a continuation of the curve of the top of the bowl, Rule 4a; the tops of the handles are continuations of the horizontal line in the top contour of the bowl, while the lower portions of the handles seem to spring or grow from the lower part of the bowl with a tangential curve.

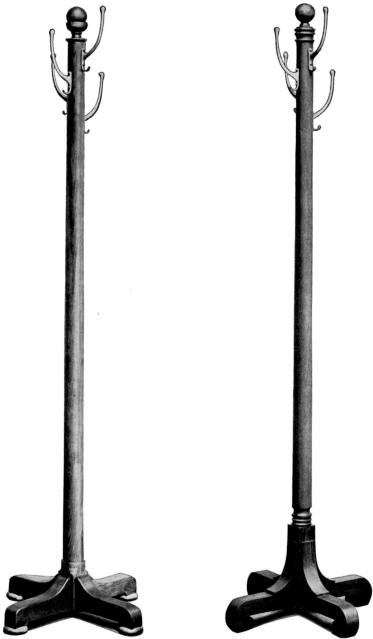

Courtesy of Berkey and Gay

FIGURE 41b   FIGURE 41c

Figure 44 is a horizontal primary mass with the horizontal subdivision in the upper section of that mass. The spout and handle spring naturally from the body and balance each other in proportion, while the cover handle rises smoothly from the primary mass. The horizontal character of the primary mass is consistently carried out in the appendages.

The handle, in Figure 45, leaving the body at a tangent, rises with a long straight curve to turn suddenly and join the pitcher in harmony with its top. The apparent abruptness of the junction is softened by the rounded corners typical of clay construction.

The Rookwood set, Figure 42, represents three similar primary masses. The proportionate ratios and the horizontal subdivisions are the same throughout. The handle for the teapot has been curved in the center to give variety to the handle. This variation is a difficult thing to manage without consequent loss of unity as by this variation Rule 4a is violated. One thing may be said in its favor. It brings the hand closer to the spout and thus supports the pouring weight. But the unusual in design is to be discouraged until sufficient skill in simple designing has been acquired.

In designing handle appendages for clay, they should be so placed that they readily control the weight of the material in the container and afford room for the fingers. Thus, it is better to have the larger portion of the handle opening at the top of the primary mass. The spout in all instances should continue sufficiently high to allow the container to be filled to its full capacity without danger of the contents running out of the spout. The glaze runs into rounded corners much more freely than into square ones, hence it is preferable to use rounded corners wherever possible.

It is the unexpected curve that is welcome in all designing, provided it supports the structure and conforms to established rules. After completing a design involving appendages it should be checked from three points of view; (1) service, (2) unity between the primary mass and the appendages, and (3) variety of curvature. On this last point it is needless to say that compass curves are not desirable except in rounding small corners or in using fillets. It is well known that compass curves are difficult to assimilate into pleasing tangential effects. They are inclined to be monotonous and regular with a

APPENDAGES INDICATED
BY · A · INCLUDE LIDS ·
SPOUTS AND HANDLES ·

A VARIATION OF THE
SYMMETRICAL HANDLE ·
SEE TEXT ·

FIG · 42 · INCLUDES THREE PIECES ·
NOTE THE SIMILARITY OF THE
PRIMARY MASSES ·

CONTINUITY OF
CURVATURE

NOTE THE RELATION
BETWEEN THE STRAI-
GHT LINE OF THE HAN -
DLE TOP AND THE TOP
OF THE BOWL · NOTE
THE TANGENTIAL UNION
OF THE LOWER END OF
HANDLE AND BOWL ·

FIG · 43 ·

FIG · 45 ·

FIG · 44 ·

EXAMPLES OF APPENDAGES IN CLASS 2
(POTTERY) ADDED TO THE PRIMARY MASS FOR
UTILITARIAN PURPOSES · THE PLASTICITY OF
CLAY ALLOWS A PERFECT TANGENTIAL UNION WITH THE BODY

PLATE 17

"made by the thousand" appearance to them. One should trust to freehand sweeps, drawn freely with a full arm movement when possible. All curves should spring naturally from the primary mass. Blackboard drawing is excellent practice for the muscles used in this type of designing. In a short time it will be found possible to produce the useful long, rather flat curve with its sudden turn (the curve of force) that will make the compass curve tame and commonplace by comparison.

Figures 55, 56, and 57, Plate 18, show the close bond between the appearance of the appendage in clay, and the one in metal. While it is technically more difficult to adapt metal to the rules governing appendages than is the case with clay, the final results are, in most instances, equally pleasing to the eye.

In most of the figures showing examples in metal, the appendages have to be secured to the primary mass by screws, rivets, or solder, whereas in clay they may be moulded *into* the primary mass. This tends to secure a more unified appearance; but in metal, the junction of the handle and the primary mass is often made a decorative feature of the design and gives added interest and variety to the project.

The simple primary mass, Figure 58, has a horizontal space division in the lower portion of the mass. This point of variation of the contour has been used in the primary masses in Figures 55, 56, and 57, also as the starting point of that dominant appendage, the handle. Springing tangentially from the body, it rises in a straight line of extreme value in service, then with a slight turn it parallels and joins the top of the bowl, thus fulfilling the design functions of an appendage from both points of service and beauty. The spout and lid, Figure 55, may be likewise analyzed.

The points of tangency, in Figure 54, become a decorative feature of the design. The handles in the parts of the fire set, Figures 48 and 49, offer different problems. It is difficult to analyze the latter figures to determine the appendages as they are in such thorough unity with the handles and are practically subdivisions of the primary mass. But referring to the rule stating the fact that the appendages are subordinated to and attached to the primary mass, it may justly be stated that the shovel portion of the design may

Freehand Curves

Appendages in Metal

Tangential Junctions

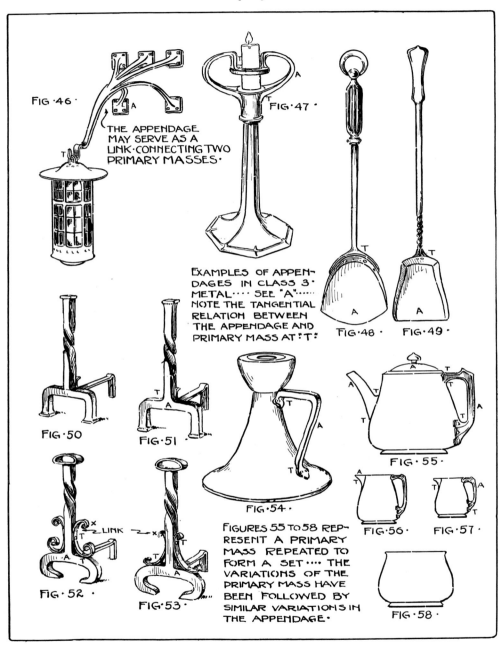

FIG·46·

THE APPENDAGE
MAY SERVE AS A
LINK·CONNECTING TWO
PRIMARY MASSES·

FIG·47·

EXAMPLES OF APPEN-
DAGES IN CLASS 3·
METAL···· SEE "A"·····
NOTE THE TANGENTIAL
RELATION BETWEEN
THE APPENDAGE AND
PRIMARY MASS AT ∶T∶

FIG·48· FIG·49·

FIG·50 FIG·51

LINK

FIG·52· FIG·53·

FIG·54·

FIG·55·

FIG·56· FIG·57·

FIGURES 55 TO 58 REP-
RESENT A PRIMARY
MASS REPEATED TO
FORM A SET···· THE
VARIATIONS OF THE
PRIMARY MASS HAVE
BEEN FOLLOWED BY
SIMILAR VARIATIONS IN
THE APPENDAGE·

FIG·58·

PLATE 18

legitimately be classed as an appendage. This will explain the need of a curve at the junction points and the feature of the decorative twists in Figure 49. Both designs may be analyzed into three horizontal divisions.

The andirons, Figures 50 to 53, illustrate interesting transitions in wrought iron from the primary mass to the appendage. The vertical shaft of wrought iron has been treated as a primary mass while the feet may be classed as appendages. In Figure 50 we have an example of a frankly square junction point. Figure 51 discloses a weld with rounded corners, forming a more pleasing junction than does the abrupt angle of Figure 50. This conforms to Rule 4b. The appendage legs echo or repeat the vertical lines of the primary mass and there is consequently a sense of unity between them.

Andiron Design

In Figure 52 the appendage foot is curved, and the primary mass has a similar curve on the top of the vertical column to apply Rule 4c to repeat the curve. The small links at X indicate an attempt to make the junction point more pleasing to the eye, but the link is too large to accomplish the desired result successfully. In Figure 53 the links have been materially reduced in size and in the amount of curvature. In this example the eye goes unhampered from appendage to primary or back again, without perceptible interruption and the unity of the mass, seriously threatened in Figure 52, is restored in Figure 53.

In Figure 46 there is an example of a link becoming large enough to be classed as an appendage connecting two primary masses, *e.g.*, the lantern and the wall. Under these conditions, one end of the appendage harmonizes with the lantern and the other end with the wall. Figure 47 shows a cast brass candlestick which is an excellent example, from the Studio, of tangential junction.

Clay may readily stand as the most adaptable material for appendages, with metal ranking second, and wood third. The grain of wood seems to interfere with the tangential junction of the appendage and primary mass. Appendages of wood are, however, quite necessary at times. Their use is merely a matter of lessening the contrast of conflicting lines in an addition of this nature.

Influence of Tools and Materials

The band and bracket saws are required in many instances to construct the connecting link between opposing masses of wood.

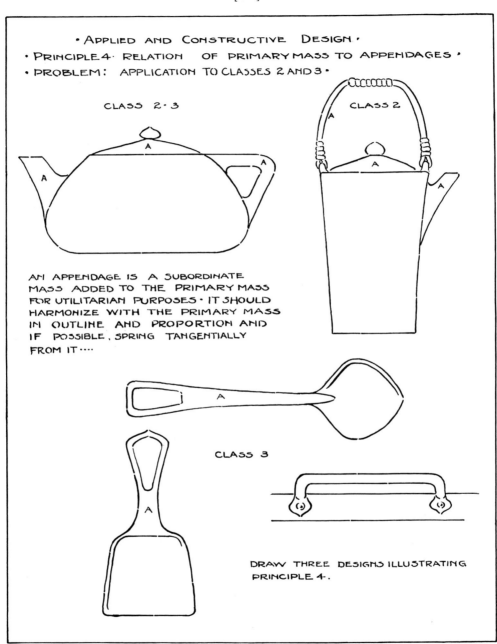

· APPLIED AND CONSTRUCTIVE DESIGN ·
· PRINCIPLE 4· RELATION OF PRIMARY MASS TO APPENDAGES ·
· PROBLEM: APPLICATION TO CLASSES 2 AND 3 ·

CLASS 2·3

CLASS 2

AN APPENDAGE IS A SUBORDINATE
MASS ADDED TO THE PRIMARY MASS
FOR UTILITARIAN PURPOSES · IT SHOULD
HARMONIZE WITH THE PRIMARY MASS
IN OUTLINE AND PROPORTION AND
IF POSSIBLE, SPRING TANGENTIALLY
FROM IT ····

CLASS 3

DRAW THREE DESIGNS ILLUSTRATING
PRINCIPLE 4.

PLATE 19

Hand building or casting is the means used to construct the append-ages in plastic materials. Appendages in cement are seen in the uprights for cement seats and are generally translated into the primary mass by means of mouldings or curves.

Forging or thin and raised metal construction affords many examples of the adaptability of material in constructing appendages. Rivets form decorative features at the junction points and should be placed with great care and relation to the decoration and the point of tangency.

INSTRUCTION SHEET FOR CLASS PRESENTATION

The typical views to be used in classroom work, with the ordinary range of problems, are shown on Plate 19. These typical views should be supplemented by dimensions, cross sections, and other views whenever necessary. Wood construction has been omitted from this sheet, but its development in design is quite similar to the steps indicated in the summary.

SUMMARY OF DESIGN STEPS

(*a*) Draw the primary rectangle.

(*b*) Subdivide the rectangle into two or three horizontal and, if necessary, vertical divisions.

(*c*) Estimate the dimensions of the appendage necessary to perform the desired service in the best manner.

(*d*) If the appendage is a handle, place it in such a position that it not only appears to but actually does support the weight of the primary mass.

(*e*) Complete the contour curves of the primary mass based upon the horizontal division which acts as a unit of measurement or a turning point.

(*f*) Join the appendages to the primary mass by means of tangential curves.

(*g*) Establish unity between the primary mass and the appendages by applying Rules 4a, 4b, and 4c.

(*h*) Dimension and otherwise prepare the drawing for shop use. See Plate 26.

SUGGESTED PROBLEMS

Design a sugar bowl, cream pitcher, and teapot. Consider them as different members of one set.

Design a sideboard 3 feet 3 inches high with plate rack, the design to contain two vertical and two horizontal divisions exclusive of the appendage.

SUMMARY OF RULES

Rule 4a. *The appendage should be designed in unity with, and proportionately related to, the vertical or horizontal character of the primary mass, but subordinated to it.*

Rule 4b. *The appendage should have the appearance of flowing smoothly and, if possible, tangentially from the primary mass.*

Rule 4c. *The appendage should, if possible, echo or repeat some lines similar in character and direction to those of the primary mass.*

REVIEW QUESTIONS

1. State the nature and use of the appendage.
2. What is the relation of the size of the appendage to the size of the primary mass?
3. How should the appendage be attached to the primary mass?
4. How does Rule 4c help to secure unity between the appendage and the primary mass?
5. Are compass curves permissible in appendage design?
6. State influence of tools and materials upon appendage design.

CHAPTER VI

ENRICHMENT OF THE CONTOURS OR OUTLINES
OF DESIGNS IN WOOD

With this chapter we introduce contour enrichment, the second major division of industrial arts design.

A critic of furniture designed by the average manual arts student has stated frankly that while it might have been honestly constructed it was, in the first place, too heavy for a woman to move about the house and, in the second place, it represented a decidedly uneconomical use of that valuable material, wood. That there is a basis in fact for this statement cannot be denied. Is it true, then, that furniture must of necessity be clumsy and heavy when it is sufficiently simplified in constructive processes for school work? We may say emphatically, "No!"

Need and Value of Enrichment

One may correct the proportions of an object and reduce the size of the materials in it to a minimum but still fail to secure the desirable elements of lightness and interest. The object may still *look* heavy and remain a box-like structure void of the grace synonymous with the best in design. It is, however, possible to correct the clumsy and heavy appearances by imparting to the design elements of grace and lightness. Two methods may be used, singly or together: (1) Enrichment of the Functional Outlines or Contours; (2) Surface Enrichment sometimes called Space Filling. These may be roughly classified respectively as three and two dimension enrichment.

The first, or outline enrichment, concerns itself with the structural lines. As all designing processes should start with the structure, it will be our policy to do so. The present chapter will deal only with enrichment of outlines of wood projects.

Contour Enrichment

Rule 5a. *Outline enrichment should be subordinated to and support the structure.*

Rule 5b. *Outline enrichment should add grace, lightness, and variety to the design.*

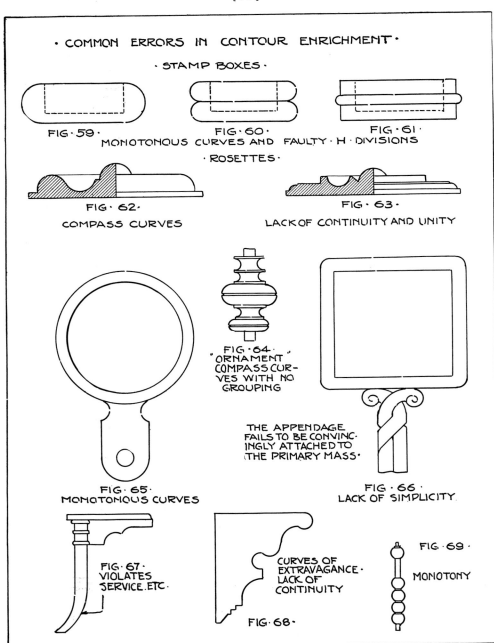

· COMMON ERRORS IN CONTOUR ENRICHMENT ·

· STAMP BOXES ·

FIG · 59 ·   FIG · 60 ·   FIG · 61 ·

MONOTONOUS CURVES AND FAULTY · H · DIVISIONS

· ROSETTES ·

FIG · 62 ·   FIG · 63 ·

COMPASS CURVES   LACK OF CONTINUITY AND UNITY

FIG · 64 ·
" ORNAMENT "
COMPASS CUR-
VES WITH NO
GROUPING

THE APPENDAGE
FAILS TO BE CONVINC-
INGLY ATTACHED TO
THE PRIMARY MASS·

FIG · 65 ·
MONOTONOUS CURVES

FIG · 66 ·
LACK OF SIMPLICITY.

FIG · 67 ·
VIOLATES
SERVICE . ETC .

CURVES OF
EXTRAVAGANCE ·
LACK OF
CONTINUITY

FIG · 68 ·

FIG · 69 ·

MONOTONY

PLATE 19a

It is the purpose of enrichment to add to the problem (1) grace; (2) lightness; (3) variety; (4) unity. If it is applied in a proper manner it should likewise add to the apparent structural strength. We should carefully guard the design, therefore, against (1) enrichment that has a tendency to obscure or destroy the structural lines; in other words, enrichment that is not subordinated to the structure, and (2) enrichment that adds nothing to the structure by its application; that is, one which does not increase either the apparent strength or the beauty of the object.

As an example of this first point, the turned candlestick with the candle supported by a stack of turned balls alternating with tauri or thin discs tends to obscure completely the sense of support. Again, the landscape gardener feels that he is violating a fundamental principle in design if by planting vines to grow around a building, he obscures the foundation, and the roof appears, consequently, to rest on and be supported by the stems and leaves of the vines. Thus it is seen that the eye registers a sense of structural weakness when the main supports of an object disappear and are no longer to be traced under the enrichment.

Under the second point falls the indiscriminate placing of unrelated objects in the contour enrichment. Naturalistic objects similar to the claw foot and the human head, for example, should give way to natural curves that add to the appearance of total strength. Where are we to find these curves suited to our purpose?

Up to this point emphasis has been placed upon straight and curved lines immediately connected with pure service. For grace and lightness it is necessary to depart at times from the rigidity of straight lines. To understand the character of this departure let us consider a simple bracket as a support for a shelf.

This bracket acts as a link, connecting a vertical wall or leg with a horizontal member or shelf. A bracket shaped like a 45-degree triangle, Figure 10, page 24, gives one the sense of clumsiness. If the feeling of grace is to be imparted the eye must move smoothly along the outline of the bracket, giving one a sensation of aesthetic pleasure. A curved line will produce this effect more completely than will a straight line. One must likewise get the feeling that the curve of the bracket is designed to support the shelf.

Purpose of Contour Enrichment

Requirements of Contour Enrichment

Valuable Curves for Outline Enrichment

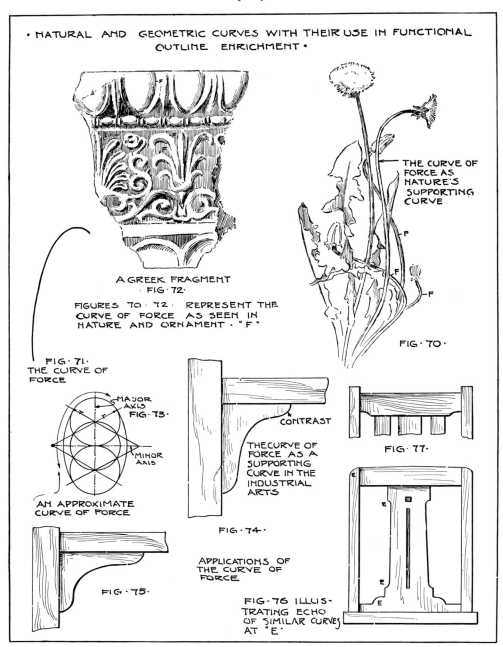

• NATURAL AND GEOMETRIC CURVES WITH THEIR USE IN FUNCTIONAL OUTLINE ENRICHMENT •

A GREEK FRAGMENT
· FIG · 72 ·

FIGURES 70 · 72 · REPRESENT THE CURVE OF FORCE AS SEEN IN NATURE AND ORNAMENT · ".F"

THE CURVE OF FORCE AS NATURE'S SUPPORTING CURVE

FIG · 70 ·

FIG · 71·
THE CURVE OF FORCE

MAJOR AXIS
FIG · 73 ·
MINOR AXIS

AN APPROXIMATE CURVE OF FORCE

CONTRAST

THE CURVE OF FORCE AS A SUPPORTING CURVE IN THE INDUSTRIAL ARTS

FIG · 74 ·

FIG · 77 ·

APPLICATIONS OF THE CURVE OF FORCE

FIG · 75 ·

FIG · 76 ILLUS- TRATING ECHO OF SIMILAR CURVES AT "E·"

PLATE 20

The Curve of Force

Turning to Figure 70, Plate 20, we find that whenever nature desires to support a weight she is inclined to use a peculiar curve seen at *F*. Possibly through continued observation the eye has associated this curve with strength or supporting power. Figure 71 has detailed this curve. It is found to consist of a long, rather flat portion with a quick and sudden turn at its end. The curve is known to designers as the Curve of Force and is most valuable in all forms of enrichment. Designers even in early ages used it in some form as will be noted from the fragment of Greek sculpture in Figure 72. Its beauty rests in its variety. A circle has little interest due to its rather monotonous curvature. The eye desires variety and the curve of force administers to this need and gives a sense of satisfaction. As designers on wood, how are we to utilize this curve for purposes of outline enrichment?

Valuable Curves

For approximate similarity of curvature an ellipse constructed as shown in Figure 73 will be found convenient. By drawing several ellipses of varying sizes upon sheets of tin or zinc, a series of templates of utmost practical value may be formed and used as was done in securing the curves of force in Figures 74 and 75. If the rail or shelf is longer than the post, measured downward from the rail to the floor or to the next shelf, the ellipse should be used with its major axis placed in a horizontal position, Figure 75. If, on the contrary, the post is longer than the shelf the ellipse should have its major axis in a vertical position, Figure 74. Figures 76 and 77 show other instances of the use of the approximate curve of force. Many similar practical applications will occur to the designer.

An Approximate Curve of Force

We have classed the bracket as a link connecting a vertical and horizontal structure. Mouldings may likewise be considered as links connecting similar horizontal or vertical surfaces by bands of graded forms. Inasmuch as they effect the outline they are considered in this chapter. As the mouldings are to assist the eye to make the jump from one surface to another by easy steps, the position from which the mouldings are to be seen determines to some extent their design.

Mouldings

Figure 78 shows the relation of the spectator to three types of mouldings at *A*, *B*, and *C*. The top or *crown* (*A*) is to be seen from

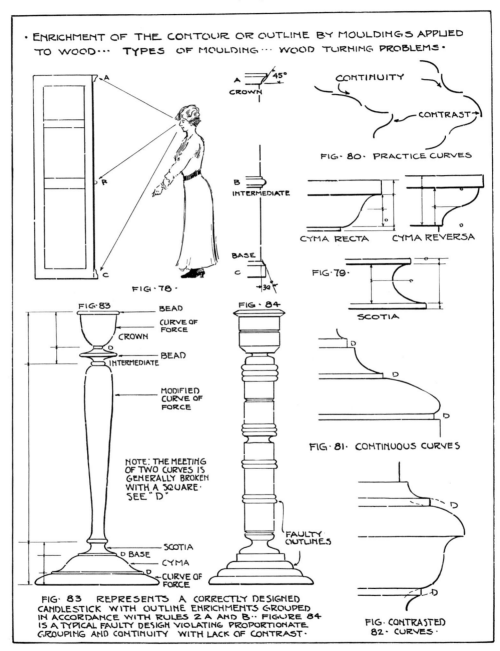

• ENRICHMENT OF THE CONTOUR OR OUTLINE BY MOULDINGS APPLIED TO WOOD··· TYPES OF MOULDING··· WOOD TURNING PROBLEMS·

A 45° CROWN

CONTINUITY

CONTRAST

FIG· 80· PRACTICE CURVES

A CROWN

B INTERMEDIATE

BASE C

CYMA RECTA   CYMA REVERSA

FIG· 79·

SCOTIA

FIG· 78·

FIG· 83   BEAD
CURVE OF FORCE
CROWN
BEAD
INTERMEDIATE

MODIFIED CURVE OF FORCE

NOTE: THE MEETING OF TWO CURVES IS GENERALLY BROKEN WITH A SQUARE. SEE "D".

SCOTIA
D BASE
CYMA
CURVE OF FORCE

FIG· 84

FAULTY OUTLINES

FIG· 81· CONTINUOUS CURVES

FIG· 82· CONTRASTED CURVES·

FIG· 83   REPRESENTS A CORRECTLY DESIGNED CANDLESTICK WITH OUTLINE ENRICHMENTS GROUPED IN ACCORDANCE WITH RULES 2 A AND B·· FIGURE 84 IS A TYPICAL FAULTY DESIGN VIOLATING PROPORTIONATE GROUPING AND CONTINUITY WITH LACK OF CONTRAST·

PLATE 21

below. On a large project the angle of the mouldings with the body of the object should be approximately 45 degrees. The *intermediate* moulding (*B*) is lighter than the crown and forms a transitional link that may be seen from either above or below. The lower or *base* moulding (*C*) is the widest member of the group as demanded by our sense of stability. It is seen from above. Both for sanitary and structural reasons it projects but slightly from the base. With this grouping in mind it is needless to say that a faulty moulding is one, some portion of which, hidden by intervening moulding, cannot be seen by the spectator.

Mouldings
(Continued)

Architectural design and history have formulated a series of curves, geometric in character, that are regarded as standards in the Industrial Arts. Some of the more prominent curves with their constructions are shown in Figure 79. The horizontal divisions are analyzed in accordance with Rules 2a and 2b. It is noticed that the Scotia possesses a curve having the shape of the curve of force, while the two Cymas are saved from monotonous division by means of their reversed curves, illustrating the contrast of direction. The curves of Figure 80 are excellent lines for freehand practice in designing mouldings and will develop the principle of continuity of curvature or the smooth transition of one curve into the next.

To keep this continuity from the monotony of a Marcel Wave it is customary to break continuous curves by a fillet such as a straight line as shown at *D*, Figures 81, 82, and 83. When the desired outside diameter has been reached, contrast of direction is necessary and pleasing as a return, Figure 82. A glance at the curves so far considered will quickly determine whether they are fitted for the crown, intermediate or base mouldings. A curve should join a straight line with either a tangential or right angle junction, which makes for positiveness in contour expression.

Continuity and Contrast

Application of these curves to outline enrichment for wood turning projects is to be governed by a strict adherence to Rules 2a or 2b, otherwise confusion and lack of unity will result. Figure 83 shows a major grouping under Rule 2b with the subdivisions and minor curves arranged under Rules 2a and 2b. Figure 84 shows a disregard for rules and the result is an undesirable monotony of contour. If smooth and even continuity of curvature is given

Grouping of Curves

FIGURE 85.— Modern Candlesticks

FIGURE 86.— Modern Book Trough

considerable thought, together with that for systematic grouping and variety, a pleasing result from wood turning (a much abused but pleasing form of outline enrichment) may be secured. Figures 85 and 86 are illustrations from the industrial field with moulding curves grouped, following and supporting the structural lines of the object. The columns in Figure 86 might, however, be advantageously reversed.

Materials

Large objects designed to be seen from a distance require larger space divisions for their mouldings than do small objects seen from a nearer point. Material affects the curve somewhat. Smaller mouldings are more suited to the expensive woods like mahogany while larger curves may be used in pine or oak.

Evolution of Enriched Outline Design

We now have at our command a number of interesting and serviceable curves suited to the material. Plate 22 is a sheet of applications. Figures 87 to 94 deal with the book-rack end and in this, as in the initial chapter, architecture is referred to as the source for many laws of industrial design. It has seemed wise to illustrate some of these important parallels as follows:

We will assume the type of joint construction of the book-rack end as settled and the question of enrichment to be under consideration.

Figure 87 is a simple primary mass without enrichment. It is comparable to the plain box-like structure with monotonous outline and without interest. The eye follows the outline in the direction of the arrows, pausing at the square corners, which interrupt a free movement by a harsh right angle. The base (an appendage) repeats in each instance the lines of the primary mass.

Figure 88. Round corners, by freeing the design from the right angles, accelerate the eye movement and give a sense of added interest and grace to the contour.

Figure 89. The cornice of a building suggests a similar arrangement which may be added to the primary mass. It adds the element of contrast of direction and variety of widths.

Figure 90. The main primary mass of a building with two equal appendages will suggest the enrichment of the outline in sympathy with three vertical divisions. Rule 3b. The rounded corners again assist the eye to travel freely around the contours, thus giving a sense of unity to the entire form.

Variations

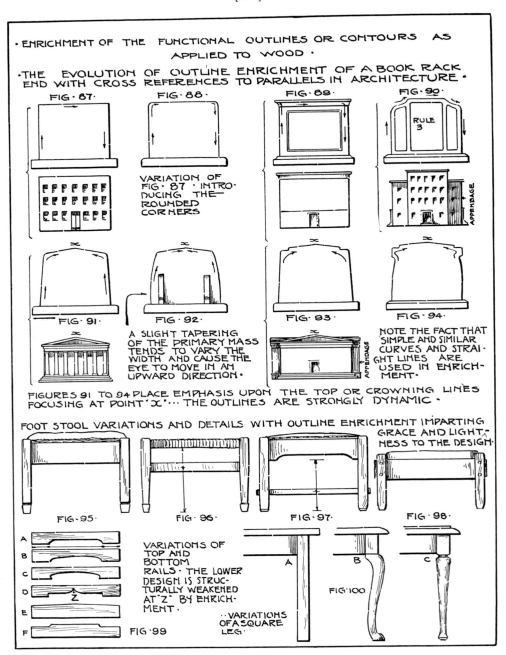

· ENRICHMENT OF THE FUNCTIONAL OUTLINES OR CONTOURS AS APPLIED TO WOOD ·

· THE EVOLUTION OF OUTLINE ENRICHMENT OF A BOOK RACK END WITH CROSS REFERENCES TO PARALLELS IN ARCHITECTURE ·

FIG · 87 ·

FIG · 88 ·

FIG · 89 ·

FIG · 90 ·

RULE 3

VARIATION OF FIG · 87 · INTRODUCING THE ROUNDED CORNERS

APPENDAGE.

FIG · 91 ·

FIG · 92 ·

FIG · 93 ·

FIG · 94 ·

A SLIGHT TAPERING OF THE PRIMARY MASS TENDS TO VARY THE WIDTH AND CAUSE THE EYE TO MOVE IN AN UPWARD DIRECTION ·

APPENDAGE

NOTE THE FACT THAT SIMPLE AND SIMILAR CURVES AND STRAIGHT LINES ARE USED IN ENRICHMENT ·

FIGURES 91 TO 94 PLACE EMPHASIS UPON THE TOP OR CROWNING LINES FOCUSING AT POINT "X" ··· THE OUTLINES ARE STRONGLY DYNAMIC ·

FOOT STOOL VARIATIONS AND DETAILS WITH OUTLINE ENRICHMENT IMPARTING GRACE AND LIGHTNESS TO THE DESIGN ·

FIG · 95 ·

FIG · 96 ·

FIG · 97 ·

FIG · 98 ·

A
B
C
D
E
F

VARIATIONS OF TOP AND BOTTOM RAILS · THE LOWER DESIGN IS STRUCTURALLY WEAKENED AT "Z" BY ENRICHMENT ·

FIG · 99 ·

A

B

C

FIG · 100

·· VARIATIONS OF A SQUARE LEG ·

PLATE 22

FIG·102 EXTRAVAGANT
CURVES· DISREGARDING
ECONOMY OF MATERIAL··
IT IS CLUMSY AND LACK-
ING DIVISIONAL HOR-
IZONTAL GROUPING (2)

FIG·101 REPRESENTS CONFUSED OUTLINE ENRICH-
MENT·· THE CURVES ARE UNRELATED TO AND DESTROY
THE STRUCTURAL LINES··· USELESS SURFACE OR-
NAMENT TENDS TO ACCENTUATE THE OTHERWISE
FAULTILY ENRICHED OUTLINE···

FIGURES 101 and 102

Figure 91. The pediment of a Greek temple with the interest
centered at the top of the pediment (x) causes a similar concentration
of interest in the book-rack end. The slight inclination of the sides
supplies variety of widths. The architect considers an object with
the interest centered in this manner in the upper portion, as possessing
more individuality than a motive with purely horizontal lines
across the top boundary.

FOLDING SCREEN.

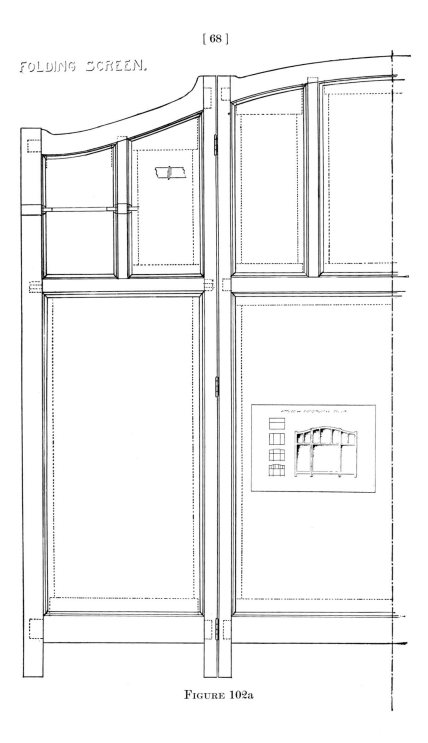

FIGURE 102a

FIGURE 103.— A Modern Telephone Stand and Stool

Courtesy of Berkey and Gay

FIGURE 104.— Modern Chair

Figure 92. In this figure the curved inclination facilitates the upward movement of the eye, at the same time supplying variety of width.

Figure 93. The addition of an appendage to the outline of the Greek temple suggests a slight drop or variation in the top edge of the book-rack end which gives increased interest and grace through variety.

Figure 94. Contrast of direction is supplied in this suggestion but it is questionable whether we are adding much to the interest by the corner.

FIGURE 105.— A Modern Serving Table

Figures 95 to 98 are variations of one theme, the foot stool, and Figure 99 adds suggestive designs for rails. *D* in Figure 99 shows the enrichment line cut to a depth which threatens the structural value of the rail. This is corrected in Figure 103. Figure 100 is an application of the curve of force to a chair leg *B*, with other possi-

Figure 105a

Courtesy of Berkey and Gay

FIGURE 106.— Sheraton Table

bilities at *A* and *C*. Numerous applications of the varied curves under consideration are found throughout this sheet.

Before closing with enriched outlines it is well to consider flagrant violations of this enrichment now on the market. Figure 101 shows a typical example of complete lack of unity and simplicity. It is a type of design often associated with cheaply constructed furniture. It is an ornate parody on outline enrichment. The curves of extravagance are well shown in Figure 102 where large bulbous curves with no systematic grouping combine disastrous waste of material with lack of grace or lightness. It is excellent practice to redesign such examples as those shown in Figures 101 and 102 with special reference to Rule 5c.

Rule 5c. *Outline enrichment, by its similarity, should give a sense of oneness or unity to the design, binding divergent members together.*

· INSTRUCTION SHEET · · CONTOUR ENRICHMENT
OF WOOD ·

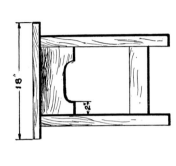

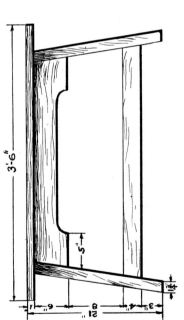

DRAWN AND DESIGNED
BY JEANNETTE E · FITCH
U · OF · W

PLATE 23

Illustrations 103 to 106 are typical forms of present day outline enrichment. Limitations of space will not permit reference to the use of Period furniture. Sheraton and Hepplewhite designs are most adaptable for school uses as may be seen by comparing the Sheraton desk (Figure 106) with the foot stool in Figure 96.

INSTRUCTION SHEET

Figure 83 and Plates 22 and 23 are indicative of what might be obtained from a class. The problem represented on Plate 23 is advantageously colored with the intended stain and with a small section of side wall and trim visible. See Chapter 16, Figures 458 to 463. Figure 102a shows the method of enlarging a design into a full size working drawing for shop purposes.

SUMMARY OF DESIGN STEPS

(a) Draw the primary rectangle.
(b) Subdivide the rectangle into vertical and horizontal divisions.
(c) Determine parts to be treated by contour enrichment.
(d) Determine method suited to the project: wood turning, moulding, etc.
(e) Group the wood turning curves under a definite system included under Rules 2a and 2b. Group the mouldings under crown, intermediate, and base classifications. Add this enrichment to the primary mass or make other simple variations that will not destroy the unity of the project.
(f) Dimension and otherwise prepare the drawing for shop use.
(g) Construct the project.

Note.— If the designer is not properly equipped to prepare his own mouldings, he should consult moulding catalogs or the stock of some local lumber company.

ADDITIONAL SUGGESTED PROBLEMS

Design a wood pedestal with the curves grouped into three horizontal divisions.

Design a hall table 2 feet 10 inches high and add simple contour enrichment.

SUMMARY OF RULES

Rule 5a. Outline enrichment should be subordinated to and support the structure.

Rule 5b. Outline enrichment should add grace, lightness, and variety to the design.

Rule 5c. Outline enrichment, by its similarity, should give a sense of oneness or unity to the design, binding divergent members together.

REVIEW QUESTIONS

1. State nature and need of enrichment.
2. What two forms of enrichment are commonly used in industrial arts design?
3. What four qualities are added to industrial design by contour enrichment?
4. What disturbing elements should be guarded against in the application of contour enrichment?
5. Describe the curve of force and its function in the contour enrichment of wood.
6. What are mouldings? Name three types of mouldings, their positions with relation to the eye level, and some curves used in their design.
7. Give examples of curves of continuity and contrast. By what means should two contrasting curves be separated?
8. How should a curve join a straight line?
9. Explain the grouping of contour curves in wood turning projects similar to a round leg or candlestick.
10. Present five designs for book-racks, enriched by changes of the contour. Give architectural cross references for each design.
11. Present three well designed table or chair legs and top and bottom rails and assemble one of these in a design.

Chapter VII

ENRICHMENT OF THE CONTOURS OR OUTLINES OF DESIGNS IN CLAY

In the medium we are now about to consider there is a tendency for the enthusiastic beginner to over-elaborate the outline into meaningless forms. This possibly is due to the ease with which clay is manipulated. It would be well then to ask two questions before starting with the work of enriching the simple structure. First, why should it be enriched — is there a positive gain by so doing? Second, (if the decision is favorable to enrichment) where should it be enriched? Let us co-ordinate the parts to assist in this process. **Need of Enrichment**

Rule 5d. *Parts of one design differing in function should differ in appearance but be co-ordinated with the entire design.* As a suggestion to guide one in enriching an object it is necessary to consider that parts differing in function may differ in appearance, but as members of one family they should still be related to the whole. For example, a spout, handle, and lid may differ in design from that of the body of a pitcher because they differ from it in function. Again, the rim and foot of a vase may be slightly changed or individually accented because of their respective duties. The base and holder of a candlestick may vary in design from the central part or handle, as each has a special function to perform. This rule of the change of appearance with the change of functional service (Rule 5d), is found throughout architectural design. The variation in design in the base, shaft, and capital of a column is possibly one of the most common examples. While differing in function they still *must have unity and "hold together."* **Parts Differing in Function** **Unity**

These functional parts of one design, differing in service rendered, form centers of construction and may receive emphasis in outline enrichment. Corners and terminal points are likewise available for decoration and will be discussed at length later.

FIGURE 107.— Clay Outline Enrichment in the Rookwood Potteries

Enrichment in clay and metal generally means a substitution of curved for straight lines in the enriched portions of the design. These curves have the ability to impart grace, lightness, and variety to an object provided they are based upon constructive features of the problem. They must have a unit of measurement and must likewise be appropriate to the material. It is therefore necessary to deal with clay in this chapter and follow with a consideration of metal in another chapter.

In Figures 109 to 123, Plate 24, we have a number of examples of variation of practically the same primary enclosing rectangle. Figure 108 represents a "squarely" proportioned circular bowl lacking both refinement of proportion and enrichment. Figure 109 has added refinement of proportions. Figures 110 and 111 have introduced an outline enriched to the extent of a simple curve. The base is the dominant width in the first, and the top dominates in width in the second. The outline in Figure 112, while similar to 110 for a portion of its length, departs at a stated point and by curving in toward the base supplies more variety to the contour. We have already said that this outline curve should have a unit of measurement and by referring to Rules 2a and 2b we are able to formulate the following:

Rule 5e. *In cylindrical forms outline curves with a vertical tendency should have their turning points or units of measurement in accordance with the horizontal divisions of Rules 2a and 2b.* Figures 112 and 113 have as their unit of measurement two horizontal spaces formed in accordance with Rule 2a, while Figures 116 and 117 have still more variety by the addition of a compound curve with its turning points or unit of measurement based upon Rule 2b. Figures 114 and 115 with outlines similar to those in Figures 112 and 113, respectively, have an additional enrichment, the foot and rim accentuation.

Unit of
Measurement
for Curves
in Outline
Enrichment

The new element of enrichment consists of accenting by adding to the design a modeled rim and a base or foot, as it is technically known. This not only strengthens the structure at these two functional points but, by adding a small section of shadow, it tends to break up the surface, Figure 127, and add to the variety of enrichment. Figures 124 to 127 show the building processes connected with this interesting and constructive addition.

Accentuation
of Functional
Parts in Clay

Figures 116 to 119 show variations of the preceding figures while Figures 120 to 123 introduce the appendages to preceding figures. As in the designing of all appendages, discussed in Chapter V, it is the designer's intention to balance spout and handle to avoid a one-sided or top-heavy appearance.

Appendages

One of the principal difficulties that confronts the amateur designer is the failure to secure variety while retaining unity. This is largely due to a lack of ideas upon the subject and a marked lack of systematic development of one theme.

Attention is directed to the diagram in the lower portion of Plate 24. The idea is to start with some simple form in columns *A*, *B*, *C*, *D*, *E*, *F*, Figure 128. Figure 129 introduces *two* horizontal divisions. Rule 2a. The *black* portion is the dominant section.

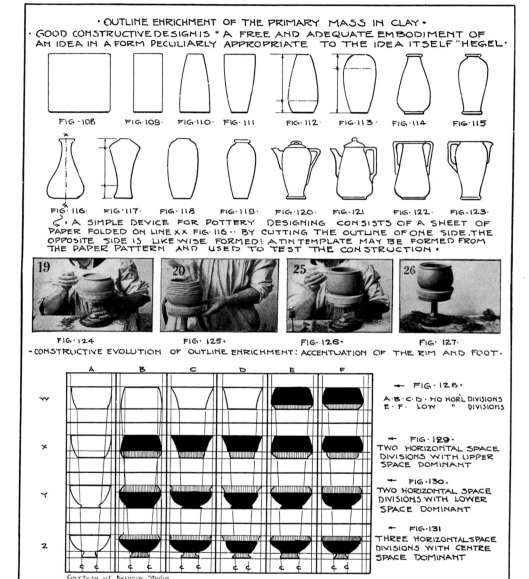

· OUTLINE ENRICHMENT OF THE PRIMARY MASS IN CLAY ·
· GOOD CONSTRUCTIVE DESIGN IS " A FREE AND ADEQUATE EMBODIMENT OF AN IDEA IN A FORM PECULIARLY APPROPRIATE TO THE IDEA ITSELF "HEGEL·

FIG·108   FIG·109   FIG·110   FIG·111   FIG·112   FIG·113   FIG·114   FIG·115

FIG·116   FIG·117·   FIG·118   FIG·119   FIG·120   FIG·121   FIG·122·   FIG·123·

⚲ · A SIMPLE DEVICE FOR POTTERY DESIGNING CONSISTS OF A SHEET OF PAPER FOLDED ON LINE XX FIG·116 ·· BY CUTTING THE OUTLINE OF ONE SIDE, THE OPPOSITE SIDE IS LIKEWISE FORMED; A TIN TEMPLATE MAY BE FORMED FROM THE PAPER PATTERN AND USED TO TEST THE CONSTRUCTION ·

FIG·124   FIG·125·   FIG·126·   FIG·127·

· CONSTRUCTIVE EVOLUTION OF OUTLINE ENRICHMENT: ACCENTUATION OF THE RIM AND FOOT·

← FIG·128·
A·B·C·D· NO HORL DIVISIONS
E · F· LOW " DIVISIONS

← FIG·129·
TWO HORIZONTAL SPACE DIVISIONS WITH UPPER SPACE DOMINANT

← FIG·130·
TWO HORIZONTAL SPACE DIVISIONS WITH LOWER SPACE DOMINANT

← FIG·131
THREE HORIZONTAL SPACE DIVISIONS WITH CENTRE SPACE DOMINANT

Courtesy of Keramic Studio

ENRICHMENT OF THE SIMPLE FORMS ON LINE "W" BY COMBINING TWO PROCESSES:
1· VARYING THE POSITION AND NUMBER OF THE HORIZONTAL DIVISIONS (RULES 2A AND B) AND
2· BY SYSTEMATICALLY VARYING THE BASE OR FOOT WIDTHS FROM "W" TO "Z" BY MEANS OF THE CONVERGING LINES "C". THE WIDTH AND HEIGHT OF THE PRIMARY MASS IS CONSTANT·

PLATE 24

Notice the change in outlines based upon this division. Figure 130 raises the division point of the two subdivisions into the upper half of the object. This brings out the need of an accented foot which is, however, not of sufficient prominence to be considered as a horizontal spacing. Figure 131 raises the horizontal division points, again causing the introduction of a larger foot and now qualifying it as a division of the whole mass. This then makes our design a three-division problem, Rule 2b, and places it under the restrictions of Rule 5e.

Systematic Development of Outline Enrichment in Clay

The feet of all of the bowls have been systematically decreased in width by the converging lines *C-C* while the tops have been maintained constant in width. By this simple diagram an infinite number of designs may be formed and the choice of selection from the series, thoughtfully exercised, will supply the ideal bowl, ready to be translated into a full size working drawing. It is not the idea, however, to guarantee a perfect design in each one of these divisions as that would be practically impossible, but we have systematically applied a method of determination for stimulating the imagination. A series of articles by F. H. Rhead in the Keramic Studio first suggested the system of development by means of graded rectangles.

Plate 25 shows a further elaboration of the succeeding themes. The candlestick series, Figures 132 to 138, introduces two or three-space division problems with contour turning points at *A*, Rule 5e, and with accented or embryonic feet and rims. The change from the purely functional and unenriched member of Figure 132 through the series shows the enrichment changing slightly to meet the needs of the three functional parts: the base, the handle, and the candle socket. Rule 5d.

Candlesticks

Figure 139 shows a series of illustrations representing variations for containers. The first figure is without enrichment, followed by variations of the outline in the manner already suggested.

Containers

Figure 140 indicates a series of pourers with the least attractive design on the left end. This unsatisfactory design is found, upon analysis, to be due to centrally placed horizontal division violating Rule 2a. The design of the appendages in this series will again be found to conform with the rules in Chapter V. The units of measurement for the curves may be readily ascertained from observation.

Pourers

• OUTLINE ENRICHMENT OF THE PRIMARY MASS IN CLAY WITH METHODS OF SECURING VARIETY •

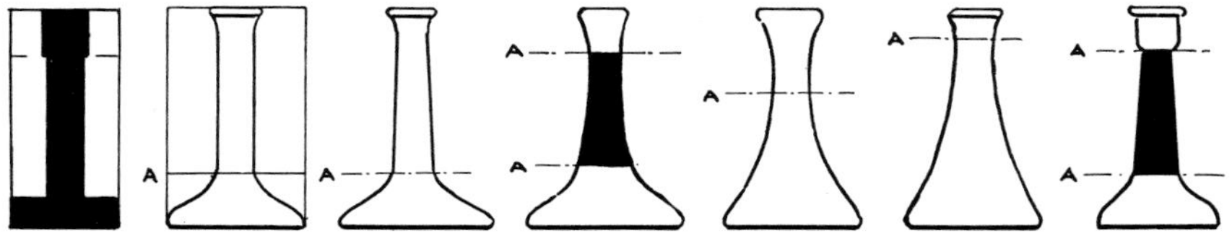

FIG·132·   FIG·133·   FIG·134·   FIG·135·   FIG·136·   FIG·137·   FIG·138·

UNENRICHED CANDLE STICK (FIG·132) WITH SIX POSSIBLE VARIATIONS OF CURVED OUTLINE ENRICHMENT

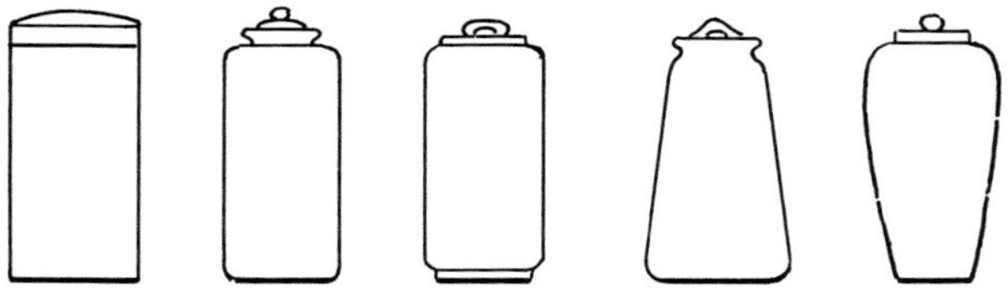

FOUR VARIATIONS OF CONTAINER WITH SLIGHT CHANGE OF PROPORTIONS
FIG· 139·

VARIATIONS OF POURER WITH APPENDAGES
FIG· 140·

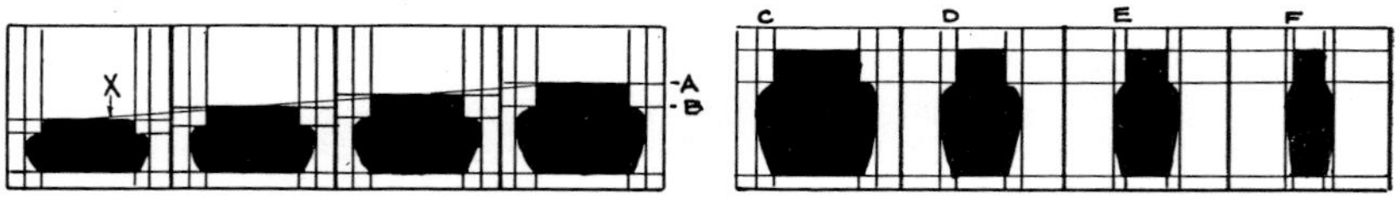

FORMS WITH THE SAME WIDTHS BUT VARYING IN HEIGHT ·

FORMS WITH THE SAME HEIGHT BUT VARYING IN WIDTH

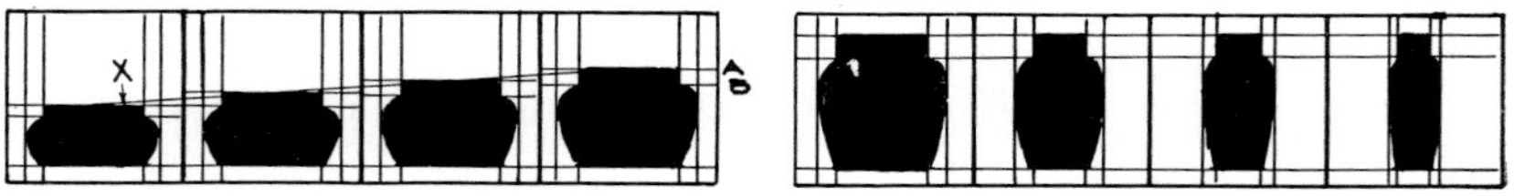

FIG·141· ·HORIZONTAL P·M·   FIG· 142 ·VERTICAL P·M·

FIGURES 141 AND 142 ILLUSTRATE A METHOD OF SYSTEMATICALLY DESIGNING A SERIES OF FORMS SIMILAR IN OUTLINE BUT VARYING IN THE PROPORTIONS OF THE PRIMARY MASSES · SELECTION OF THE MOST PLEASING DESIGN SHOULD BE FOLLOWED BY A FULL SIZE WORKING DRAWING·

PLATE 25

Figure 141 is useful for the following purpose. It is desirable at times to develop a number of similar forms for a set, with a gradually increasing ratio of proportions, either in height or width. Figure 141 shows how the *height* may be increased while maintaining a common width. Notice the gradual proportionate increase of the height of the neck *A-B* as well as that of the body. The line *X* is of the utmost value in ascertaining the height of the intermediate bowls. The eye should now be so trained that the height of the neck *A-B* on the last bowl can be readily proportioned by *eye measurement* to that of the first bowl. A line similar to *X* will give the intermediate points.

Figure 142 varies the *width* in a similar manner. Notice the gradually decreasing distances *C-D-E-F*, the spaces for which may be determined by the eye.

Similarity
with Varying
Primary
Masses

INSTRUCTION SHEET

Plate 26 suggests the sequential progression of steps leading to the potter's working drawing.

SUMMARY OF DESIGN STEPS

(*a*) Draw the primary rectangle.
(*b*) Add limits of functional parts: handle, spout, cover, etc.
(*c*) Establish unit of measurement for primary rectangle contour curves.
(*d*) Design contour of primary mass and add the appendages to it, observing the rules pertaining to appendages and unit of measurement.
(*e*) Dimension and otherwise prepare the drawing for the potter's use. This includes the planning of a working drawing, one-eighth larger in all directions than the preliminary design, to allow for the shrinkage of the clay body. The working drawing should also be in partial sections to show the construction of the interior of the ware.

SUGGESTED PROBLEM

Design a teapot, tea caddy, and cup showing a common unity in contour design. (Plate 82.)

SUMMARY OF RULES

Rule 5d. *Parts of one design differing in function should differ in appearance but be co-ordinated with the entire design.*
Rule 5e. *In cylindrical forms outline curves with a vertical tendency should*

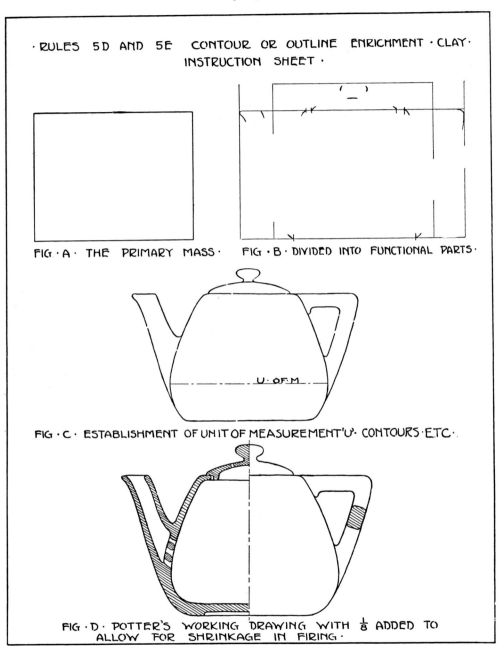

· RULES 5 D AND 5 E · CONTOUR OR OUTLINE ENRICHMENT · CLAY · INSTRUCTION SHEET ·

FIG · A · THE PRIMARY MASS ·   FIG · B · DIVIDED INTO FUNCTIONAL PARTS ·

FIG · C · ESTABLISHMENT OF UNIT OF MEASUREMENT 'U' · CONTOURS · ETC ·

FIG · D · POTTER'S WORKING DRAWING WITH $\frac{1}{8}$ ADDED TO ALLOW FOR SHRINKAGE IN FIRING ·

PLATE 26

have their turning points or units of measurement in accordance with the
horizontal divisions of Rules 2a and 2b.

REVIEW QUESTIONS

1. Give and illustrate the rule governing the change in the appearance of
   the design with the change of functional service.
2. What is the aesthetic value of curves in outline enrichment?
3. Correlate the rule governing the unit of measurement for vertical contour
   curves with the rules controlling horizontal divisions.
4. Show, by a diagram, the method of systematically varying the contours of
   circular forms: (*a*) by changing the horizontal divisions; (*b*) by varying
   the proportion of the primary mass.
5. What is the value of accenting the functional parts in clay design?

Courtesy of James Milliken University

FIGURE 142a.— Outline and Surface Enrichment in College Pottery

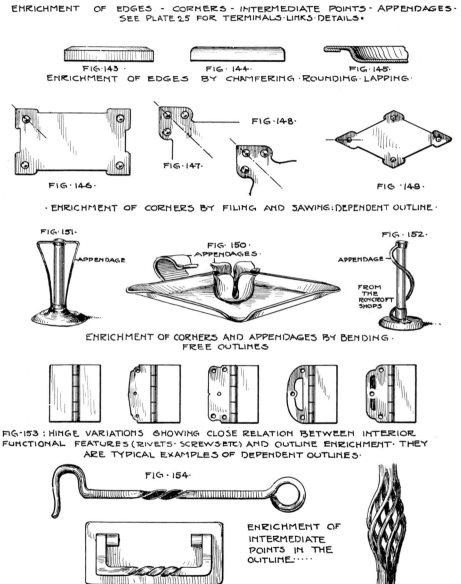

·OUTLINE ENRICHMENT OF THE PRIMARY MASSES OF THE BASER·METALS·
ENRICHMENT OF EDGES - CORNERS - INTERMEDIATE POINTS - APPENDAGES·
SEE PLATE 25 FOR TERMINALS·LINKS·DETAILS·

FIG·143 · FIG·144· FIG·145·
ENRICHMENT OF EDGES BY CHAMFERING·ROUNDING·LAPPING·

FIG·146· FIG·147· FIG·148· FIG·149·

· ENRICHMENT OF CORNERS BY FILING AND SAWING:DEPENDENT OUTLINE ·

FIG·151· FIG·150· FIG·152·
APPENDAGE APPENDAGES· APPENDAGE
FROM THE ROYCROFT SHOPS

ENRICHMENT OF CORNERS AND APPENDAGES BY BENDING·
FREE OUTLINES

FIG·153 : HINGE VARIATIONS SHOWING CLOSE RELATION BETWEEN INTERIOR
FUNCTIONAL FEATURES (RIVETS·SCREWS·ETC) AND OUTLINE ENRICHMENT· THEY
ARE TYPICAL EXAMPLES OF DEPENDENT OUTLINES·

FIG·154·

ENRICHMENT OF
INTERMEDIATE
POINTS IN THE
OUTLINE·····

FIG·155 FIG·156·

PLATE 27

CHAPTER VIII

ENRICHMENT OF THE CONTOURS OR OUTLINES OF DESIGNS IN BASE AND PRECIOUS METALS

The contours of clay forms are generally free to follow the curves and take the direction dictated by the knowledge and taste of the designer. Metal outlines are more restricted in this respect. Metal is frequently associated with service and consequently its design is often governed by its intended use. For example, if we were to design a metal drawer pull for a buffet, it would have to be considered in relation to the character and shape of the buffet. Again, the screws with which it is attached to the buffet would influence its outline design. It is, in other words, a *dependent* outline.

Enrichment of the Base Metals — Iron, Copper, Brass, Bronze

To distinguish between an unrestricted outline and one bound by other considerations we will term the restricted outline a *dependent outline*, for its enrichment must be related to other forms either within or without its surface. A *free outline* on the other hand is one in which the designer is free to use his ideas unrestricted by any other outside consideration, except service and design consistent with the material.

Free and Dependent Outlines

In order to emphasize the nature of a dependent outline we have Rule 5f. *Dependent outline enrichment should be related to essential parts of a design and influenced by their forms and functions; it must be consistent with the idea of the subject.*

We will start with the simplest form of outline enrichment of base metals, the decoration of an edge. It is contrary to the laws of service to leave sharp edges on articles intended for intimate household use, except where cutting edges are required. The rounding of sharp edges is likewise dictated by the laws of beauty. The transition from one plane surface to another is assisted by a rounded edge, as the eye takes kindly to the softened play of light and shade.

Enrichment of Edges

This gives us the simplest form of enrichment—the beveled, chamfered, or rounded edge, Figures 143 and 144, Plate 27. The rim of a

[87]

thin 18-gauge plate is likewise improved and strengthened by lapping the edge as shown in Figure 145, giving the rounded effect shown in Figure 144.

There are six important functional parts with which we are brought into common contact in industrial design of base metals. There are many more, but these are the most common and consequently are of the utmost importance to the designer as design centers. These parts are itemized as follows: (1) Corners, (2) Appendages, (3) Intermediate Points, (4) Terminals, (5) Links, (6) Details. As the decorative treatment of each part varies with the functional duty, Rule 5d, separate treatment and consideration of each part will be necessary.

Enrichment of Functional Parts

Corners, as extreme turning points of a design, are often found convenient for the location of screw holes, rivets, etc. These important construction elements become prominent functional parts of the design and by custom and the laws of design, Rule 5d, they are capable of receiving outline enrichment. But the contour of the corner must be related to the screws or rivets, particularly if they are near the edge, hence our outline becomes a *dependent outline* and as such must be related to the rivets or screws by Rule 5f.

Enrichment of Corners

Figures 146 to 149 show various arrangements of this type of design. The unity of the design is not lost, and the functional parts are enriched by contours related to the elements of service (rivets). Figure 153 shows another but slightly modified example of the same laws applied to hinge construction. The enriched outline in this case is closely associated with the holes in the hinge. The hinges in turn must be related to the object for which they are designed. Figure 150 gives a common example of corner enrichment by means of varying the edge at the corners, *i.e.*, by rounding the tray corners.

As appendages have distinct functional duties their design may vary as the design of the arm of the human figure differs from the head. Yet, as parts of the same body, they must fit the shape of the object to which they are attached. The candle holder and handle as appendages in Figure 150 are designed in sympathetic relation by means of tangential and similar curves sufficiently varied to give the eye a feeling of variety in the design. The novel single flower holders, Figures 151 and 152, with the glass test tube acting as a

Enrichment of Appendages

container show other possible forms of the appendage design. The first is informal while the second is formal, but both adhere to the first simple rules of appendage design. Rule 4a, etc.

The enrichment of center or intermediate points should be handled with great care and with a definite reason. Careless handling may cause the design to lack unity. Figures 154 and 155 show a simple twist as enrichment. The serviceable reason for this is to obtain a grip at the point of the twist. Again, it varies the character of the

Figure 156a.— Candlestick, Rendered by E. R.

straight edges and adds interest without loss of compactness or unity. If one is desirous of widening a vertical or horizontal rod, the enrichment made by welding a number of small rods together with a spreading twist gives a pleasing and serviceable handle. Figure 156.

As the public demands a happy ending to a story or a play, so does the eye demand a well-designed ending to a design. The part that terminal enrichment plays in industrial design is, therefore, to say the least, important to us as designers. Figure 157 illustrates terminals in thin metal and is shown by courtesy of the *School Arts*

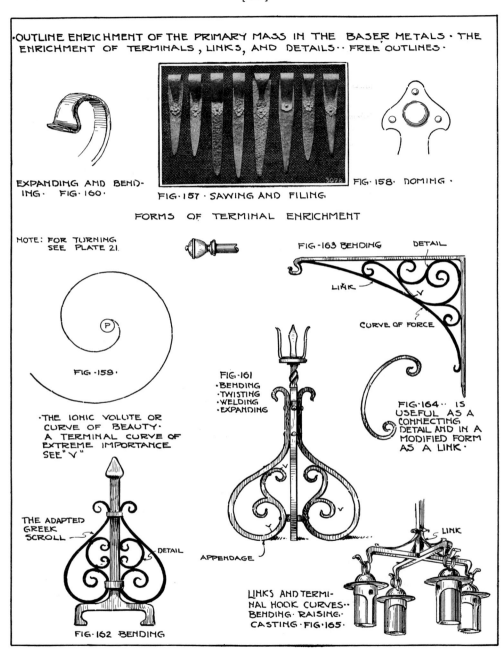

·OUTLINE ENRICHMENT OF THE PRIMARY MASS IN THE BASER METALS· THE
ENRICHMENT OF TERMINALS, LINKS, AND DETAILS·· FREE OUTLINES·

EXPANDING AND BEND-
ING· FIG·160·

FIG·157· SAWING AND FILING·

FIG·158· DOMING·

FORMS OF TERMINAL ENRICHMENT

NOTE: FOR TURNING
SEE PLATE 21.

FIG·163 BENDING

DETAIL

LINK

CURVE OF FORCE

FIG·159·

·THE IONIC VOLUTE OR
CURVE OF BEAUTY·
A TERMINAL CURVE OF
EXTREME IMPORTANCE
SEE "V"

FIG·161
·BENDING
·TWISTING
·WELDING
·EXPANDING

FIG·164·· IS
USEFUL AS A
CONNECTING
DETAIL AND IN A
MODIFIED FORM
AS A LINK·

THE ADAPTED
GREEK
SCROLL

DETAIL

APPENDAGE

LINK

LINKS AND TERMI-
NAL HOOK CURVES··
BENDING· RAISING··
CASTING· FIG·165·

FIG·162 BENDING

PLATE 28

Magazine from one of the articles by Mr. Augustus Rose. The outlines are in part dependent in character, controlled by rivets. Notice
the change of curve as the function changes from the *dependent
curve* of the rivet area to the *free outline* of the handle and again from
the handle to the cutting blade; a functional change of marked
character, but in thorough unity with the entire design. It is again
emphasized that whether the design possesses a free or a dependent
outline, or a combination of both types, all parts of the design must
be held together by entire *unity*. The rivets are occasionally placed
toward the edge and a domed boss is used to accent the center as is
shown in Figure 158.

Free and
Dependent
Contour
Enrichment

The Ionic Volute

As the Curve of Force was a valuable curve in wood construction,
so we find it an equally valuable curve for wrought metal. Its
recurrence again and again in industrial design leads us to appreciate
its value in the arts. It is the Ionic volute handed down to us in its
present form from the time of the Greeks, who developed it to a high
state of perfection.

Terminal
Enrichment
in Wrought
Metal

While its geometric development is a tedious process, it may be
easily constructed for practical purposes by the following method.
In Figure 159, *P* represents a small cylinder of wood, possibly a
dowel. A strong piece of thread, or fine wire, is wrapped around the
base of the dowel a number of times and a loop is formed in the free
end. A pencil with a sharp point is inserted in the loop and the
pencil and dowel are placed together on a sheet of paper. As the
thread unwinds from the dowel the point of the pencil will describe
a volute which may be developed indefinitely. It will be noticed
that no corresponding parts of the curve are concentric and it thus
has constant variety. It has been termed the Curve of Beauty
and is found in nature in the wonderfully designed shell of the
nautilus.

Curve of
Beauty

It is advisable to form several templates for the volute out of bent
wrought iron, of different sizes, and to practice drawing the curve
many times to accustom the hand and the eye to its changes of direction. The "eye" or center portion is sometimes terminated by
thinning and expanding in the manner shown in Figure 160.

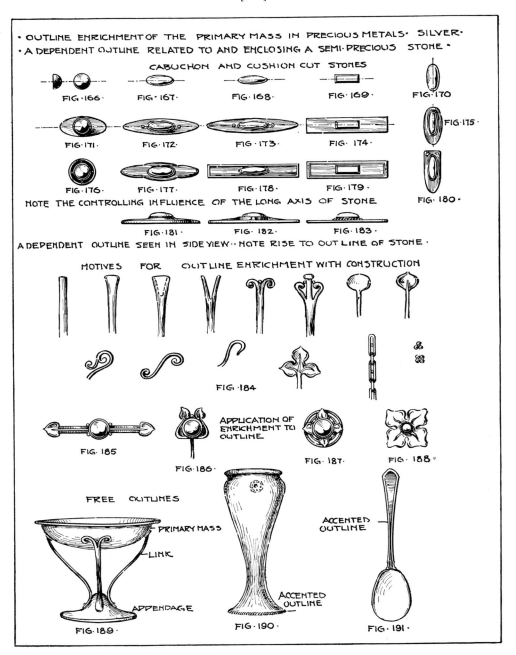

- OUTLINE ENRICHMENT OF THE PRIMARY MASS IN PRECIOUS METALS· SILVER·
- A DEPENDENT OUTLINE RELATED TO AND ENCLOSING A SEMI·PRECIOUS STONE·

CABUCHON AND CUSHION CUT STONES

FIG·166· FIG·167· FIG·168· FIG·169· FIG·170

FIG·171· FIG·172· FIG·173· FIG·174· FIG·175·

FIG·176· FIG·177· FIG·178· FIG·179·

NOTE THE CONTROLLING INFLUENCE OF THE LONG AXIS OF STONE FIG·180·

FIG·181· FIG·182· FIG·183·

A DEPENDENT OUTLINE SEEN IN SIDE VIEW·· NOTE RISE TO OUTLINE OF STONE·

MOTIVES FOR OUTLINE ENRICHMENT WITH CONSTRUCTION

FIG·184

FIG·185

FIG·186·

APPLICATION OF ENRICHMENT TO OUTLINE

FIG·187·

FIG·188·

FREE OUTLINES

PRIMARY MASS

LINK

APPENDAGE

FIG·189·

ACCENTED OUTLINE

ACCENTED OUTLINE

FIG·190·

ACCENTED OUTLINE

FIG·191·

PLATE 29

One form of application of the volute is shown in the terminal points of the candlestick in Figure 161. It is here shown combined with the second volute in the form of a reverse curve. In Figure 162, it has been combined with a smaller but reversed volute at the upper end. The entire and combined curve is commonly known as a Greek Scroll. In Figure 163 the Greek Scroll has been combined with the reverse curve of Figure 161 to form a portion of the bracket. In this figure we find the familiar curve of force faithfully serving its function as a supporting member for the top portion of the bracket.

Greek Scroll

A link is a convenient filler in connecting parts of a right angle. It likewise serves as a brace in connecting several disconnected parts and is useful in maintaining the unity of a design. Figure 164 shows a common form of link with its ends thinned and expanded as shown in Figure 160. This construction may, however, be disregarded as it is technically quite difficult to accomplish.

Enrichment of Links

Details are the smaller portions of a design and are similar to the trimmings and minor brackets of a building in relative importance. They enter to a considerable extent into wrought metal grille design, and are generally formed of the link, Greek scroll, or the Ionic volute, so as to be in harmony with the other parts of the design outline. Rule 5f. Their presence and use may be readily detected on Plate 28.

Enrichment of Details

Rule 5g. *A curve should join a straight line with either a tangential or right angle junction.*

As we are now familiar with continuity in wood moulding curves we should feel, in reviewing the figures in this chapter, the value of flowing continuity and tangential junction points (Rule 5g) necessary in wrought metal enrichment. The curves that we have considered are adapted to the materials and a comparatively large and new field of design is opened to the designer through a combination of curves mentioned. Plate 30 is self-explanatory and brings out the general application of the foregoing principles as applied to cast bronze hardware. It is interesting to notice the change of enrichment paralleling the change of function as outlined in Rule 5d.

Summary of Wrought Metal Free Outline Enrichment

Outline Enrichment of Precious Metals

Little has been written regarding the designing of jewelry. As can be readily seen, a semi-precious stone is the controlling factor

Outline Enrichment of Silver

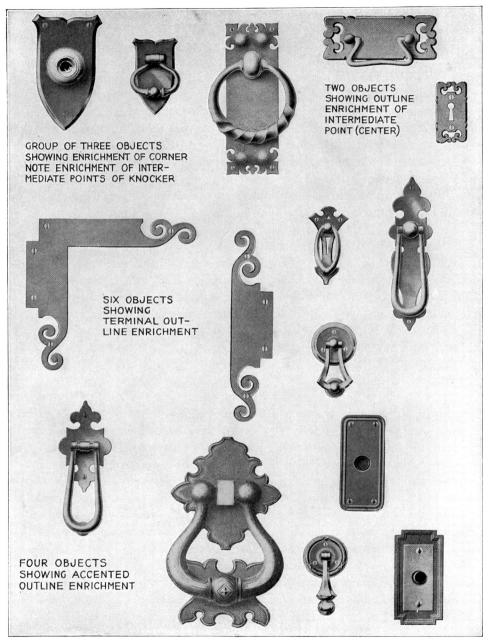

GROUP OF THREE OBJECTS
SHOWING ENRICHMENT OF CORNER
NOTE ENRICHMENT OF INTER-
MEDIATE POINTS OF KNOCKER

TWO OBJECTS
SHOWING OUTLINE
ENRICHMENT OF
INTERMEDIATE
POINT (CENTER)

SIX OBJECTS
SHOWING
TERMINAL OUT-
LINE ENRICHMENT

FOUR OBJECTS
SHOWING ACCENTED
OUTLINE ENRICHMENT

Courtesy of P. and F. Corbin

PLATE 30

in the major portion of the designs with silver as a background. Any enrichment merely accentuates the beauty of the setting. This statement would lead us to consider the outline as *dependent* in character and thoroughly related to the stone. It is necessary then to take the stone as a point of departure. The standard stone cuttings used in simple jewelry are shown in Figures 166 to 170. The first three and the last are cabochon cut, elliptical in contour with flat bottoms. The long axes have been drawn in each instance.

With Figures 171 to 174 we begin to see the close relation between the stone and its enclosing form. Rule 5f. A longer major axis in the stone calls for an increased length in the corresponding axis of the silver foundation or background. It is really a re-echo of the proportions of the primary mass of the stone in the mass of the silver. It is well for the beginner to make the axis of the stone and the silver blank coincide and to use this long axis as a basis for future enrichment. In a vertical primary mass, similar to the one shown in Figure 180, it is better design to place the stone a short distance above the geometric center of the mass as it insures a sense of stability and balance. A stone when placed toward the bottom of a design of this nature is inclined to give a feeling of "settling down" or lost balance.

Figure 176 varies the design shown in Figure 171. The two circles related to the stone are connected by four silver grains or balls. Figure 177 shows an attempt to enrich the contour of the silver, but there is a resulting tendency to detract from the simplicity of the unbroken outline and, as a result, little is gained by its attempted enrichment. Figures 178 and 179 show a better form of enrichment by accentuating the outline. This may be accomplished either by engraving a single line paralleling the contour or by soldering a thin wire around the outline.

While the top view of an article of jewelry may have been carefully designed the side view in most instances is totally neglected. The side view should show a steady graduation from the surface of the silver to the outline of the stone. This prevents the stone from bulging from the surface like a sudden and unusual growth. Doming, small wedges of silver, or a twist around the bezel may accomplish this as can be readily seen in Figures 181, 182, and 183.

· RULES 5D · 5E · 5F · 5G · CONTOUR OR OUTLINE ENRICHMENT · CLAY · METAL ·
INSTRUCTION SHEET ·

FIG · A · THE PRIMARY RECTANGLE

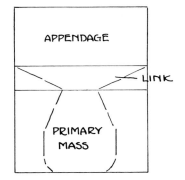

APPENDAGE

LINK

PRIMARY
MASS

FIG · B · FUNCTIONAL DIVISIONS ·

NOTE:
THIS SHEET ILLUSTRATES
THE DESIGN PROCESSES OF
A LAMP
ALL CLAY PARTS SHOULD
BE TRANSLATED INTO A
POTTER'S DRAWING ·

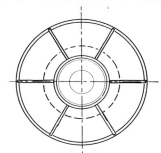

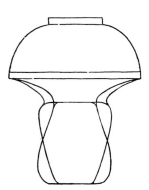

FIG · C · TWO DESIGNS FOR
CONTOUR ENRICHMENT ·

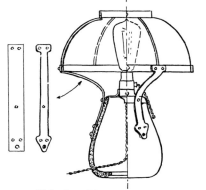

FIG · D · FINAL SELECTION FROM
"C" DEVELOPED INTO WORKING DRAWING ·

PLATE 31

While emphasis should be placed upon simplicity of outline, certain well regulated forms of enrichment may be added to the contour and enhance the beauty of the stone. Such motives with constructive steps are shown in Figure 184 and their application in Figures 185 to 188. It will be noticed that the enrichment *invariably leads up to the stone* which is the center of interest in the design. The ornament is likewise based upon the prominent axes of the stone.

Figures 189, 190, and 191 are types of beaten and raised silver work and show characteristic forms in silver, with two examples of accented outline enrichment. As they are curvilinear forms, their design is similar in many ways to clay forms of similar proportions and uses.

Motives for Outline Enrichment in Silver

Free Outline Enrichment in Silver

INSTRUCTION SHEET

Plate 31 shows the design steps necessary to the evolution of a lamp in two materials. A full size working drawing should follow Figure D.

SUMMARY OF DESIGN STEPS

(*a*) Draw the unenriched primary mass.

(*b*) For dependent contours, locate the elements of service within the primary mass. This may be interpreted to mean rivets, screw holes, semi-precious stones, etc.

(*c*) Determine upon the portion of the contours to be enriched, gauged by its need for grace, lightness, and variety. This enrichment is preferably concentrated at the following points: edges, corners, appendages, intermediate points, terminals, links, and details. These points may be combined provided the result does not violate the simplicity of the structural lines.

(*d*) Draw the enrichment in the predetermined area, causing it to be in harmony with such interior functional parts as screw holes, rivets, semi-precious stones, etc. Utilize suggested curves.

(*e*) Review all of the contour curves added to the design. Are they feeble compass curves or do they have the character of long sweeping curves with short "snappy" turns for variety?

(*f*) Test the entire design for unity. Does the eye move smoothly through all parts of the contour? Does the design "hold together"? Are all links and appendages joined to the primary mass in a graceful tangential manner?

(*g*) Dimension, add additional views, and details, if necessary, and otherwise prepare the drawing for shop use.

SUGGESTED PROBLEMS

Design an electric table lamp with square copper rod as a support, feet, and copper shade.

Design a hinge for a cedar chest.

SUMMARY OF RULES

Rule 5f. *Dependent outline enrichment should be related to essential parts of a design and influenced by their forms and functions; it must be consistent with the idea of the subject.*

Rule 5g. *A curve should join a straight line with either a tangential or right angle junction.*

REVIEW QUESTIONS

1. Contrast contour enrichment of wood, clay, and metal.
2. Define free and dependent outline in contour enrichment of base metal.
3. Describe and explain the use of the Ionic volute in contour enrichment of metal.
4. Define and present illustrations of contour enrichment designed for edges, corners, appendages, intermediate points, terminals, links, and other details in base metal.
5. Define and illustrate free and dependent contour enrichment of precious metal.

FIGURE 190a.— Union of Outline Enrichment on Clay and Metal

CHAPTER IX

SURFACE ENRICHMENT OF SMALL PRIMARY
MASSES IN WOOD

With this chapter we enter upon a consideration of the third and last major division of Industrial Arts Design, that of Surface Enrichment.

We have considered in previous chapters the subject of contour or outline enrichment. Now consider for a moment the fact that articles such as a square box, or tile, are not suited to outline enrichment, yet they have large, flat, and rather monotonous surfaces capable of decoration. It is readily seen that such surfaces will admit of further elaboration which we will distinguish from contour enrichment by using the term Surface Enrichment. As in contour enrichment, so in surface enrichment, the added element of design not only increases the beauty of the object but it likewise, if properly applied, gives apparent added strength to the structure. **Nature and Need of Surface Enrichment**

Rule 6a. *Surfaces to be enriched must admit of enrichment.*

Strictly utilitarian articles should not be ornamented by surface enrichment. As an example, a wooden mixing spoon, bowl, or wooden knife handle should not be enriched by carving, as the carving would interfere with the proper cleansing of the article. A surface exposed to considerable wear should not be enriched. Objects not strictly in the utilitarian class, such as a paper knife, book stall, envelope holder, or library table may be appropriately enriched in an unostentatious manner so that they will harmonize with their surroundings. **When and Where to Enrich a Surface** But the enrichment should first be placed upon the surface in such a manner that it will not interfere with the functional use of the article for service. Large projections upon the back of a chair or upon the handle of a paper cutter are unpleasant and interfere with intended uses.

FIGURE 191a.— Structure Obscured by Surface and Contour Enrichment

Rule 6b. *Surface enrichment must be related to the structural contours but must not obscure the actual structure.*

Careful consideration should be given to the often-mentioned law that the surface enrichment must be thoroughly related to structure and contour but not so as to obscure either. We must keep in mind the fact that it is necessary to support the structure, not to cover it up by related ornament, as in Figure 191a.

Most critics of industrial design complain of an overwhelming desire upon the part of the designer to over-decorate the structure. Surface enrichment runs wild over steam radiators, stoves, and wooden rocking chairs. Reserve is the watchword recommended as of extreme importance. The illustrations in this chapter are restricted to a limited range of design motives for the express purpose of simplifying the number of recommended methods.

Conservative Use of Ornament

Rule 6c. *The treatment must be appropriate to the material.*

The close-fibered woods with smooth, even textures are capable of more delicate enrichment than woods of coarser grain. Small articles are generally seen from a close range and should, therefore, be ornamented with finer decoration than large articles, such as a piece of furniture that is to be seen from a distance. The latter should have surface enrichment of sufficient boldness to "carry" or to be distinct from a distant point. Furthermore the enrichment should not have a "stuck on" appearance, but be an integral part of the original mass.

Relation of Enrichment to Material

There are three distinct means of ornamenting wood: (1) inlaying, depending for interest upon the difference in value and hue of the different inlaying woods used; (2) carved enrichment, depending upon line and mass for its beauty and made visible by contrasts of light and shade; (3) painting or staining of the surface with the interest dependent upon the colors or stains and their relation to each other and to the hue of the wood. It has been deemed wise to consider the first two types in the present chapter, and leave the last type for later consideration. In Chapters XV, XVI, and XVII, accentuation has been placed on wood coloring. The designer is advised to read those chapters before attempting to stain or color his problem.

Appropriate Methods of Surface Enrichment for Wood

Treating surface enrichment in its listed order we find that inlaying is one of the most common and best forms of enrichment for wood

Inlaying

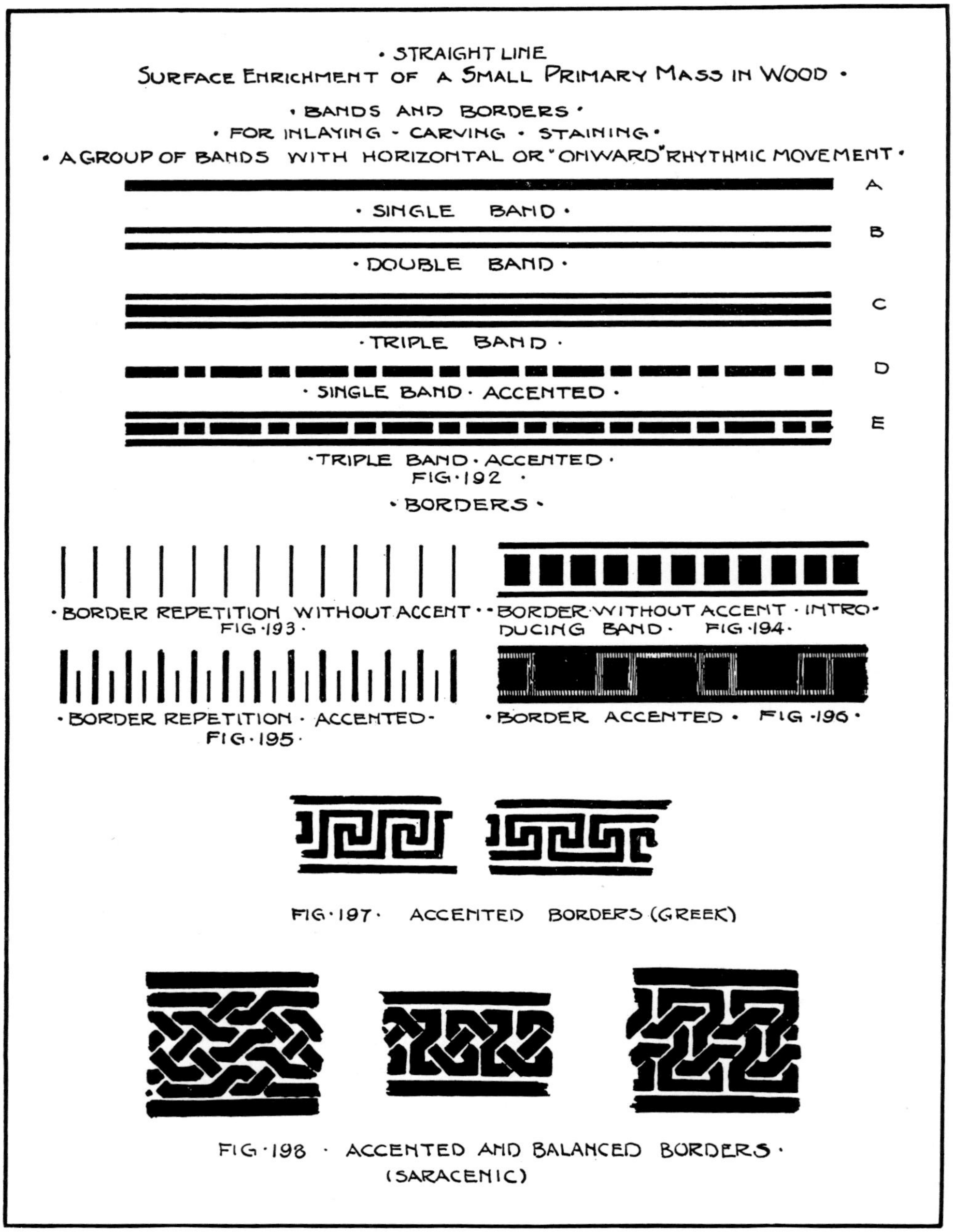

· STRAIGHT LINE

SURFACE ENRICHMENT OF A SMALL PRIMARY MASS IN WOOD ·

· BANDS AND BORDERS ·
· FOR INLAYING · CARVING · STAINING ·
· A GROUP OF BANDS WITH HORIZONTAL OR "ONWARD" RHYTHMIC MOVEMENT ·

A

· SINGLE BAND ·

B

· DOUBLE BAND ·

C

· TRIPLE BAND ·

D

· SINGLE BAND · ACCENTED ·

E

·TRIPLE BAND · ACCENTED ·
FIG·192 ·

· BORDERS ·

·BORDER REPETITION WITHOUT ACCENT ·
FIG·193·

· BORDER·WITHOUT ACCENT · INTRO-
DUCING BAND · FIG·194·

·BORDER REPETITION · ACCENTED·
FIG·195·

· BORDER ACCENTED · FIG·196·

FIG·197· ACCENTED BORDERS (GREEK)

FIG·198 · ACCENTED AND BALANCED BORDERS ·
(SARACENIC)

PLATE 32

work. As inlaying readily adapts itself to bands and borders, emphasis is placed upon them.

Rule 6i. *Inlayed enrichment should never form strong or glaring contrasts with the parent surface.*

Two conspicuous errors are often associated with inlaid designs. The first is the use of woods affording a glaring contrast with that of the project. Figure 209, Page 106. The right contrast of value is established when the inlay seems neither to rise from the surface nor sink through it. It should remain *on the surface* of the plane to be enriched, for it is surface enrichment. Figures 210, 211, and 212 are illustrative of pleasing contrasts. **Errors in Wood Inlay**

The second specific glaring error is the use of unrelated inlay. As an example, an Indian club is created by glueing many vari-colored woods around a central core. The result of the pattern so formed has little relation to the structural lines, fails entirely to support them, and, as a result, should be discarded.

Carving is difficult for the average beginner in wood working design, therefore merely the simplest forms of the craft are suggested as advisable. Figure 205a. If an elaborate design is desired (Figure 205c), it should be first drawn in outline and finally modeled in relief by Plastelene. This model is then an effective guide for the carver, supplementing the original outline drawing. **Carving**

Carving may be roughly divided into the following groups: (1) high relief carving similar to heads, human figures, and capitals; (2) low relief carving in which the planes have been flattened to a comparatively short distance above the original block of wood, such as panels, which are good examples of this group; (3) pierced carving where the background has been entirely cut away in places, such as screens, which illustrate this type; (4) incised carving in which the design has been depressed *below* the surface of the wood. Geometric chip carving is a representative type of this group. There are possible variations and combinations of these groups. **Divisions of Carving**

Rule 6j. *Carved surface enrichment should have the appearance of belonging to the parent mass.*

The central governing thought in all carved designs is to show an interesting proportion of light and shade coupled with a unity between the raised portion of the design and the background. If the carv-

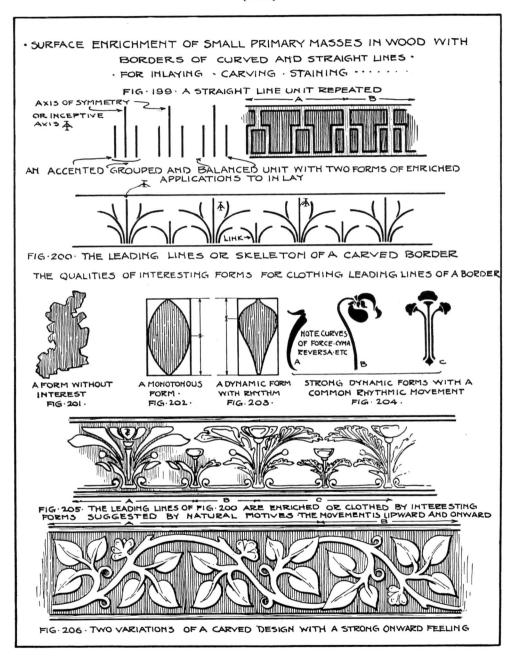

• SURFACE ENRICHMENT OF SMALL PRIMARY MASSES IN WOOD WITH
BORDERS OF CURVED AND STRAIGHT LINES •
· FOR INLAYING · CARVING · STAINING · · · · · ·

FIG · 199 · A STRAIGHT LINE UNIT REPEATED

AXIS OF SYMMETRY
OR INCEPTIVE
AXIS

AN ACCENTED GROUPED AND BALANCED UNIT WITH TWO FORMS OF ENRICHED
APPLICATIONS TO INLAY

LINK →

FIG · 200 · THE LEADING LINES OR SKELETON OF A CARVED BORDER

THE QUALITIES OF INTERESTING FORMS FOR CLOTHING LEADING LINES OF A BORDER

NOTE CURVES
OF FORCE · CYMA
REVERSA · ETC

A FORM WITHOUT
INTEREST
FIG · 201 ·

A MONOTONOUS
FORM ·
FIG · 202 ·

A DYNAMIC FORM
WITH RHYTHM
FIG · 203 ·

STRONG DYNAMIC FORMS WITH A
COMMON RHYTHMIC MOVEMENT
FIG · 204 ·

FIG · 205 · THE LEADING LINES OF FIG · 200 ARE ENRICHED OR CLOTHED BY INTERESTING
FORMS SUGGESTED BY NATURAL MOTIVES · THE MOVEMENT IS UPWARD AND ONWARD

FIG · 206 · TWO VARIATIONS OF A CARVED DESIGN WITH A STRONG ONWARD FEELING

PLATE 33

ing has a glued on appearance it becomes mechanical and resembles a stamped or machine-produced ornament.

A typical carved enrichment is carried through four steps: (1) the design is transferred to the wood surface by means of carbon paper; (2) the design is "set in" or separated from the ground by means of a grooved chisel; (3) the wood is cut away from the back of the design by a process of grounding; (4) the leaves and flowers or other elements of the design are modeled. The designer should keep these processes in mind when developing his design.

Steps Taken in Carving

It is now essential to find the extent of the vocabulary possible for the designer of surface enrichment. He has three large sources of information: first, geometric forms and abstract spots; second, natural organic objects such as flowers, leaves, animals, etc.; third, artificial objects, pots, jars, ink bottles, and other similar objects.

The Designer's Vocabulary

He may assemble or group these objects or elements for future designs into four typical systems: first, bands or borders; second, panels; third, free ornament; and fourth, the diaper or all-over patterns.

DESIGNING BANDS ON BORDERS

Rule 6d.   *Bands and borders should have a consistent lateral, that is, onward movement.*

Rule 6e.   *Bands and borders should never have a prominent contrary motion, opposed to the main forward movement.*

Bands are particularly suitable for inlaying. They are composed of straight lines arranged in some orderly and structurally related manner. They are used for bordering, framing, enclosing, or connecting. They give a decided *onward* motion which tends to increase the apparent length of the surface to which they are applied. Referring to Plate 32, Figure 192, we find three typical bands, *A*, *B*, and *C*. It is often the custom to limit the width of the inlayed bands to the width of the circular saw cut. To secure unity, the center band in *C* is wider than the outside sections.

Bands

A possible variation of motive in band designing may be secured by accenting. The single band has been broken up at *D* into geometric sections of pleasing length. But while this design gives variety, it also destroys the unity of a single straight line. Unity

Accenting

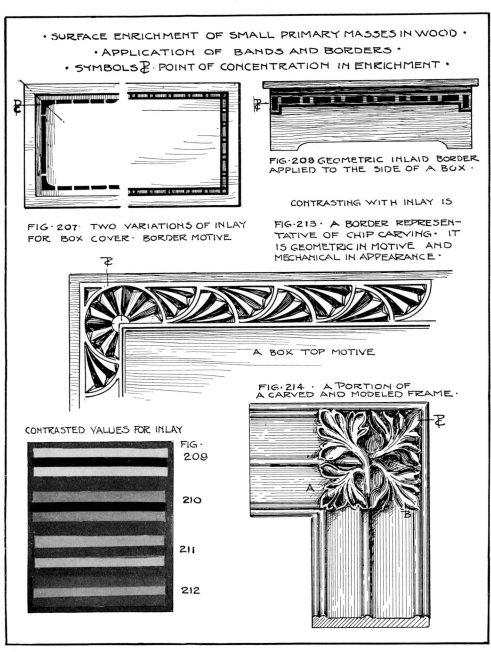

· SURFACE ENRICHMENT OF SMALL PRIMARY MASSES IN WOOD ·

· APPLICATION OF BANDS AND BORDERS ·

· SYMBOLS Ⓟ · POINT OF CONCENTRATION IN ENRICHMENT ·

FIG·208 GEOMETRIC INLAID BORDER APPLIED TO THE SIDE OF A BOX ·

FIG·207· TWO VARIATIONS OF INLAY FOR BOX COVER · BORDER MOTIVE

CONTRASTING WITH INLAY IS

FIG·213 · A BORDER REPRESEN-TATIVE OF CHIP CARVING · IT IS GEOMETRIC IN MOTIVE AND MECHANICAL IN APPEARANCE ·

A BOX TOP MOTIVE

FIG·214 · A PORTION OF A CARVED AND MODELED FRAME ·

CONTRASTED VALUES FOR INLAY

FIG· 209

210

211

212

PLATE 34

may, however, be restored by the addition of the top and bottom bands at *E*. This method of restoring unity is of extreme value in all border arrangements and is constantly used by the designer.

Rule 6f. *All component parts of a border should move in unison with the main movement of the border.*

Bands, as has just been stated, give distinctly "onward" movement. Borders are merely bands combined with other motives from the designer's vocabulary. As will be seen, bands, by their onward movement, tend to hold the other elements of the border together. Figure 193 is a border design without variety, unity, or interest. Figure 194 has added unity to a similar border by the addition of the double bands, but monotony is still present. Figure 195 suggests a method of relieving the monotony by accentuating every other repeat, thus supplying variety and creating an analogy to march-time music. Figure 196 has accentuated the monotonous border in Figure 194 by omitting every other square. This makes a simple and effective inlay pattern and suggests a large number of possible variations that could be applied to accented band motives. **Borders**

Figures 197 and 198 are border motives of geometric derivation taken from the historic schools of ornament. Figure 198 illustrates the "strap ornament" of the Moorish school. The simple underlying geometric net upon which these designs are based may be found in Meyer's Handbook of Ornament. **Moorish Ornament**

Inceptive Axes

Rule 6h. *Borders intended for vertical surfaces may have a strongly upward movement in addition to the lateral movement, provided the lateral movement dominates.*

In addition to the purely onward borders we now come to a variety with a distinctly *upward* movement as well. While this new feature adds materially to the interest of the border, it also adds to the difficulty of designing. The upward movement is often centered about an axis termed the Axis of Symmetry or Inceptive Axis, about which are grouped and balanced the different elements from the designer's vocabulary. When both sides are alike, the unit so formed is called a *bilateral unit*. Figure 199 shows the formation of a bilateral unit by means of grouping, accenting, and balancing straight lines **Upward and Onward Borders**

FIGURE 215.— Inlaid Band Border

over an inceptive axis. By adding bands above and below and doubling these vertical lines to gain width, we form at *A* and *B*, Figure 199, inlaid designs with an upward and onward tendency or movement.

The introduction of curved lines and natural units allows us to add more grace to these combined movements. The leading lines of a small border, designed to be seen at close range, are planned in

FIGURE 216.— Single and Double Band Inlaid Border

Courtesy of C. E. Partch

FIGURE 216a.— Work of High School Students

Figure 200. The central line or inceptive axis is repeated at regular intervals and the leading or skeleton lines are balanced to the right and left of this axis. These leading lines, as can be readily seen, have an upward and onward movement. To insure continuity, a small link and the top and bottom bands have been added to complete the onward movement.

Material for straight borders may be derived from geometry, nature, or artificial forms, but for borders designed in curves, nature is generally selected as a source.

Figure 201 illustrates a crude and uninteresting form, unsuited to outline enrichment. Figure 202 has brought Figure 201 into some semblance of order, but as can be readily seen by the primary outline which encloses it, the widest point occurs exactly midway from top to bottom, which makes the form monotonous. This defect has been remedied in Figure 203 and an interesting and varied area appears for the first time. What Dr. Haney calls "the feebly flapping curve" of Figure 202 has been replaced by the vigorous and "snappy" curve of Figure 203, which gives what is termed a dynamic or rhythmic value in surface enrichment.

Courtesy of C. E. Partch

FIGURE 216b.— Work of High School Students

Rule 6g. *Each component part of a border should be strongly dynamic and, if possible, partake of the main movements of the border.*

Any form which causes the eye to move in a given direction is strongly *dynamic*, and is opposed to the *static* form which does not cause a marked eye movement. A circle is symbolic of the static form, while a triangle is dynamic. In the designer's nomenclature, the term "rhythmic" may be used synonymously with "dynamic."

Dynamic areas or forms should carry out the upward and onward movement of the leading lines. Figure 204 shows how closely dynamic areas are connected with nature's units for design motives. A slight change in the contour may transform a leaf into excellent material with which to clothe the leading lines. The curve of force, the cyma, and other curves described in previous chapters should be recognized by the designer and utilized in the contours of dynamic forms.

Courtesy of C. E. Partch

FIGURE 216c.— Instruction Sheet Problem

The leading lines of the border in Figure 200 are shown clothed or enriched in Figure 205. Vigorous dynamic spots, conventionalized from natural units, continue the upward and onward movement of the original leading lines. As will be noted, the background has been treated to allow the spots to appear in relief. Small "fussy" spots or areas have been omitted and the units, varied in size and strongly dynamic in form, balance over an inceptive axis. The small link reaches out its helping hand to complete the onward movement without loss of unity, while the bands above and below bind the design together and assist in the lateral movement. Figure 205 shows three methods of treatment: simple spots without modeling, from *A* to *B*; slight indications of modeling, from *B* to *C*; full modeling of the entire unit at *C*. The choice of treatment depends, of course, upon the skill of the craftsman.

FIGURE 217.— Carved and Accented Border and Triple Carved Band

Figure 206 shows a design varied from formal balance over a central axis of symmetry or an inceptive axis. It has a decided onward movement with the leaves balanced above and below the stem which is the axis. The "repeat" has been reversed at *B* and is more pleasing than the portion at *A*. The area of the background, in its relation to that used for ornamentation or "filling," cannot be predetermined with exactness. There should be no blank spaces for the eye to bridge. Some designers allow about one-third ground

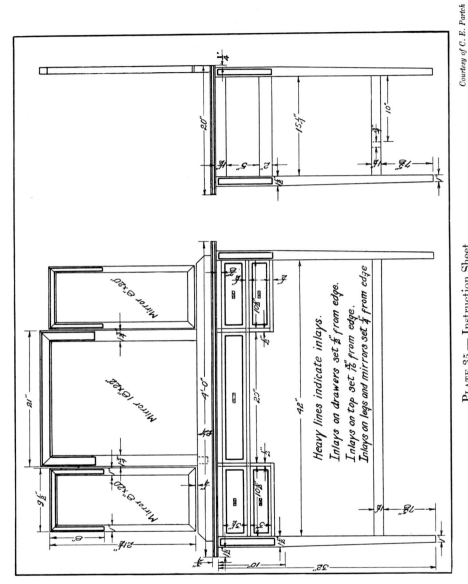

PLATE 35.— Instruction Sheet

Heavy lines indicate inlays.
Inlays on drawers set ¼″ from edge.
Inlays on top set ⁵⁄₁₆″ from edge.
Inlays on legs and mirrors set ¼″ from edge

Mirror 8″x20″

Mirror 16″x28″

Mirror 8″x20″

for two-thirds filling or enrichment. This proportion gives a full and rich effect and may be adopted in most instances as satisfactory.

When a border is used to parallel a rectangle it is customary to strengthen the border at the corners for two reasons: first, to strengthen, apparently, the structure at these points; second, to assist the eye in making the sudden turn at the corner. The corner enforcement affords momentary resting points for the eye, and adds pleasing variety to the long line of border. The strengthened point is called the *point of concentration* or point of force. Its presence and effect may be noted by the symbol P. C. in Figures 207, 208, 213, and 214.

Point of Concentration —Effect upon Structure

Figure 213 represents the rather angular and monotonous chip carving motive. It is, however, a simple form of carved enrichment for wood construction. Figure 214 shows the more rhythmic flow of a carved and modeled enrichment. Two methods of leaf treatment are given at *A* and *B*.

Chip Carving

Figures 215, 216, and 217 are industrial and public school examples of the forms of surface enrichment treated in this chapter.

INSTRUCTION SHEET

Plate 35 shows the necessary working drawings for wood inlay and is supplied as a typical high school problem by Mr. C. E. Partch of Des Moines, Iowa. See Figure 216c.

SUMMARY OF DESIGN STEPS

(a) Draw the primary rectangle, appendage, etc.
(b) Subdivide the rectangle into its horizontal and vertical subdivisions.
(c) Design very simple contour enrichment.
(d) Determine the location of zone of enrichment, and the amount and method of enriching the surface.
(e) Make several preliminary sketches to determine the best design and add the one finally selected to the structure. Correlate with contour enrichment.
(f) Add additional views, dimension, and otherwise prepare the drawing for shop use.

SUGGESTED PROBLEM

Design a walnut side table 3 feet high and enrich with a double band inlay of ebony.

SUMMARY OF RULES

Rule 6a. *Surfaces to be enriched must admit of enrichment.*

Rule 6b. *Surface enrichment must be related to the structural contours but must not obscure the actual structure.*

Rule 6c. *The treatment must be appropriate to the material.*

Rule 6d. *Bands and borders should have a consistent lateral, that is, onward movement.*

Rule 6e. *Bands and borders should never have a prominent contrary motion, opposed to the main forward movement.*

Rule 6f. *All component parts of a border should move in unison with the main movement of the border.*

Rule 6g. *Each component part of a border should be strongly dynamic and, if possible, partake of the main movement of the border.*

Rule 6h. *Borders intended for vertical surfaces may have a strongly upward movement in addition to the lateral movement, provided the lateral movement dominates.*

Rule 6i. *Inlayed enrichment should never form strong or glaring contrasts with the parent surface.*

Rule 6j. *Carved surface enrichment should have the appearance of belonging to the parent mass.*

REVIEW QUESTIONS

1. Give the reasons why surface enrichment may be used as decoration.
2. State an original example illustrating when and where to use surface enrichment.
3. Name an object from the industrial arts in which the structure has been weakened or obscured by the application of surface enrichment. Name an example of the correct use of surface enrichment and state wherein it has been correctly applied.
4. How should surface enrichment of small masses differ from that applied to larger masses; in what manner does the fiber of the wood affect the design?
5. Name three means of enriching the surface of wood. Briefly describe the processes of inlaying and carving, with the design restrictions governing each.
6. Give three sources of ornament open to the designer of surface enrichment.
7. Draw an accented triple band motive for inlay.
8. What is the inceptive axis; a bilateral unit? What are leading lines; dynamic forms; points of concentration?
9. Design an upward and onward continuous carved border for wood and base it upon a vertical inceptive axis. Treat as in A, Figure 205.
10. Illustrate the manner in which structure may be apparently strengthened by a band or border.

CHAPTER X

SURFACE ENRICHMENT OF SMALL PRIMARY MASSES IN WOOD—Continued

ENCLOSED AND FREE ORNAMENT

Chapter IX dealt with methods of developing continuous or repeating ornament (bands or borders). This leaves enclosed and free forms of surface enrichment to be considered in this chapter.

Enclosed Ornament (Panels)

As an enclosed form, a panel may be enriched by geometric, natural, or artificial ornament. It is enclosed in a definite boundary of bands or lines and may be a square or other polygon, circle, ellipse, lunette, spandrel, lozenge, or triangle. As the decoration does not have the continuous repeating movement of the border and as it covers an enclosed area, it is necessarily treated in a different manner from either band or border. Its object is to decorate a plane surface. The enrichment may be made by means of carving, inlaying, or painting.

Free ornament means the use of motives not severely enclosed by bands or panels. Free ornament is generally applied to centers or upper portions of surfaces to relieve a monotonous area not suited to either panel or border treatment. It may have an upward or a radial movement dependent upon the character of the member to be enriched.

Free Ornament

We then have three forms of possible surface enrichment: repeating or continuous motives, enclosed motives, and free motives. Our next point is to consider where the last two may be used appropriately in surface enrichment.

Summary

The panel of a small primary mass of wood may be enriched at any one of three places: first, at the margins; second, at the center; third, over the entire surface. The exact position is a matter to be determined by the structural design and the utilitarian requirements of the problem. For example, a bread board or taboret top would require the enrichment in the margin with the center left free. A table leg might require an enrichment in the center of the upper portion of the leg, while a square panel to be inserted in a door, Figure 233, Page 124, might require full surface treatment.

Zone of Enrichment

Each area of panel enrichment should have one or more accented points known as points of concentration. The design should become more prominent at these places and cause the eye to rest for a moment before passing to the next point of prominence. The accented portion of the design at these points should be so related to the structure that it apparently reinforces the structure as a whole. Corners, centers of edges, and geometric centers are salient parts of a structure; we shall therefore be likely to find our points of concentration coinciding with them. Let us then consider the first of these arrangements as applied to enclosed enrichment.

Structural Reinforcement

Marginal Panel Enrichment

Enclosed Enrichment for Partly Enriched Surfaces

Rule 7a. *Marginal panel enrichment should parallel or be related to the outlines of the primary mass and to the panel it is to enrich.*

Rule 7b. *Marginal points of concentration in panels should be placed (1) preferably at the corner or (2) in the center of each margin.*

Rule 7c. *To insure unity of design in panels, the elements composing the points of concentration and the links connecting them must be related to the panel contour and to each other.*

Marginal Zone Enrichment

The marginal method of enrichment may be used when it is impossible to enrich the entire surface because the center is to be used for utilitarian purposes or because it would be aesthetically unwise to enrich the entire surface. The marginal zone is adapted to enriching box tops, stands, table tops, and similar surfaces designed preferably with the thought of being seen from above. We shall call such surfaces horizontal planes.

As the design is to be limited to the margin, the panel outline is bound to parallel the contours, or outlines, of the surface to be enriched. It is well to begin the design by creating a panel parallel to the outlines of the enriched surface. Figure 218. The next step is to place the point of concentration in the marginal zone and within this figure. Common usage dictates the *corners* as the proper points.

It may be the designer's practice to use the single or double bands, Figures 218, 219, 220, with a single accentuation at the corners. The spots composing the point of concentration must have unity with the enclosing contours and with the remainder of the enrichment. Figure 220 is, in this respect, an improvement over Figure 219. But these examples are not *true* enclosed panel enrichment. They are the borders of Chapter IX acting as marginal enrichment. It is not until we reach Figure 221 that the true enclosed enrichment appears, when the panel motive is clearly evident. In this figure a single incised band parallels the contours of the figure until the corner is reached. Here we find it turning, gracefully widening to give variety, and supporting the structure by its own increased strength. The single band in Figure 221 acts as a bridge, leads the eye from one point of concentration to the next similar point, forms a compact mass with the point of concentration, and parallels the enclosing contours of the enriched surface.

Points of Concentration

Points of Concentration in the Corner of Margin

In Figure 222 the point of concentration is to be found in the *center* of each margin. This bilateral unit is clearly designed on and about the center lines of the square panel. These points of concentration take the place of previous concentrations at the *corners* which were based upon the square's diagonals. While accenting based upon the center lines is acceptable, this means of concentration does not seem so successfully to relate the accented part to the structural outlines as that of concentration based upon the diagonals. The latter, therefore, is recommended for beginners. The corners of Figure 222 are, however, slightly accented by means of the bridging spots *x-x*.

Points of Concentration in the Center of Margin

The diagonals and center lines of the surface enriched squares of Figures 221 and 222 and similar structural lines are *inceptive axes*, as they are center lines for new design groups. It may then be said that a strong basic axis or similar line depending upon the structure, may become the center line or inceptive axis upon which to construct a bilateral design. It is only necessary to have this inceptive axis pass through the enrichment zone of the panel. Hereafter in the drawings, inceptive axes will be designated by the abbreviation I. A. while the point of concentration will be indicated by the abbreviation P. C.

Inceptive Axes or Balancing Lines

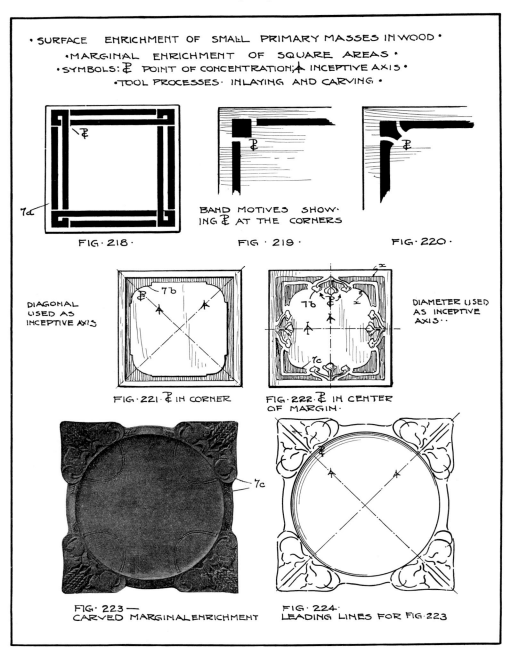

• SURFACE ENRICHMENT OF SMALL PRIMARY MASSES IN WOOD •
• MARGINAL ENRICHMENT OF SQUARE AREAS •
• SYMBOLS: ℗ POINT OF CONCENTRATION; ⚹ INCEPTIVE AXIS •
• TOOL PROCESSES · INLAYING AND CARVING •

FIG · 218 ·

BAND MOTIVES SHOW-
ING ℗ AT THE CORNERS

FIG · 219 ·

FIG · 220 ·

DIAGONAL
USED AS
INCEPTIVE AXIS

FIG · 221 ℗ IN CORNER

DIAMETER USED
AS INCEPTIVE
AXIS · ·

FIG · 222 ℗ IN CENTER
OF MARGIN ·

FIG · 223 —
CARVED MARGINAL ENRICHMENT

FIG · 224 ·
LEADING LINES FOR FIG · 223

PLATE 36

The strongest plea for the inceptive axis is the fact that it inter-locks surface enrichment with the structure, insuring a degree of unity that might otherwise be unattainable.

The carved enrichment of Figure 223 fully illustrates this point. The analytical study of Figure 224 shows the diagonal used as an inceptive axis, with the leading lines grouped about it at the corner point of concentration.

Inceptive
Axis

FREE ENRICHMENT

Rule 8a.   *Free ornament for partly or fully enriched surfaces should be based and centered upon an inceptive axis of the structure.*

Rule 8b.   *Free ornament should be related and subordinated to the structural surfaces.*

Rule 8c.   *Points of concentration in free enrichment of vertically placed masses are usually located in and around the inceptive axis and above or below the geometric center of the design.*

This method of surface enrichment is used to relieve the design of heavy members in the structure or to distribute ornament over the surface of lighter parts in a piece of furniture. An example is noted in Figure 246, Page 128, where the upper portion of the legs has center enrichment. As can be readily seen, the enrich-ment is generally free in character with little or no indication of enclosure. Figure 225 shows the application of free enrichment to a paneled screen or hinged door. The P. C. is in the upper portion of the door and is re-echoed in the door frames, while the ornament itself is strongly dynamic in movement with a decided upward tendency in sympathy with the proportions of the door. This motive might be developed by inlay, carving, or paint.

Center
Zone
Enrichment

Figure 226 is a carved Gothic leaf, appropriately used as enrich-ment of heavy furniture. The unit may be raised above the surface or, even more easily, depressed or incised into the surface. The small corner spot is added with the intention of bringing the leaf into sympathetic conformity with the contours. Note how the center line of both units in Figures 225 and 226 coincides with the inceptive axis of the structure. Let it again be reiterated that this binding of the surface enrichment to the structure by means of the coincidence

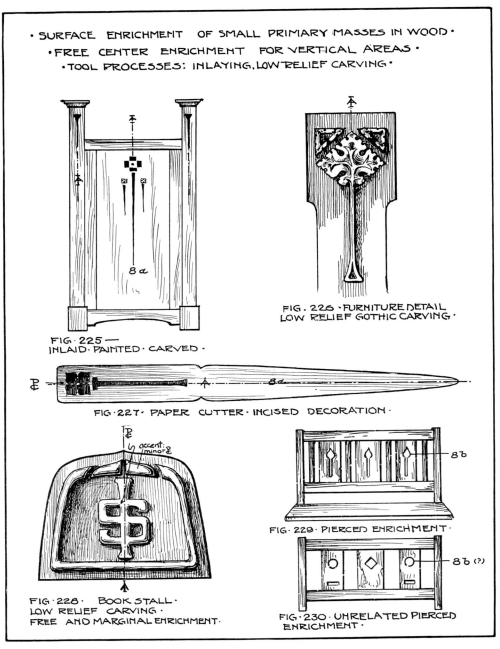

• SURFACE ENRICHMENT OF SMALL PRIMARY MASSES IN WOOD •
• FREE CENTER ENRICHMENT FOR VERTICAL AREAS •
• TOOL PROCESSES: INLAYING, LOW RELIEF CARVING •

FIG · 225 —
INLAID · PAINTED · CARVED ·

FIG · 226 · FURNITURE DETAIL
LOW RELIEF GOTHIC CARVING ·

FIG · 227 · PAPER CUTTER · INCISED DECORATION ·

FIG · 228 · BOOK STALL ·
LOW RELIEF CARVING ·
FREE AND MARGINAL ENRICHMENT ·

FIG · 229 · PIERCED ENRICHMENT ·

FIG · 230 · UNRELATED PIERCED
ENRICHMENT ·

PLATE 37

of the axes of symmetry and the inceptive axes causes the most positive kind of unity. No part of this form of enrichment should be carved sufficiently high to give it the appearance of being separated from the main surface.

Figures 227 and 228 are additional examples of free enrichment. Figure 228 has introduced by its monogram the individual touch of ownership so essential to the success of school designing. The monogram represents free enrichment while the border is marginal decoration with the point of concentration in the center of the top edge. Both types of enrichment are related to each other and to the structural contours.

Figure 229 is typical free *pierced* enrichment. The wood in the enriched portion is removed and the resulting figure supplies added lightness of construction and variety to the surface. One encounters this form of enrichment in the average school project with greater frequency than either inlaying or carving. It is with the thought of adding to the possibilities of school project decoration that the latter forms have been introduced. A word regarding the errors often encountered in pierced enrichment of the character of Figure 229 may not be amiss. Pupils, believing the square to be the last word in this form of enrichment, place the figure on the member to be enriched with little thought of its possible relation to the structural contours; the result is the un-unified design illustrated in Figure 230. To correct this, reference should be made to Rule 8b.

Full Panel Enrichment

Rule 7d. *The contours of fully enriched panels should parallel the outlines of the primary mass and repeat its proportions.*

This is the richest and most elaborate form of enrichment when carried to its full perfection. It generally takes the form of a panel filled with appropriate design material. This panel may be used to enrich the plain end of a project such as a book stall and thus cover the entire surface, or it may be inserted into a large primary mass and accentuate its center as in a door, in a manner similar to Figure 233. Its use, whatever its position, leads us to the consideration of methods of designing full panels.

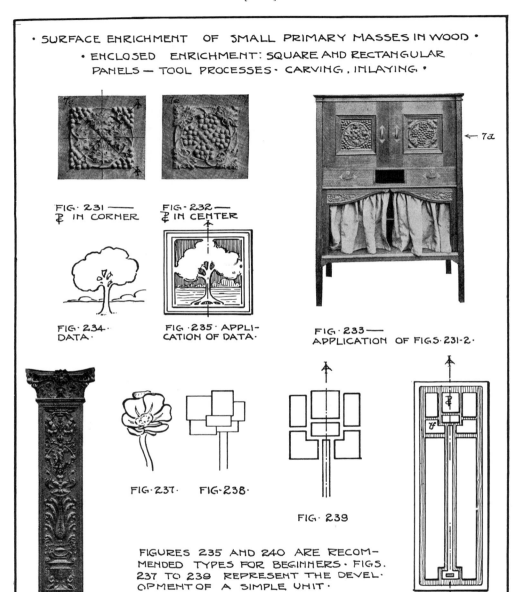

SURFACE ENRICHMENT OF SMALL PRIMARY MASSES IN WOOD ·
· ENCLOSED ENRICHMENT: SQUARE AND RECTANGULAR
PANELS — TOOL PROCESSES · CARVING , INLAYING ·

FIG· 231 ——
℞ IN CORNER

FIG· 232 ——
℞ IN CENTER

FIG· 234·
DATA·

FIG ·235· APPLI-
CATION OF DATA·

FIG· 233 ——
APPLICATION OF FIGS· 231-2·

← 7a

FIG· 237·

FIG· 238·

FIG· 239

FIGURES 235 AND 240 ARE RECOM-
MENDED TYPES FOR BEGINNERS · FIGS·
237 TO 239 REPRESENT THE DEVEL·
OPMENT OF A SIMPLE UNIT ·

FIG· 240·

FIG· 236·

PLATE 38

Rule 7e. *The points of concentration for a fully enriched square panel may be in its center or in its outer margin.*

In planning designs for full panels, it would be well to consider: first, square panels; second, rectangular panels; third, varied panels. The point of concentration may be kept in the *corners* of a square panel, as designed in Figure 231, or it may be placed in the *center*, as shown in Figure 232. The effects, when assembled, are indicated in Figure 233.

To secure these effects, a square panel is commonly divided into quarter sections by center lines. The diagonals of each quarter should be drawn before proceeding with the details of the design. These diagonals and center lines are the building lines or leading *axes* of the pattern. The *leading lines and details* are then grouped around these center and diagonal axes in a manner quite similar to the method used in Figures 223 and 224. These leading lines are then *clothed with enrichment* by applying the processes indicated in Chapter IX.

Without going into detail we may say that it is good practice: first, to draw the square panel; second, to draw the center lines and diagonals; third, to locate points of concentration; fourth, to make the leading lines move inwardly to center concentration or outwardly to corner concentration; fifth, to clothe these lines with ornament having strongly dynamic movement corresponding to the leading lines; sixth, to fill in remaining space with ornament, supporting the movement toward points of concentration, even though slight and minor contrasts of direction are added to give variety. When the entire design is completed one should ask the following questions: Does the design have unity? Does it seem too thin and spindling? And most of all, do the points of concentration and shape of the panel fit the structural outlines and proportions? We cannot fit a square peg into a round hole; neither can we fit a square panel into a circular or rectangular mass without considerable change to the panel.

Figures 234 and 235 have been drawn with the idea of suggesting a simple and modified form of panel enrichment which may be readily handled by the beginner. The tree as a decorative symbol is appropriate to wood, and its adaption to a square panel is drawn at Figure 235.

Square Panels

Steps in Panel Designing

· SURFACE ENRICHMENT OF SMALL PRIMARY MASSES IN WOOD ·

· ENCLOSED PANEL ENRICHMENT — FORMAL AND FREE BALANCE ·

· APPLICATION OF NATURAL AND ARTIFICIAL MOTIVES ·

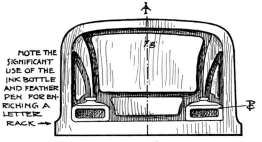

NOTE THE SIGNIFICANT USE OF THE INK BOTTLE AND FEATHER PEN FOR EN-RICHING A LETTER RACK →

· FIG· 241· LETTER RACK· FORMAL BALANCE ·

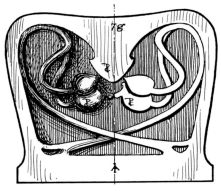

· FIG· 242· BOOK STALL· FORMAL BALANCE·
FLAT AND MODELED TREATMENT.

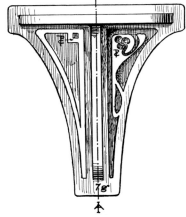

· FIG· 243· BRACKET SHOW-ING MARGINAL AND PANEL TYPES ·

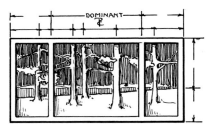

· FIG· 244· TRIPTYCH· FREE BALANCE·
THREE VERTICAL DIVISIONS.

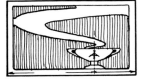

FIG· 245· BOUILLON CUP· FREE BALANCE MOTIVE FOR RECTAN-GULAR SERVING TRAY · · · ·

PLATE 39

While a rectangular panel may be divided into sections by a number of different methods, it is well for the beginner in design to treat it as a vertical mass, designed to enrich a vertical surface. This vertical panel may then be divided into halves by the axis of symmetry, which should coincide with an inceptive axis, but it is not essential to balance the enrichment exactly in each half. Small deviations from exact symmetry sometimes give added variety to the design.   Figure 235.

Rule 7f.   *The points of concentration for a fully enriched vertical panel should be in the upper portion of the panel.*

The point of concentration in vertical panels should be in the upper portion, and all parts of the design, both leading lines and clothing, should have a strong upward tendency.   Figure 236 is a vertical panel from historic ornament.   The heavier parts have been designed at the bottom for stability and the lighter and more intricate members have been placed at the top.

Rule 7g.   *The fully enriched panel and its contents should be designed in unified relation to the structural outlines, with the center line of the panel coinciding with the inceptive axis of the structure.*

To see how to apply rectangular panels to wood surfaces, let us look at Figure 240.   This is a simple design with an incised background and might be used for enriching a narrow paneled door, newel post, or frame.   The large areas are at the bottom; the point of concentration is at the top, and the entire design balances over the inceptive axis.   The point of concentration consists of the geometrically treated small flower form, with its original lines modified to simplify the carving processes.   The stem coincides with the inceptive axis, while narrow and sympathetically related minor panels fill in the background and keep the design from appearing weak and thin.

Figure 237 is an accurate rendering of the flower form and is the *data or record of facts* for Figure 240.   Figure 238 introduces the method of plotting the areas from these facts.   Variety of form and area is, at this stage, desirable.   Figure 239 has assembled these areas into orderly balance over the axis of symmetry.   Figure 240 has again slightly modified them to apply to the vertical panel in wood.

Courtesy of Berkey and Gay

FIGURE 246.— Example of Free and Marginal Enrichment

VARIED PANELS

The panels under consideration up to this time have been designed to harmonize with square and rectangular contours. The panel may, however, become a most flexible and sympathetic element, changing its form to suit the ever-changing contours. But though change of shape affects the contents of the panel to a certain extent the points of concentration and the inceptive axes still act as our guide. Objects are arranged formally on each side of the inceptive axes and the space filling is approximately the same as in former examples. **Panels of Varied Shapes**

The still life sketches of the art class may be conventionalized into appropriate motives for utilitarian objects as shown in Figure 241. This use of still life suggests a most desirable correlation and a welcome one to many drawing teachers. Three points should be kept in mind: first, adaptability of the object, its decorative possibilities, and appropriateness to service; second, adjustment of the panel to contours; third, adjustment of the object to the wood panel. **Use of Artificial Objects**

Some portion of the object should be designed to parallel the panel. Small additional spots may assist in promoting harmony between the object and the panel boundary. These three considerations are essentially necessary factors in the design of enclosed enrichment. Figures 242 and 243 are other adaptations of panel design to varied contours.

In the foregoing examples the designs are more or less rigidly balanced over the inceptive axis or axis of symmetry. Imaginary axis it is, but, acting with the panel, it nevertheless arbitrarily limits the position of all parts within the panel. By removing this semblance of formal balance, we approach what is termed *free balance*. In this we find that the designer attempts to balance objects informally over the geometric center of the panel or combined panels. As the arrow points in Figure 244 indicate, the problem is to balance the trees in an informal and irregular manner, avoiding "picket fence" regularity. In all of this freedom there is a sense of order, since a mass of trees on one side of the geometric center is balanced by a similar mass on the other side. Indeed, in Figure 244 this may be carried even to the point of duplicating in reverse order the outside panels of the Triptych. **Free Balance**

·RULES 7D TO 7E·· ENCLOSED SURFACE ENRICHMENT WITH
APPLICATION OF STILL LIFE TO A FULLY ENRICHED SURFACE·

·INSTRUCTION SHEET·

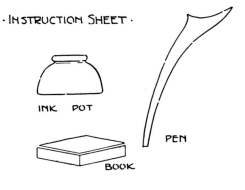

INK POT

PEN

BOOK

FIG·A· STILL LIFE GROUP·

FIG·B· STILL LIFE GROUP ANALYZED
AND RESOLVED INTO DESIGN
ELEMENTS ADAPTED TO MATERIAL·

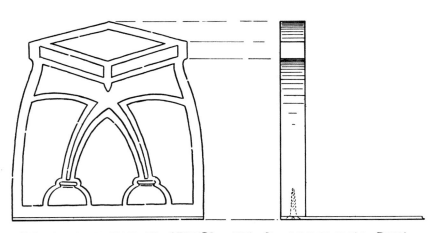

FIG·C· ADAPTATION TO STAINED
SURFACE ENRICHMENT OF· A
BOOK STALL·

FIG·D· ADDITIONAL DATA
·SUPPLIED FOR CONSTRUCTIVE
PURPOSES·

PLATE 40

Figure 245 again reverts to artificial motives, illustrated in free balance. The jet of steam is the unifying factor which brings the cup into harmony with the enclosing space. Figure 246 shows illustrations of free balance and border enrichment from the industrial market.

INSTRUCTION SHEET

Plate 40 indicates the necessary design steps for a panel surface enrichment correlating with still life drawing. Note the connection between the ink bottle, pen, and book as used to decorate a book stall.

SUMMARY OF DESIGN STEPS
For Square Panel Surface Enrichment

(a) Draw the primary rectangle of the principal surface, appendages, etc.
(b) Subdivide into major vertical and horizontal divisions.
(c) Design simple contour enrichment. Determine location of zone of enrichment (the panel), the amount and method of enriching the surface.
(d) Draw outline of the panel which should be sympathetically related to the contours.
(e) Draw diameters, diagonals, or center lines of the panel. Regard these as possible inceptive axes.
(f) Locate points of concentration on either diameters, diagonals, or center lines.
(g) Draw leading lines in sympathy with the contours of the panel, the inceptive axis, and the point of concentration.
(h) Clothe the leading lines with enrichment that shall be appropriate to the structure, the material, and the intended service. Note the result. Is the panel agreeably filled without appearing overcrowded or meager? Several preliminary sketches should be made.
(i) Add additional views, dimension, and otherwise prepare the drawing for shop use.

SUGGESTED PROBLEM

Design a glove box and enrich the cover with a simple carved panel with marginal panel enrichment.

SUMMARY OF RULES
Enclosed Surface Enrichment for Partly Enriched Panels

Rule 7a. *Marginal panel enrichment should parallel or be related to the outlines of the primary mass, and to the panel it is to enrich.*

Rule 7b. *Marginal points of concentration in panels should be placed (1) preferably at the corners or (2) in the center of each margin.*

Rule 7c. *To insure unity of design in panels, the elements composing the points of concentration and the links connecting them must be related to the panel contour and to each other.*

ENCLOSED SURFACE ENRICHMENT FOR FULLY ENRICHED PANELS

Rule 7d. *The contours of fully enriched panels should parallel the outlines of the primary mass and repeat its proportions.*

Rule 7e. *The points of concentration for a fully enriched square panel may be in its center or in its outer margin.*

Rule 7f. *The points of concentration for a fully enriched vertical panel should be in the upper portion of the panel.*

Rule 7g. *The fully enriched panel and its contents should be designed in unified relation to the structural outlines, with the center line of the panel coinciding with the inceptive axis of the structure.*

FREE SURFACE ENRICHMENT

Rule 8a. *Free ornament for partly or fully enriched surfaces should be based and centered upon an inceptive axis of the structure.*

Rule 8b. *Free ornament should be related and subordinated to the structural surfaces.*

Rule 8c. *Points of concentration in free enrichment of vertically placed masses are usually located in and around the inceptive axis and above or below the geometric center of the design.*

Postulate: *Surface enrichment should be inseparably linked to the surface and to the outlines or contours.*

REVIEW QUESTIONS

1. What is a panel?
2. State three sections or areas at which a panel may be enriched. Give reasons for selecting a given area.
3. Explain relation of point of concentration to each section.
4. In marginal enrichment, is it preferable to locate the point of concentration in the center or corner of the margin? Why?
5. What is the value of an inceptive axis with relation to the unity of a design? What is its relation to the structure?
6. Give the characteristics and use of free enrichment.
7. State the use of full panel enrichment.
8. Where may the point of concentration be located in full square panel enrichment?
9. Name six steps essential to the designing of a square panel.
10. For what specific purpose is a vertical rectangular panel adapted?
11. Where should the point of concentration be located in a vertical rectangular panel?
12. Draw a flower form and adapt it to a carved enrichment in wood.
13. To what uses are panels of varied shapes adapted?
14. How may artificial objects be adapted to surface enrichment?
15. Explain the term "free balance."

CHAPTER XI

SURFACE ENRICHMENT WITH MINOR SUBDIVISIONS
OF LARGE PRIMARY MASSES IN WOOD

This article is, in part, a brief summary and review of Rules 2a, 2b, 3a, 3b, 3c (vertical and horizontal major divisions) with application to minor subdivisions. By minor spacings or subdivisions in wood work we refer to the areas occupied by drawers, doors, shelves, and other small parts subordinated in size to the large or major divisions such as large front or side panels, etc. These smaller or minor subdivisions in wood work are bounded by runners, rails, guides, and stiles depending upon the form of construction and character of the minor subdivision. Major divisions are often bounded by legs, table tops, and principal rails.

Minor Subdivisions

It is an interesting and useful fact that rules governing major divisions generally apply equally well to minor ones. There are a few exceptions and additions to be noted in their appropriate places.

When minor subdivisions are well planned they supply one of the most interesting forms of surface enrichment or treatment, for if we consider paneling an appropriate form of decoration, we are equally privileged to feel that each small drawer or door adds its quota of interest to the sum total of the entire mass. We are equally justified in accenting these drawers or doors with panel decoration or other forms of surface enrichment provided that harmony is maintained.

These minor subdivisions, properly enriched, may become equalizers, or elements which adjust the design to the character of the surroundings destined to receive the project of which they are a part.

With reference to the illustrations, Figure 247, Plate 41, shows a simple minor panel treatment falling under Rule 3a. Single or preferably double band inlay might have been suitably substituted for the sunken panels. As many craftsmen are not properly equipped

Vertical Sections and Their Divisions

[133]

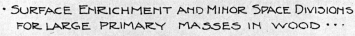

· SURFACE ENRICHMENT AND MINOR SPACE DIVISIONS ·
FOR LARGE PRIMARY MASSES IN WOOD · · ·
· ACCENTUATION OF MINOR VERTICAL DIVISIONS ·

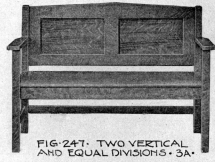

FIG · 247 · TWO VERTICAL
AND EQUAL DIVISIONS · 3A ·

FIG · 248 · THREE MINOR VER-
TICAL DIVISIONS · 3B ·

FIG · 249 · THREE VERTICAL
DIVISIONS · 3B · MINOR 3A

FIG · 250 · THREE VERTICAL
DIVISIONS · 3B · MINOR · 2A

FIG · 251 · THREE VERTICAL
DIVISIONS (WITHOUT REPETITION
IN APPENDAGE) · 4A · MINOR · 2A ·

FIG · 252 · THREE VERTICAL DIVISIONS
REPEATED IN APPENDAGE · 4C ·

PLATE 41

to produce inlays, it is practicable to use stock inlays, thus simplifying the process.

In a three-part design it is the designer's desire to gain the effect of lightness and height by the use of Rule 3b. As a simple treatment of a three-part design, Figure 248 needs little comment. Figures 249 and 250 are examples of dividing, by means of minor divisions, the outer sections of a three-part design.

The small drawers in the right and left sections of Figure 250 might have been improved in proportion by again applying Rule 2a to their design, thereby varying the measure of their heights. The enclosed panel enrichment affords pleasing variety to the otherwise unvaried front panels. Rule 7g.

Figures 251 and 252 show unbroken drawer runners continuing through all three vertical sections, thus definitely binding these sections together. It is seen that this device is conducive to unity, whenever two or three vertical divisions have been used.

Figure 252 is a repetition of Figure 251, but shows the echo or continuation of the three divisions of the primary mass into the appendage. The use of the single or double band enrichment still further binds the minor subdivisions of the primary mass into ideal unity with the appendage.

SEQUENTIAL PROGRESSION OF MINOR HORIZONTAL SPACE DIVISIONS

Rule 2c. *A primary mass may be divided into three or more smaller horizontal masses or sections by placing the larger mass or masses at the bottom and by sequentially reducing the height measure of each mass toward the smaller division or divisions to be located at the top of the mass.*

Rule 2c. Let us now imagine the center section of a three-part design to be removed and extended upward. Its transformation by this process into a cabinet or chiffonier similar to Figure 253, Plate 42, introduces the new principle of *sequential progression.* Instead of adhering to the limitation of Rules 2a and 2b, this arrangement shows that the horizontal divisions may be gradually decreased in height from the bottom toward the top of the primary mass. By this rhythmic decrease in the measure of the height, the eye is led

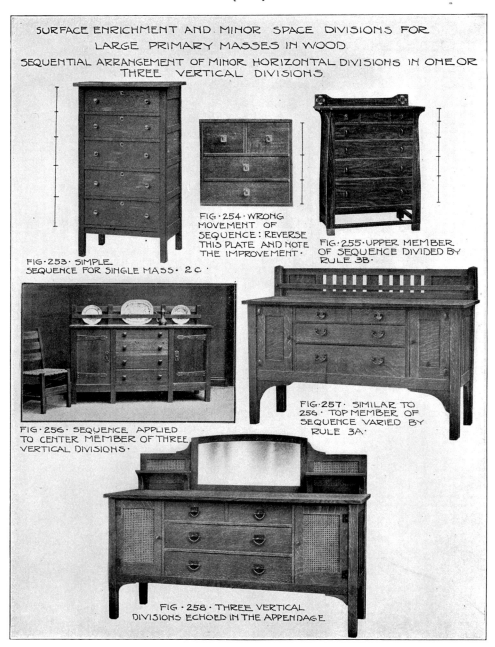

SURFACE ENRICHMENT AND MINOR SPACE DIVISIONS FOR LARGE PRIMARY MASSES IN WOOD

SEQUENTIAL ARRANGEMENT OF MINOR HORIZONTAL DIVISIONS IN ONE OR THREE VERTICAL DIVISIONS

FIG·253· SIMPLE SEQUENCE FOR SINGLE MASS· 2 C·

FIG·254·WRONG MOVEMENT OF SEQUENCE: REVERSE THIS PLATE AND NOTE THE IMPROVEMENT·

FIG·255·UPPER MEMBER OF SEQUENCE DIVIDED BY RULE·3B·

FIG·256· SEQUENCE APPLIED TO CENTER MEMBER OF THREE VERTICAL DIVISIONS·

FIG·257· SIMILAR TO 256· TOP MEMBER OF SEQUENCE VARIED BY RULE 3A·

FIG·258· THREE VERTICAL DIVISIONS ECHOED IN THE APPENDAGE·

PLATE 42

through an orderly gradation through lesser areas to the top, thus giving a pleasing sensation of lightness and variety to the structure. By this method, also, the large areas are retained at the bottom to give stability and solidity to the structure. A quick test of these conditions may be made by reversing Figure 254, thus producing a more decidedly pleasing effect.

Sequential Arrangements— (Continued)

This orderly gradation or sequence of heights need not be carried out with absolute mathematical precision such as 7-6-5-4-3-2-1. Arrangements similar to the following progression make for equally pleasing and more varied effect: $9\frac{1}{4}$-8-$6\frac{3}{4}$-6-5-$4\frac{3}{4}$. Many designers repeat similar heights for two neighboring horizontal spaces as, 6-5-5-$4\frac{3}{4}$, but the upward gradation should be apparent. Figure 255, an Austrian motive, shows a strongly marked sequence with the top division broken by Rule 3b. It is better practice to keep such attempts confined to the bottom or top members of the sequence or loss of unity may be the final result.

By applying this principle to the center section of a three-part design, we now have illustrated in Figure 256 the new sequence in its application, and Figures 257 and 258 are variations of the same idea.

We now come to the transitional type of design where three *vertical* sections begin to lose their dominance as major divisions, but still retain their places in the design as minor sections. Replacing these in prominence is the *horizontal* major section or division. The first immediate result of this change as shown in Plate 43 is to produce a more compact surface with a greater impression of length because of the presence of strongly accented horizontal lines which are always associated with horizontal divisions. This transitional style with its minor but dominant horizontal divisions would harmonize with the long horizontal lines of a room or similar lines in the furniture. The full expression of this style or type will be readily seen by comparing Plates 43 and Figures 251 and 252, Plate 41. Several styles of period furniture have been introduced in Plate 43 to prove the universality of these principles of space divisions.

Figures 259, 260, and 262, Plate 43, are divided by three minor vertical sections cut by two minor horizontal divisions with the dominance in the *lower section*. Rule 2a. The arrangement of the small

Two
Horizontal
and Three
Vertical
Divisions

SURFACE ENRICHMENT AND MINOR SUB DIVISIONS
FOR LARGE PRIMARY MASSES IN WOOD ·
·THREE VERTICAL DIVISIONS CROSSED BY TWO HORIZONTAL DIVISIONS·

FIG·259·
SHERATON

FIG·260
ADAM

FIG·261·
SHERATON

FIG·262·
MISSION

FIG·263· THIS SEQUENTIAL
PLAN OF THE SMALL CENTER
DRAWERS WOULD HAVE INCREASED
THE INTEREST IN FIGURES
259 TO 262·

FIG·264· AN APPROACH TO THREE
HORIZONTAL DIVISIONS (PLATE 44)
NOTE PANEL ENRICHMENT WITH P
IN CENTER·

FIG·265· SEQUEN-
TIAL PLAN FOR
TWO DRAWERS·

PLATE 43

central drawers could have been more varied by the application of the principle of sequential progression. Figures 261 and 263 show similar vertical spacings with a difference in the arrangements of the horizontal divisions. In these figures the dominance has been placed in the *upper section* of the primary mass by the division created by the runner above the lower drawer. It is likewise seen that Figure 263 needs a top appendage to bind the top into closer unity with minor spacings.

In carrying the transitional type to which we have referred in the previous paragraphs from the vertical space influence toward the horizontal, we are gradually approaching *three minor horizontal divisions*, still maintaining three minor vertical divisions in a modified and less prominent form. Figure 264 is an approach toward three horizontal divisions. As only one clear-cut horizontal space division is visible, this figure is not a pure example. The upper horizontal space division is broken up into a three-part design by the drawer guides. It is not until we reach Figure 266 that three horizontal divisions are clearly evident.

Horizontal Divisions

The horizontal minor divisions in furniture are generally drawer runners and the vertical minor divisions are often drawer guides. The horizontal divisions may be arranged in either one of two ways: first, by the application of Rule 2b; or second, by applying Rule 2c, the rule of sequential progression. Figures 266, 267, and 268, Plate 44, are representative of the former while Figures 269 and 270 are typical of the latter. The result in either case is a compactly designed and solid mass of simple structural lines. On some occasions we find the three-part rule used for minor divisions within the horizontal sections, while again the two-part rule is used. The method depends upon the desired use and appearance. In either case the long areas and large masses are to be retained as far as possible near the bottom of each primary mass, as this custom tends to give a sense of solidity to the design.

Figure 271 is a rare reversion to more than three vertical divisions. In this case, Rule 3c has been observed and we find all of the panels

Marginal notes:

Dominance of Lower or Upper Sections

Transitional Types

Three Minor Horizontal Divisions Cut by Varying Numbers of Vertical Divisions

Four Vertical Divisions

· SURFACE ENRICHMENT AND MINOR SUB DIVISIONS
FOR LARGE PRIMARY MASSES IN WOOD · ·
·ACCENTED HORIZONTAL DIVISIONS (THREE) CUT BY VERTICAL DIVISIONS·

FIG · 266
RULE 2B

FIG · 267
RULE 2B

FIG · 268
RULE 2B

FIG · 269
RULE . 2C

FIG · 270
RULE · 2C ·

FIG · 271 (COLONIAL)
RULES 2B AND 3C ·

PLATE 44

are of equal size. Variety has been secured by means of the horizontal spacings.

FREE BALANCE

This form of design is inherent in the Japanese system. It consists in the planning and balancing of unequal areas over a geometric center. It is not subject to definite rules as is the more formal balancing. The reader is referred to Mr. Arthur Dow's excellent book on Composition for further discussion of the subject. Figure 272, Plate 45, is an example of partly formal and partly free balance and its method of treatment.

Figures 273 and 274 are pierced designs, thoroughly related to the structure and in no way weakening it. Figure 273 is representative of a type which, if carried to extremes, will cause the structure to become too weak for service; it is, therefore, necessary to guard and restrict this form of enrichment. The carving of Figure 275, combined with the contour enrichment, forms a pleasing variation to this common type of furniture design.

Small minor details in furniture construction should be designed with as much care as the larger major or minor parts. The larger areas or spaces in small details similar to stationery shelves and pigeon holes must harmonize in proportion with the space in which they are placed and of which they are a part.

The three-part or three-vertical division system, Rule 3b, is generally used to design the small details in furniture as may be seen in Figures 276, 277, 278, and 279; while the rule of sequence, Rule 2c, may be employed again to subdivide these small details in a horizontal direction with as much variety as is consistent with unity. Figure 280 is a leaded glass surface enrichment for doors. Note the leading lines of the enrichment as they parallel the dominant proportions of the panel opening.

Free Minor Space Treatment

Free Balance

Carving and Piercing as Applied to Large Masses

Small Minor Details of Large Primary Masses

INSTRUCTION SHEET

Plate 46 is a typical high school sheet of design problems, with the masses accentuated by pen shading. See Plate 15.

SUMMARY OF DESIGN STEPS

(*a*) to (*e*). See similar steps in Chapter IV.

· SURFACE ENRICHMENT AND MINOR SUB DIVISIONS
FOR LARGE PRIMARY MASSES IN WOOD ·
·FREE MINOR SPACINGS · APPENDAGES · PIERCED AND CARVED ENRICHMENT·

FIG ·273·
PIERCING·

FIG·272· FREE MINOR SPACE TREATMENT·
COURTESY INTERNATIONAL
STUDIO

FIG·275·
CARVING·
COURTESY INT· STUDIO·

FIG · 274 ·
PIERCING·

FIG ·276·
MINOR SPACES·

FIG · 278 ·

FIG·277· MINOR SPACING
RULE 3 B ·

FIG· 280·

FIG · 279·
RULES 3 B· C · ETC.

PLATE 45

SUGGESTED PROBLEM

Design a sideboard 3 feet 3 inches high with plate rack. The primary mass should have three minor horizontal divisions and three minor vertical divisions, with the horizontal divisions accented.

SUMMARY OF RULES

Sequential Progression of Minor Horizontal Space Divisions

Rule 2c. *A primary mass may be divided into three or more smaller horizontal masses or sections by placing the larger mass or masses at the bottom and by sequentially reducing the height measure of each mass toward the smaller division or divisions to be located at the top of the mass.*

REVIEW QUESTIONS

1. What are minor subdivisions in wood construction?
2. What is the effect of a design with dominant vertical major divisions? State its use.
3. Show some customary methods of dividing three vertical major divisions into minor subdivisions.
4. State the rule of sequential progression. Give illustrations from the industrial arts.
5. Describe the transitional stage between the point where the dominance of the vertical motive ceases and the horizontal influence begins.
6. What is the effect of a design with dominant horizontal major divisions? State its use.
7. Show some customary methods of subdividing horizontal major divisions into minor subdivisions.
8. What should be the relation in a design between the details of a project and the divisions of the primary mass?

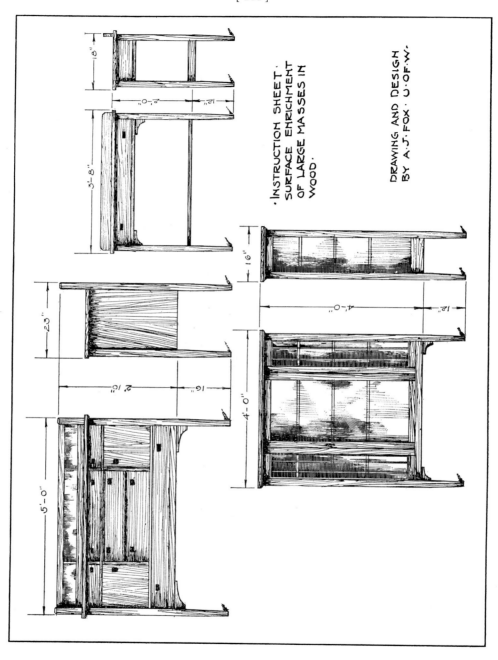

· INSTRUCTION SHEET ·
SURFACE ENRICHMENT
OF LARGE MASSES IN
WOOD ·

DRAWING AND DESIGN
BY A·J·FOX· U·OF·W·

PLATE 46

Chapter XII

SURFACE ENRICHMENT OF CLAY

In some respects the surface enrichment of clay is similar to that of wood as, for example, the similarity produced by inlays in clay and in wood. On the other hand the enrichment of clay is unhampered by the restricting effects of unequal resistance of the material, such as the grain of wood. Again it *is* limited to those effects or forms of enrichment that are capable of withstanding the intense heat to which ceramic decoration is subjected. See Frontispiece.

Limitations for Surface Enrichment

Courtesy of the Rookwood Potteries

FIGURE 281.— Filling the Saggars before Firing

Before proceeding with a design it is well for one to understand clearly the possibilities of clay enrichment. He must know what kind of designs are best suited to clay as a medium, to the intended service, and to the ultimate application of the heat of the pottery kiln. Without entering into technicalities let us briefly discuss the follow-

Decorative Processes of Surface Enrichment

FIGURE 282.— Stacking the Kiln

ing processes. The first three deal with finger and tool manipulation of the clay body and are consequently the simpler of the processes. The last five are concerned chiefly with the addition of coloring pigments either to the clay or to the glaze and are, therefore, more complex in character.

Forms of Manipulation

PROCESSES

Rule 9a. Surface enrichment of clay must be so designed as to be able to withstand the action of heat to which all ware must be submitted.

Rule 9b. Incised, pierced, and modeled decoration in clay should be simple and bold and thus adapted to the character of the material.

1. This is the simplest form of enrichment, a process familiar to the earliest primitive potters and appropriate now for beginners. It consists of the process of lowering lines or planes into the clay body to the depth of from one-sixteenth to one-eighth of an inch. These lines or planes should be bold and broad. They may be made with a blunt pencil or a flat pointed stick. A square, rectangular, or round stick may be used as a stamp with which to form a pattern for incising. Illustrations of simple incising may be found in Figures 283, 284, 295, 319, 330. The tiles shown are about six inches square.

Incising

2. This process is less common and, as its name implies, is carried out by cutting through the clay. It may be done with a fine wire. Either the background or the design itself may be thus removed. The effect produced is that of lightening an object such as the top of a hanging flower holder, a window flower box, or a lantern shade.

Piercing

3. By adding clay to the main body, and by working this clay into low relief flower or geometric forms, one has the basic process of modeling. The slightly raised areas of clay form a pleasing play of light and shade that varies the otherwise plain surface of the ware. The process should be used with caution, for over-modeling, Figure 325, will obstruct the structural outlines and, because of its over prominence as decoration, will cease to be *surface enrichment*. In the technical language of the designer over-modeling is an enrichment which is not subordinated to the surface. In articles intended for service this high relief modeling is unsanitary and unsatisfactory.

Modeling

Figures 286 and 287 show incising with slight modeling, while 324, 328, and 329 are examples of more complex enrichment.

· SURFACE ENRICHMENT OF CLAY ·
· RECTANGULAR AND SQUARE AREAS ·

· KEY TO ZONES OF ENRICHMENT ·
A · MARGIN OF SURFACE ·
B · CENTER OF SURFACE ·
C · FULL HORIZONTAL
   SURFACE
D · FULL VERTICAL
   SURFACE
E · FREEBALANCE ON
   FULL SURFACE
F · ACCENTED CONTOUR

FIG · 283 · C · 1 ·
FIG · 284 · A · 1 · 4 ·
FIG · 285 · B · 1 · 4 ·
FIG · 286 · A · 1 ·
FIG · 287 · A · 1 · 3 ·
FIG · 288 · A · 3 ·
FIG · 289 · C · 3 ·
FIG · 292 · D · 3 ·
FIG · 290 · D · 5 ·
FIG · 291 · C · 5 ·
FIG · 293 · E · 5 · 6 (MATT)
FIG · 295 · E · 1 ·
FIG · 294 · E · 5 · 6 · MATT
FIG · 296 ·
FIG · 297 · APPLICATION
OF THE DECORATIVE
MOTIVE OF FIG · 296
TO AN OVERMANTLE · E ·
5 · 6 (MATT)
FIG · 298 · E ·
5 · 6 · (MATT)

PLATE 47

With the introduction of the second group comes an added interest and difficulty, that of the introduction of color. Pigments that will withstand the application of heat are suggested at different points. Introduction of Coloring Pigments

4. This process consists of removing certain areas from the clay body to the depth of one-eighth inch and filling in the depression with tinted clay. Tints formed by the addition of ten per cent or less of burnt umber or yellow ochre to the modeling clay will give interesting effects. Figures 284, 285, 320, and 321 show forms which may be developed by this process. Inlay

Sgraffito, an Italian process, is more difficult than inlaying, but the effect is similar. A thin layer of colored clay is placed over the natural clay body, and the design is developed by cutting away this colored coating in places, thus exposing the natural clay body. Figure 306. There are variations of this plan that may be attempted by the advanced designer.

5. Slip is clay mixed with water to the consistency of cream. For slip painting this mixture is thoroughly mixed with not more than ten per cent of coloring pigment as represented by the underglaze colors of the ceramist. This thick, creamy, colored slip is then painted on the surface of the clay body while damp, much as the artist would apply oil colors. The ware, when thoroughly dried, is glazed and fired, which produces the effect shown in Figures 290, 291, and 327. The color range is large; almost any color may be used with the exception of reds and strong yellows. A colorless transparent glaze should be used over beginner's slip painting. Slip Painting

6. This process refers to the direct introduction of the colored pigment into the glaze. By varying the glaze formula we may have a clear, transparent, or glossy glaze similar to Figure 317, a dull surfaced opaque effect, termed a matt glaze, Figure 332; or a glossy but opaque faience glaze similar to the blue and white Dutch tiles. There are other forms such as the crystalline and "reduced" glazes, but these as a rule are far beyond the ability of the beginning craftsman in ceramics. Colored Glazes

It is possible to use these three types of glazed surface in various ways. For example, a vase form with an interesting contour may be left without further surface enrichment except that supplied by clear glaze or by a colored matt similar to certain types of Teco Ware. Combinations

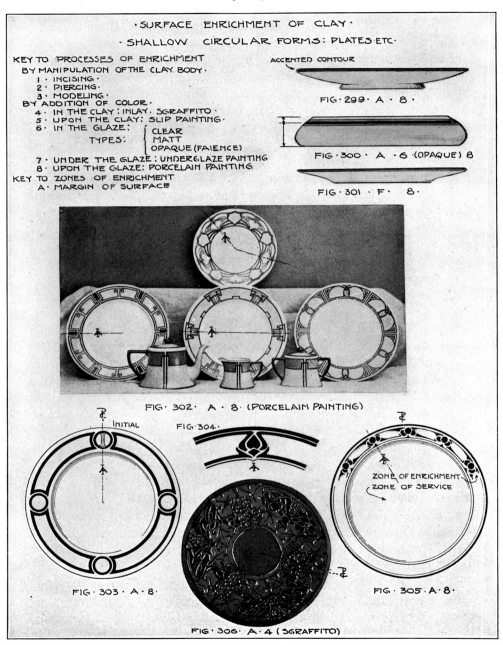

· SURFACE ENRICHMENT OF CLAY ·

· SHALLOW CIRCULAR FORMS: PLATES ETC ·

KEY TO PROCESSES OF ENRICHMENT
  BY MANIPULATION OF THE CLAY BODY ·
    1 · INCISING ·
    2 · PIERCING ·
    3 · MODELING ·
  BY ADDITION OF COLOR ·
    4 · IN THE CLAY : INLAY. SGRAFFITO ·
    5 · UPON THE CLAY: SLIP PAINTING ·
    6 · IN THE GLAZE: CLEAR
                        MATT
              TYPES: OPAQUE (FAIENCE)
    7 · UNDER THE GLAZE : UNDERGLAZE PAINTING
    8 · UPON THE GLAZE: PORCELAIN PAINTING
KEY TO ZONES OF ENRICHMENT
  A · MARGIN OF SURFACE

ACCENTED CONTOUR

FIG · 299 · A · 8 ·

FIG · 300 · A · 6 (OPAQUE) 8

FIG · 301 · F · 8 ·

FIG · 302 · A · 8 · (PORCELAIN PAINTING)

INITIAL

FIG · 304 ·

ZONE OF ENRICHMENT
ZONE OF SERVICE

FIG · 303 · A · 8 ·

FIG · 306 · A · 4 (SGRAFFITO)

FIG · 305 A · 8 ·

PLATE 48

It is likewise possible to apply transparent glazes over incised designs, inlay or slip painting, increasing their beauty and the serviceability of the ware. A semi-transparent glaze is sometimes placed over slip painting giving the charm inherent to the Vellum Ware of the Rookwood Potteries. Figure 332. Greens, blues, yellows, and browns, with their admixtures, are the safest combinations for the craftsman who desires to mix his own glazes.

7. This process may be seen in the examples of Newcomb Pottery illustrated particularly in Figure 314 or 326. The underglaze pigment is thinly painted upon the fired "biscuit," or unglazed ware. A thin, transparent glaze is then placed *over* the color, and in the final firing the underneath color shows through this transparent coating, thus illustrating the origin of the name underglaze or under-the-glaze painting. Sage-green and cobalt-blue underglaze colors are frequently used in Newcomb designs with harmonious results. The outline of the design is often incised and the underglaze color, settling into these channels, helps to accentuate the design. Figure 314.

Underglaze Painting

8. This is popularly known as china painting and consists of painting directly upon the glazed surface of the ware and placing it in a china kiln where a temperature between 600 degrees and 900 degrees C. is developed. At this point the coloring pigment melts or is fused into the porcelain glaze, thus insuring its reasonable permanence. Figure 302.

Porcelain or Overglaze Painting

The eight processes briefly described may be readily identified on the plates by referring to the figures corresponding to those which number the processes and are added to each figure number. Two processes are sometimes suggested as possible for one problem.

Different clay forms require different modes of treatment. To simplify these treatments will now be our problem. It has been found convenient to form four divisions based upon the general geometric shape of the ware. The first, Plate 47, includes rectangular and square areas; the second, Plate 48, shallow and circular forms; the third, Plate 49, low cylindrical forms; and the fourth, Plate 50, high cylindrical forms. The first three divisions have distinct modes of design treatment, while the fourth interlocks to a considerable extent with the third method. We shall now consider each plate with reference to its use and possible forms of enrichment. For the

Classification of Structural Clay Forms

· SURFACE ENRICHMENT OF CLAY ·
· LOW CYLINDRICAL FORMS ·

CF:
FOR ADDITIONAL
LOW BOWL SUG-
GESTIONS · SEE
PLATE 3 ·

NOTE:
THE LETTER
FOLLOWING EACH
NUMBER SHOWS THE
ZONE OF ENRICHMENT · THE
FIGURE SUGGESTS ENRICHMENT

FIG 307 · D · 8

FIG · 308 · A · 6 OR 8

ELEMENT

FIG · 309 · A · 6 OR 8 ·

FIG · 310 · A · 8 ·

FIG · 311 · A · 6 OR 8 ·

FIG 313 A · 1 + 6 (MATT)

FIG 312 · A · 6 OR 8 ·

FIG · 314 · D · 1 + 7

FIG · 315 · E · 6 · MATT ·

FIG · 316 · A · 7 ·

FIG · 317 · D · 1 + 7

FIG · 318 · IS THE
APPROACH TO
HIGHER FORMS ·
NOTE THE IM-
PORTANCE OF
FIG · 318 · D   THE VERTICAL
1 + 7   LINE · · ·

PLATE 49

sake of brevity, the results have been condensed into tabulated forms.

Each geometric form or type on these plates has not only distinctive methods of design treatment but characteristic locations for placing the design as well. These places or zones of enrichment have been indicated in the following tabulated forms by the letters in parentheses. There are a number of zones for each plate. For example, Plate 47 has its distinctive problems as tiles, weights, etc., and five characteristic zones of enrichment described on pages 153-155 and indicated by the letters A, B, C, D, E, followed by a brief description of that zone. Each zone is still further analyzed into its accompanying type of design, inceptive axis, point of concentration, and illustrations. Each plate has the proper zone of enrichment immediately following the figure number and in turn followed by the process number.

Problems: Tiles for tea and coffee pots, paper weights, window boxes; architectural tiles for floors, and fire places.

Square and Rectangular Areas, Plate 47

(*A*) *Zone of Enrichment:* In the margin.
    Reason for Choice: Central area to be devoted to zone of service requiring simplicity in design.
    Type of Design: Bands or borders.
    Inceptive Axis: For corners; the bisector of the angle.
    Points of Concentration: The corners and, if desired, at equal intervals between the corners.
    Illustrations: Figures 283, 284, 286, 287, 288.

Marginal Enrichment

(*B*) *Zone of Enrichment:* center of surface, free ornament.
    Type of Design: Initials, monograms, street numbers, geometric patterns, and other examples for free ornament. A star or diamond is *not* appropriate enrichment for a square area unless properly related to the contour by connecting areas.
    Inceptive Axes: Vertical or horizontal diameters or diagonals.
    Points of Concentration: Center of embellishment.
    Illustrations: Figure 285.

Center Enrichment

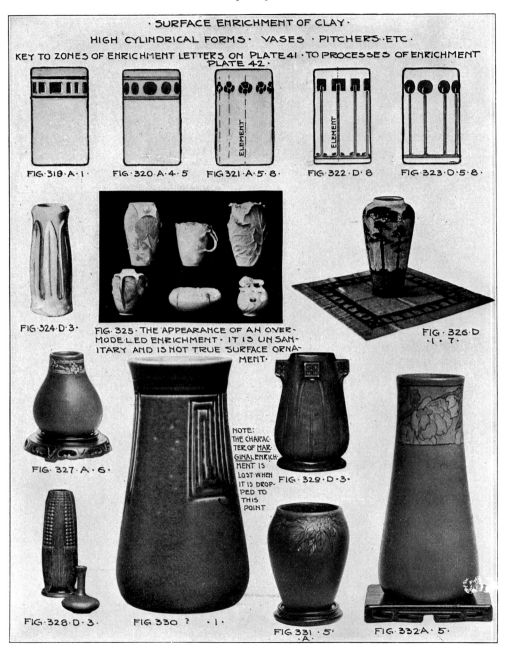

· SURFACE ENRICHMENT OF CLAY ·

HIGH CYLINDRICAL FORMS · VASES · PITCHERS · ETC ·

KEY TO ZONES OF ENRICHMENT LETTERS ON PLATE 41 · TO PROCESSES OF ENRICHMENT PLATE 42 ·

FIG · 319 · A · 1 ·

FIG · 320 · A · 4 · 5

FIG · 321 · A · 5 · 8 ·

FIG · 322 · D · 8

FIG · 323 · D · 5 · 8 ·

FIG · 324 · D · 3 ·

FIG · 325 · THE APPEARANCE OF AN OVER-MODELLED ENRICHMENT · IT IS UNSANITARY AND IS NOT TRUE SURFACE ORNAMENT ·

FIG · 326 · D · 1 · 7 ·

FIG · 327 · A · 6 ·

NOTE: THE CHARACTER OF MARGINAL ENRICHMENT IS LOST WHEN IT IS DROPPED TO THIS POINT

FIG · 329 · D · 3 ·

FIG · 328 · D · 3 ·

FIG · 330 ? · 1 ·

FIG · 331 · 5 · A

FIG · 332 A · 5 ·

PLATE 50

(*C*) *Zone of Enrichment:* full surface enrichment in a horizontal position.

Type of Design: A symmetrical pattern generally radiating from the geometric center of the surface and covering at least two-thirds of the surface.

Inceptive Axes: Diameters or diagonals of the area.

Points of Concentration: At the corners or the center of the outer margin; at geometric center, as in a rosette.

Illustrations: Figures 283, 289, and 291.

Full
Horizontal
Surface
Enrichment

(*D*) *Zone of Enrichment:* full surface enrichment in a vertical position.

Type of Design: A symmetrical pattern with a strong upward movement and covering more than one-half of the surface.

Inceptive Axis: The vertical center line.

Point of Concentration: Upper section of the surface.

Illustrations: Figures 290 and 292.

Full
Vertical
Surface
Enrichment

(*E*) *Zone of Enrichment:* free balance over full surface.

Type of Design: Semi-decorative motive preferably covering the entire surface.

Inceptive Axis: Masses freely balanced over the geometric center of the area.

Point of Concentration: Near, but not in the exact center.

Illustrations: Figures 293, 294, 295, 296, 297, 298.

Note: The points of concentration should be accented by slight contrast of value and hue. See chapters on color.

Free
Balance

Problems: Plates, saucers, ash trays, card receivers, almond and candy bowls.

Shallow
Circular
Forms,
Plate 48

(*A*) *Zone of Enrichment:* margin of interior surface; margin of exterior surface.

Type of Design: Bands or borders thoroughly related to the structural contours. Bands for exterior enrichment may be placed directly on the contour, Figures 299 and 301, thus forming an

12

· Applied and Constructive Design ·

· RULE 9 : ENRICHMENT OF THE PRIMARY MASS BY A BORDER ·
· PROBLEM: ENRICHMENT OF CLASS 2 (POTTERY) ·

BORDERS ARE WELL ADAPTED TO THIS CLASS AND MUST ECHO
OR PARALLEL A DOMINANT PROPORTION · THE BORDER MUST
CAUSE THE EYE TO TRAVEL IN THE DIRECTION OF THIS PROPORTION
HENCE · ALL OF ITS COMPONENT PARTS MUST POSSESS CONCERTED
ACTION IN THIS DIRECTION OR RHYTHM · RHYTHM IS THE CONSISTENT CO-
ORDINATION OF PARTS THAT ASSISTS THE EYE TO FIND ITS WAY THROUGH
ALL DETAILS OF THE DESIGN ·

FORMAL BI SYMMETRICAL REPETITION   FREE REPETITION

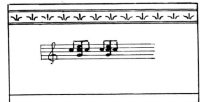

SKELETON BORDERS FOR WALL SURFACES WITH MUSICAL ANALOGIES

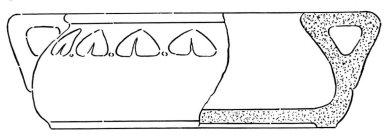

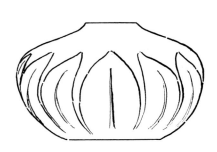
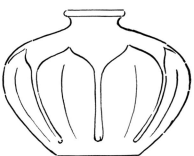

· DRAW TWO DESIGNS ILLUSTRATING THIS FORM OF ENRICHMENT ·

PLATE 51.— Instruction Sheet

accented contour (F) or slightly removed from it, as in Figure 300.

Inceptive Axes: For interior surfaces, the radii of the contour circle generally supply the axes of symmetry.

Points of Concentration: For interior surfaces, the points of concentration may be placed in or near the radii of the area.

Illustrations: Figures 302, 303, 304, 305, 306.

Marginal Enrichment

Problems: Cups, pitchers, steins, nut and rose bowls, low vase forms.

(A) Zone of Enrichment: upper margin of exterior.

Type of Design: Borders of units joining each other or connected by bands or spots acting as connecting links. Rule 9c.

Inceptive Axes: Vertical elements of the exterior surface. Elements are imaginary lines dividing the exterior surface into any given number of vertical sections. Elements used as center lines form the axes of symmetry about which the butterfly of Figure 308 and similar designs are constructed.

Points of Concentration: On each vertical element.

Illustrations: Figures 308, 309, 310, 311, 312, 316.

Low Cylindrical Forms, Plate 49

Marginal Enrichment

(D) Zone of Enrichment: full vertical surface.

Type of Design: Extended borders with strongly developed vertical lines or forms. Less than one-half of the surface may be covered.

Inceptive Axes: Vertical elements.

Points of Concentration: In upper portion of vertical elements, hence in upper portion of area.

Illustrations: Figures 307, 314, 317, 318.

Full Vertical Surface Enrichment

(E) Zone of Enrichment: free balance of full surface. (See *D*, above).

Illustration: Figure 315.

Problems: Vases, jars, pitchers, tall flower holders, covered jars for tea, crackers, or tobacco.

High Cylindrical Forms, Plate 50

**Marginal
Enrichment**

(*A*) *Zone of Enrichment:* margin of exterior.

Type of Design: Borders of geometric units, freely balanced floral units, and other natural motives placed in upper margin of mass.

Inceptive Axes: Vertical elements of cylinder.

Points of Concentration: In upper portion of vertical elements.

Illustrations: Figures 319, 320, 321, 327, 331, 332.

**Full
Surface
Enrichment**

(*D*) *Zone of Enrichment:* full surface of exterior.

Type of Design: Free of formal conventionalized unit repeated on each vertical element. The units may be juxtaposed or may be connected by bands or similar links.

Inceptive Axes: Vertical elements of cylinder.

Point of concentration: In upper portion of vertical elements.

Illustrations: Figures 322, 323, 324, 326, 328, 329.

**Types of
Commercial
Pottery**

The reader should carefully consider the postulate and various divisions of Rule 7 and try to apply them to the material now under consideration. Acknowledgment is made for material supplied by the Rookwood Potteries for Figures 288, 289, 292, 293, 294, 297, 298, 315; 327 and 332; Newcomb Potteries, Figures 314, 316, 317, 318, 326; Teco Potteries, 329; Keramic Studio Publishing Company, 302, 307, 308, 310, 312.

INSTRUCTION SHEET

Plate 51 illustrates the marginal surface enrichment of low cylindrical forms, with part surface enrichment of two higher forms.

SUMMARY OF DESIGN STEPS

(*a*) Draw primary mass:

For square or rectangular areas draw square rectangle, etc.

For shallow circular forms draw a circle.

For low cylindrical forms draw a rectangle; subdivide this if desired by a unit of measurement into two horizontal divisions.

For high cylindrical forms draw a rectangle; subdivide this if desired by a unit of measurement into two or three horizontal divisions.   Rule 5e.

(*b*) Design simple contour enrichment based upon these units of measurement.

(*c*) Locate zone of enrichment.

(*d*) Draw inceptive axes:

For square or rectangular areas draw diameters, diagonals, or both.

For shallow circular forms draw radii of the primary circle; concentric circles for bands.

For low cylindrical forms draw the elements of the underlying cylindrical form for extended borders or lines paralleling the top or bottom of the primary mass for bands.

For high cylindrical forms draw inceptive axes similar to low cylindrical forms.

(e) Locate points of concentration in these inceptive axes.

(f) Determine manner and amount of surface enrichment.

(g) Add leading lines and develop these into surface enrichment.

(h) Make potter's working drawing, full size (See Plate 26). Add the necessary amount for shrinkage and otherwise prepare the drawing for potter's use.

(i) Make a paper tracing of the surface enrichment for transfer to clay body and cut a zinc or tin template as a contour guide in building the form.

SUGGESTED PROBLEMS

Design a cider or chocolate set with appropriate surface enrichment.

Design an architectural tile 6 in. by 9 in. for accenting a brick fireplace in the home.

SUMMARY OF RULES

Rule 9a. *Surface enrichment of clay must be so designed as to be able to withstand the action of heat to which all ware must be submitted.*

Rule 9b. *Incised, pierced, and modeled decoration in clay should be simple and bold and thus adapted to the character of the material.*

Rule 9c. *A border should not be located at the point of greatest curvature in the contour of a cylindrical form. The contour curve is of sufficient interest in itself at that point.*

REVIEW QUESTIONS

1. Compare the surface enrichment of clay with that of wood.
2. State a major requirement of a good pottery design.
3. Give the broad divisions into which it is possible to divide the decorative processes of clay surface enrichment.
4. Name and briefly describe eight methods of enriching the surface of clay.
5. What precautions should be exercised with regard to the use of incised, pierced, and modeled decoration?
6. Should a border be placed at the point of greatest curvature of the contour? Give reasons.
7. Name method of classifying structural forms in clay into four groups.
8. State problems and possible zones of enrichment in each group. Give reasons for choice.
9. State type of design unit, conventionalized, natural or artificial forms, location of inceptive axis, points of concentration, and process for each zone of enrichment.
10. What is an element of a cylindrical surface?

Chapter XIII

SURFACE ENRICHMENT OF PRECIOUS METALS

Small Flat Planes

Base and Precious Metals

Chapter XII referred to clay as a free and plastic material adapted to a wide range of surface enrichment processes. Metal as a more refractory material offers greater resistance to the craftsman and is relatively more limited in its capacity for surface enrichment. As was the case in the consideration of contour enrichment for designing purposes, it is necessary in the consideration of surface enrichment to divide metal into two groups: precious and base metals. As the field of design in both base and precious metals is large, we shall consider the surface enrichment of *precious metals only* in this chapter.

Divisions for Enrichment

Following an order similar in character to that used in clay designing, problems in both base and precious metals may be divided into four classified groups as follows: flat, square, rectangular, or irregular planes; shallow circular forms; low cylindrical forms; high cylindrical forms. Designs included in the first group, flat planes, comprise such problems as are typically represented by tie pins, fobs, rings, and pendants. The design problems presented by these examples are so important that it is wise to restrict this chapter to *flat planes*.

Rule 10g. *The inceptive axis should pass through and coincide with one axis of a stone, and at the same time be sympathetically related to the structure.*

Rule 10h. *The position of the inceptive axis should be determined by: (1) use of the project as ring, pendant, or bar pin, (2) character of the primary mass as either vertical or horizontal in proportion.*

The semi-precious or precious stone is commonly found to be the point of concentration of these designs. The inceptive axes of tie pins, pendants, and fobs are generally vertical center lines because of the vertical positions of the objects when worn. The inceptive axes, moreover, should pass through the point of concentration and, at the same time, be sympathetically related to the structure. Rings and bar pins are frequently designed with horizontal inceptive axes, so determined by their horizontal characteristics and positions.

The point of concentration for tie pins, pendants, and fobs in formal balance, in addition to coinciding with the inceptive axis, is generally located above or below the geometric center of the primary mass. The point of concentration for rings and bar pins is placed in the horizontal inceptive axis and centrally located from left to right.

As a step preliminary to designing, and in order that the enrichment may be conventionalized or adapted to conform to the requirements of tools, processes, and materials, it is now imperative to become familiar with a number of common forms of surface enrichment in metal. There are eight processes frequently encountered in the decoration of silver and gold: piercing, etching, chasing or repousséing, enameling, inlaying, stone setting, building, carving. To these may be added planishing, frosting or matting, and oxidizing as methods employed to enrich the entire surface. Economy of material is of prime importance in the designing of precious metal and, particularly in gold projects, conservation of the metals should be an urgent consideration in all designs.

Rule 10a. *Designs in precious metals should call for the minimum amount of metal necessary to express the idea of the designer for two reasons: (1) good taste; (2) economy of material.*

A non-technical and brief description of each process follows. All designs in this chapter may be identified by referring to the process numbers after the figure description as 1, 3, 5; 2, 4, 6, corresponding to the key numbers on Plate 52. A design to be submitted to the craftsman should be a graphic *record of technical facts* in addition to good design, which requires that we should have an expressive *technical means of rendering each process.* The last column, on Plate 52, indicates this rendering. In addition to this rendering each one of the eight technical processes has been carried through three design steps. 1. (first column, Plate 52) Planning the original primary mass, with its inceptive axis suggested by the structure and intended use. It passes through the point of concentration. 2. (second

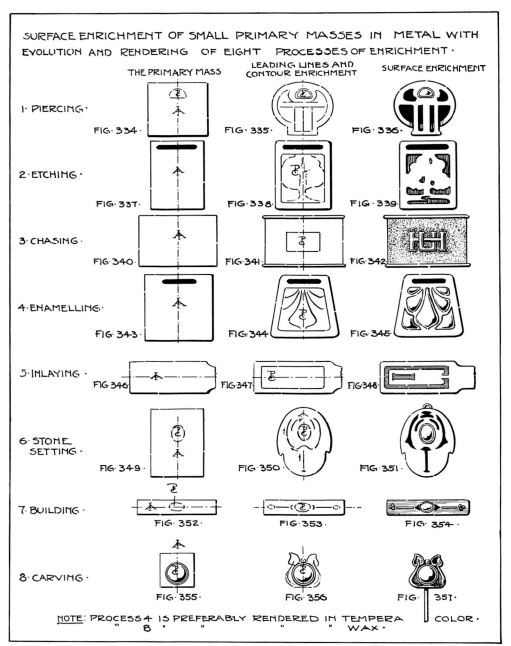

SURFACE ENRICHMENT OF SMALL PRIMARY MASSES IN METAL WITH EVOLUTION AND RENDERING OF EIGHT PROCESSES OF ENRICHMENT.

THE PRIMARY MASS | LEADING LINES AND CONTOUR ENRICHMENT | SURFACE ENRICHMENT

1· PIERCING·
FIG· 334·   FIG· 335·   FIG· 336·

2· ETCHING·
FIG· 337·   FIG· 338·   FIG· 339·

3· CHASING·
FIG· 340·   FIG· 341·   FIG· 342·

4· ENAMELLING·
FIG· 343·   FIG· 344·   FIG· 345·

5· INLAYING·
FIG· 346·   FIG· 347·   FIG· 348·

6· STONE SETTING·
FIG· 349·   FIG· 350·   FIG· 351·

7· BUILDING·
FIG· 352·   FIG· 353·   FIG· 354·

8· CARVING·
FIG· 355·   FIG· 356·   FIG· 357·

NOTE: PROCESS 4 IS PREFERABLY RENDERED IN TEMPERA COLOR·
" 8 · " " " " WAX ·

PLATE 52

column, Plate 52). The division of the primary mass into zones of service and enrichment with the suggestion of the leading lines which, at some points, are parallel to the contours and lead up to the point of concentration. The contours in this column have, in several instances, been changed to add lightness and variety to the problem. 3. The last step (column three, Plate 52) shows the design with graphic rendering suggestive of the completed process.

Technical Processes and Methods of Illustrating Same in a Design

1. Removal of design unit or background by means of the jeweler's saw. Bridges of metal should be left to support firmly all portions of the design. Test this by careful study of the design. Rendering — shade all pierced portions of the design in solid black. Slightly tint portions of the design passing *under* other parts. Illustration, Figure 336. **Piercing**

Rule 10j. *All surface enrichment should have an appearance of compactness or unity. Pierced spots or areas should be so used as to avoid the appearance of having been scattered on the surface without thought to their coherence.*

2. Coating either design or background with an acid resistant, to be followed by immersion of the article in an acid bath. Allow the unprotected portion to be attacked and eaten by the acid to a slight depth. Rendering — slightly tint all depressed or etched parts of the design. Illustration, Figure 339. **Etching**

3. The embossing and fine embellishment of a metal surface by the application of the hammer and punches. The work is conducted mainly from the top surface. Rendering — stipple all parts of the background not raised by the process. Chasing should seem an integral part of the background and not appear stuck upon it. Illustration, Figure 342. Rule 10k. **Chasing or Repousséing**

4. A process of enameling over metal in which the ground is cut away into a series of shallow troughs into which the enamel is melted. Exercise reserve in the use of enamel. Over-decoration tends to cheapen this valuable form of decoration. Rendering — shade the lower and right-hand sides of all enameled areas to suggest relief. Illustration, Figure 345. If possible render in tempera color. **Enameling (Champleve)**

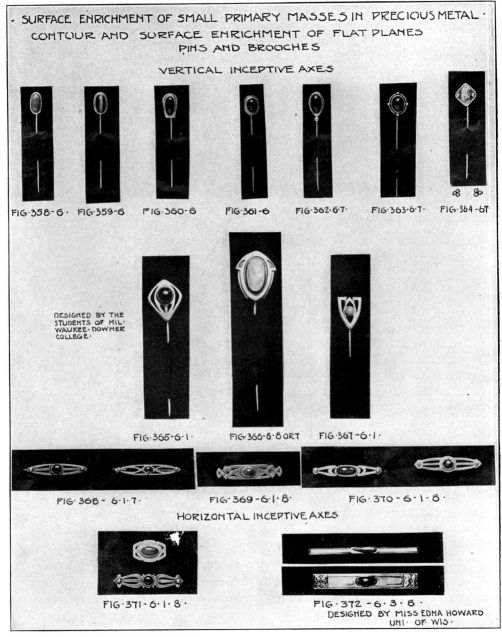

SURFACE ENRICHMENT OF SMALL PRIMARY MASSES IN PRECIOUS METAL ·
CONTOUR AND SURFACE ENRICHMENT OF FLAT PLANES
PINS AND BROOCHES

VERTICAL INCEPTIVE AXES

FIG·358·6·   FIG·359·6   FIG·360·6   FIG·361·6   FIG·362·6·7·   FIG·363·6·7·   FIG·364·6T·

DESIGNED BY THE
STUDENTS OF MIL·
WAUKEE-DOWNER
COLLEGE·

FIG·365·6·1·   FIG·366·6·8 ORT   FIG·367·6·1·

FIG·368·6·1·7·   FIG·369·6·1·8·   FIG·370·6·1·8·

HORIZONTAL INCEPTIVE AXES

FIG·371·6·1·8·   FIG·372·6·3·8·
DESIGNED BY MISS EDNA HOWARD
UNI· OF WIS·

PLATE 53

Rule 10i. *Caution should be exercised with regard to the use of enamel. Over-decoration by this material tends to cheapen both process and design.*

Rule 10l. *The lanes or margins between enameled spots should be narrower than the lane or margin between the enamel and the contour of the primary mass.*

5. The process of applying wire, etc., to an incision on metal either by burnishing or fusing the metal into the cavities. Rendering — tint the darker metal or, if possible, render in color. Illustration, Figure 348.

Inlaying

6. An enrichment of the surface by the addition of semi-precious or precious stones. Other enrichment is generally subordinated to the stone which then becomes the point of concentration. All enrichment should lead toward the stone. Small stones may, however, be used to accentuate other points of concentration in surface enrichment. Rendering—shade the lower and right-side of the stone to suggest relief. Pierced subordinate enrichment should be shaded in solid black. A concentric line should be drawn outside of the contour of the stone to designate the thin holding band, or bezel, enclosing the stone on all sides. Illustration, Figure 351.

Stone Cutting

Rule 10d. *Surface enrichment should at some point parallel the contours of both primary mass and point of concentration, especially whenever the latter is a stone or enamel.*

Rule 10e. *In the presence of either stone or enamel as a point of concentration, surface enrichment should be regarded as an unobtrusive setting, or background.*

Rule 10f. *Stone or enamel used as a point of concentration should form contrast with the metal, either in color, brilliancy, or value, or all three combined.*

7. The process of applying leaves, wire, grains, and other forms of surface enrichment to the plane of the metal. These may afterwards be carved or chased. Rendering — shade the lower and right-hand lines; slightly tint the lower planes of the metal. Illustration, Figure 354.

Building

8. The process of depressing or raising certain portions of the metal surface by means of chisels and gravers. By the use of these tools the surface is modeled into planes of light and shade, to which

Figure 372a.— Tie Pins

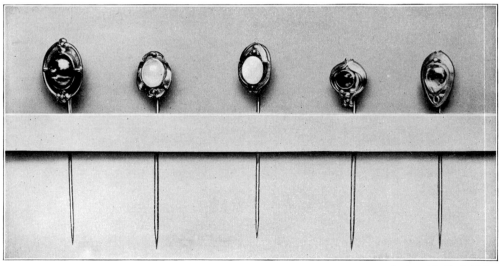

FIGURE 372b.— Tie Pins

interest is added if the unaggressive tool marks are permitted to remain on the surface. Rendering—shade the raised and depressed portions to express the modeling planes. As this is a difficult technical process the designer is advised to model the design in plastelene or jewelers' wax first. Illustration, Figure 357. **Carving**

Rule 10k. *Built, carved, and chased enrichment should have the higher planes near the point of concentration. It is well to have the stone as the highest point above the primary mass. When using this form of enrichment, the stone should never appear to rise abruptly from the primary mass, but should be approached by a series of rising planes.*

9. The process of smoothing and, at the same time, hardening the surface of the metal with a steel planishing hammer. The hammer strokes give an interesting texture to the surface which may be varied, from the heavily indented to the smooth surface, at the will of the craftsman. The more obvious hammer strokes are not to be desired as they bring a tool process into too much prominence for good taste. Rendering — print desired finish on the drawing. **Planishing**

10. A process of sand blasting or scratch brushing a metal surface to produce an opaque or "satin" finish. Rendering — similar to planishing. **Frosting**

11. A process of darkening the surface of metal by the application of chemicals. Potassium sulphite will supply a deep, rich black to silver and copper. Rendering — see Planishing. **Oxidizing**

The eleven processes mentioned above are among those which, by recent common practice, have become familiar to the craftsman in precious metals. While they do not cover the entire field, they at least give the beginner an opportunity to design intelligently in terms of the material. **Design of Pins and Brooches**

Plate 53 is mainly the enrichment of the flat plane by the addition of semi-precious stones (process six). Whatever surface enrichment is added to this design becomes *dependent* enrichment and quite analogous to *dependent* contour enrichment, Plate 29, inasmuch as it has to be designed with special reference to the shape and character of the stone. Figures 358 to 363 are examples of *dependent contour* enrichment; Figures 364 to 371 are examples of *dependent surface* enrichment. Figures 358 to 367 are based upon *vertical* inceptive axes as appropriate to their intended service. The point of con- **Dependent Surface Enrichment for Pins**

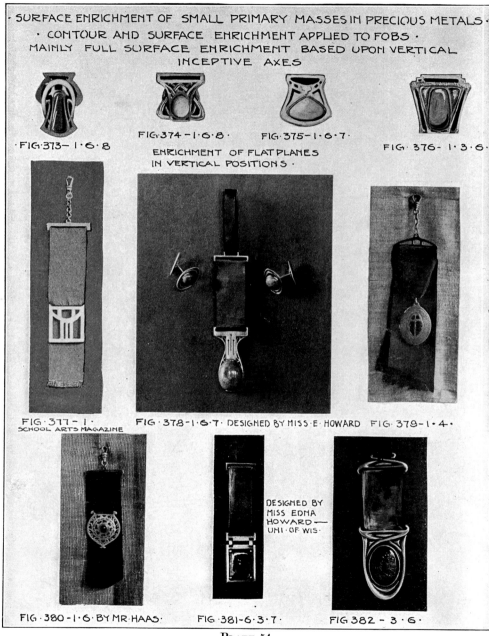

SURFACE ENRICHMENT OF SMALL PRIMARY MASSES IN PRECIOUS METALS ·
· CONTOUR AND SURFACE ENRICHMENT APPLIED TO FOBS ·
MAINLY FULL SURFACE ENRICHMENT BASED UPON VERTICAL
INCEPTIVE AXES

· FIG · 373 — 1 · 6 · 8

FIG · 374 — 1 · 6 · 8 ·

FIG · 375 — 1 · 6 · 7 ·

FIG · 376 — 1 · 3 · 6

ENRICHMENT OF FLAT PLANES
IN VERTICAL POSITIONS ·

FIG · 377 — 1 ·
SCHOOL ARTS MAGAZINE

FIG · 378 — 1 · 6 · 7 · DESIGNED BY MISS E · HOWARD

FIG · 379 — 1 · 4 ·

FIG · 380 — 1 · 6 · BY MR · HAAS ·

FIG · 381 — 6 · 3 · 7 ·

DESIGNED BY
MISS EDNA
HOWARD —
UNI · OF · WIS ·

FIG · 382 — 3 · 6 ·

PLATE 54

centration may be located at practically any point on this inceptive axis, provided the major axis of the stone coincides with the inceptive axis. The best results are obtained by placing the stone a little above or below the exact geometrical center of the primary mass.

Figures 368 to 372 show articles based upon a horizontal inceptive axis. The stone, in accordance with formal balance, is in the geometric center from left to right. One notices the important fact that the surface enrichment must bring the stone and contour together in sympathetic relation and, at the same time, be related to both stone and contour. This again brings out the meaning of *dependent* surface enrichment. The contour enrichment is to be kept as simple as possible and the interest concentrated upon the surface enrichment. The *accentuation of both surface and contour enrichment* in a single design marks the height of bad taste in design.

Inceptive Axes for Pins

Rule 10b. *Contour and surface enrichment should never appear to compete for attention in the same design.*

Plate 54 shows flat planes, the service of which suggests vertical inceptive axes. Figure 380 is noted as an exception to this vertical inceptive axis as it possesses a vertical primary mass but with radial inceptive axes. The interesting manner by which the dynamic leaves of the outer border transmit their movement to the inner border, which in turn leads toward the point of concentration, is worthy of attention. The points of concentration in other designs on this plate are all contained in the vertical inceptive axes.

Fobs

Plate 55, at first thought, would seem to fall under the classification of low cylindrical forms but when reference is made to Figure 385 it is readily seen that the ring has to be first developed as a flat plane, to be afterwards bent into the required form. Care should be taken to keep the design narrow enough to be visible when the ring is in position on the finger.

Rings

The long horizontal band of the ring supplies the motive for the horizontal inceptive axis as a common basis or starting point for a large number of designs. If the designer so desires, the vertical axis of the finger is authority for an elliptical stone to be placed with its major axis as a vertical line in harmony with the finger axis. In any instance the designer seeks to lead the eye from the horizontal portion of the ring (the finger band) toward the point of concentra-

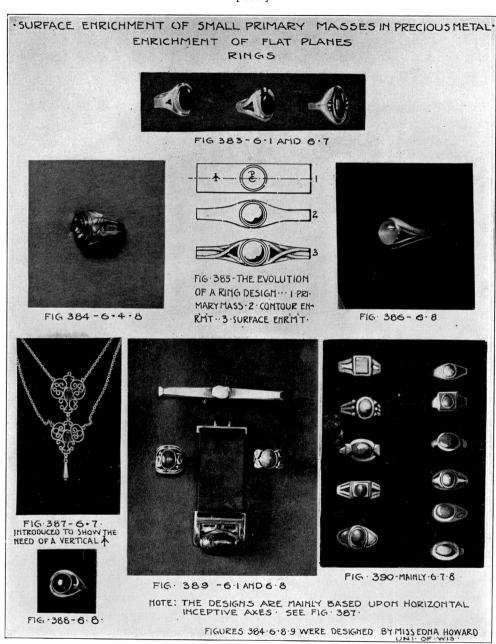

·SURFACE ENRICHMENT OF SMALL PRIMARY MASSES IN PRECIOUS METAL·

ENRICHMENT OF FLAT PLANES

RINGS

FIG 383 — 6·1 AND 6·7

FIG·385 — THE EVOLUTION OF A RING DESIGN ··· 1·PRIMARY MASS·2·CONTOUR ENR'MT··3·SURFACE ENR'M'T·

FIG 384 — 6·4·8

FIG·386 — 6·8

FIG·387 — 6·7· INTRODUCED TO SHOW THE NEED OF A VERTICAL ↑

FIG·388 — 6·8·

FIG· 389 — 6·1 AND 6·8

FIG·390·MAINLY·6·7·8

NOTE: THE DESIGNS ARE MAINLY BASED UPON HORIZONTAL INCEPTIVE AXES· SEE FIG· 387·

FIGURES 384·6·8·9 WERE DESIGNED BY MISS EDNA HOWARD UNI· OF WIS·

PLATE 55

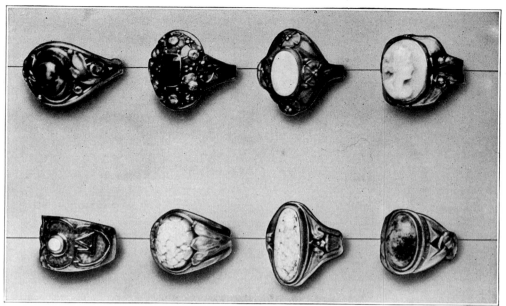

FIGURE 390a.— Rings

tion (the stone), by means of surface enrichment. A long sloping contour curve helps, as a transition line in the boundary, to carry the attention from the stone to the finger band. A great number of devices are used to complete a similar transition in the surface enrichment. Figure 390a. Too much piercing weakens the structure, and it is therefore to be avoided.

Plate 56 suggests some vertical flat planes for pendants. While no definite rule can be stated for the location of the stone, from past experience, it is easier for beginners to place the stone on the vertical inceptive axis slightly above the geometric center of the primary mass. Figures 391 to 395. A design thus formed is less likely to appear heavy, although there is nothing arbitrary about the suggestion.

Rule 10c. *Parts of a design differing in function should differ in appearance but be co-ordinated with the entire design.*

In pendant design the surface enrichment generally carries the attention from the contour of the pendant to the stone, thus insuring

SURFACE ENRICHMENT OF SMALL PRIMARY MASSES IN PRECIOUS METAL·
ENRICHMENT OF FLAT PLANES OF
PENDANTS · CHAINS · LOCKETS ·

FIG· 391 — 6·2·

FIG· 392 — 6·2·
FOB

FIG· 393 — 6·1·

FIG· 394 — 6·1·

FIG· 395 — 6·1·
DESIGNED BY MISS E· ROSENCRANZ
· UNI· OF WIS·

FIG· 396 — 2·3·

FIG· 398 — 6·8·
DESIGNED BY MISS E· HOWARD
UNI· OF WIS·

FIG· 397 — 6·1·
NOTE FIG· 387·

FIG· 399 — 6·3·8·
DESIGNED BY MISS E· HOWARD

FIG· 400 — 6·8·

FIG· 401 — 6·1·7·
DESIGNED BY STUDENTS OF MILWAUKEE · DOWNER COLLEGE

PLATE 56

unity at this point, while the contour lines often lead the attention from the pendant to the chain. The eye should move in unbroken dynamic movement from pendant to chain. The chain may have points of accent designed to vary the even distribution of the links. These accents are frequently composed of small stones with surface enrichment sympathetically designed in unity with pendant, chain, and stone. Figure 401 shows examples of this arrangement and similarly the need of a horizontal inceptive axis to harmonize with the length of the chain. These small accents are quite similar in design to bar pin motives.

Pendants and Chains

Rule 10m. *Transparent and opaque stones or enamel should not be used in the same design.*

For the designer's purposes we may consider two kinds of stones, the transparent and the opaque. These should not be mixed in one design. The most favorable stones are those forming contrasts of value or brilliancy with the metal as, for example, the amethyst, lapis lazuli, or New Zealand jade, with silver; or the dark topaz, or New Zealand jade, with gold. Lack of these contrasts gives dull, monotonous effects that fail to make the stone the point of concentration. Figure 467. These effects may be partially overcome by frosting, plating, or oxidizing the metal, thus forming stronger contrasts of value

Relation of Stones to Metal

INSTRUCTION SHEET

Plates 52 and 57 are representative of the steps, processes, and problems for school use.

SUMMARY OF DESIGN STEPS

(a) Draw the primary mass.

(b) Locate the inceptive axis in this primary mass with its direction determined by the ultimate use or position of the primary mass and its general shape.

(c) Locate zone of enrichment.

(d) Locate point of concentration in the zone of enrichment and in the inceptive axis.

(e) Design simple contour enrichment.

(f) Design leading lines in sympathy with the contour and leading toward the point of concentration.

(g) Elaborate the leading lines in sympathy with the material, the type of enrichment, the contours, and the inceptive axis.

(h) Render in the technical manner suggested by Plate 52, dimension the primary mass, and otherwise prepare the drawing for shop use.

Courtesy of the Elverhoj Colony

FIGURE 401a.—Pendants

CHAPTER XIV

SURFACE ENRICHMENT OF LARGE PRIMARY MASSES
IN BASE AND PRECIOUS METALS

The surface enrichment of small, flat primary masses treated in Chapter XIII emphasized the designer's tendency for *full* surface enrichment of small areas. Such treatment has proved satisfactory because the eye can readily and immediately observe and comprehend or assimilate an enrichment upon a small area. For larger enriched areas considered in this chapter, full surface enrichment becomes a questionable policy for the following reasons.

Enrichment for Small Areas

It is true that the old time craftsman with consummate skill fully enriched large surfaces, but two factors interfere with this mode of treatment today. The first factor is the decidedly practical nature of the problem. The service to which the modern industrial project is put interferes with the use of full surface enrichment. The second is the lack of skill on the part of the modern amateur designer. It is a sound policy to avoid the ornateness that frequently accompanies a large and unskillfully planned area. In place of this, we should limit the enrichment of large masses to a few salient areas which are well related to the structural lines.

Enrichment for Large Areas

Rule 11b. *Conservative application should mark the use of surface enrichment of large masses. Its use should:* (1) *lighten or soften necessarily heavy construction;* (2) *support or apparently strengthen good structure;* (3) *add interest to large unbroken and uninteresting surfaces.*

These salient areas should determine the surface enrichment appropriate to the structure, so that the enrichment: (1) will lighten or soften necessarily heavy construction as in Figure 403; (2) support or apparently strengthen good structure, Figure 413; (3) add interest to large unbroken or otherwise uninteresting surfaces as illustrated in Figure 405. To aid in producing the desired results, we have the technical processes mentioned in Chapter XIII as follows: (1) Piercing;

Essentials of Good Surface Enrichment

[179]

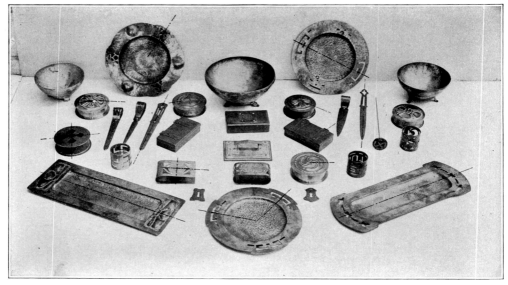

Figure 406a.— Mainly Objects Designed to be Seen from Above

(2) Etching; (3) Chasing; (4) Enameling; (5) Inlaying; (6) Stone-setting; (7) Building; (8) Carving; (9) Planishing; (10) Frosting; (11) Oxidizing. On the plates for this chapter, the figure generally following the cut number refers to the process, as: Figure 446, 3.

SURFACE DESIGN EVOLUTION

Rule 11a. *The preliminary steps toward surface enrichment should be thought out before they are drawn.*

A designer will be materially helped if he devotes a few moments of thought to his design problem before he applies the pencil to the paper. In the end the time given to thinking out his problem will gain for him both increased excellence of design and rapidity of execution, provided his thinking is systematic. A sequential order of points to be observed is given below. The object of systematic thought is to form a mental picture of the enrichment to be in full accord with the materials and construction and to be sympathetically related to the structural axes and to the contours. The unenriched mass has been designed and we are now ready for the consideration of surface enrichment in the following order.

(a) *Placing the Zone of Service.*

1. Where is the zone of service?

(b) *Classification of Form.*

1. Is the object flat, shallow and circular, low and cylindrical, high and cylindrical?

(c) *Placing the Zone of Enrichment.*

1. Is the enrichment to be seen from above or from the side? See Figure 406a.

2. What point of the structure suggested by the form needs surface enrichment? Is it the primary mass, appendages, terminals, links, or details? Let the area selected become the zone of enrichment.

(d) *Amount of Enrichment.*

1. Will the enrichment cover the full surface, part surface (center or margin), or accented outline?

(e) *Location of Inceptive Axis.*

1. Is the zone of enrichment associated with a square, rectangle, hexagon, or irregularly shaped flat plane, circular or cylindrical surface? Figure 470.

2. How should the inceptive axis be placed in the zone of enrichment to harmonize with the structural forms suggested by 1 (e) and the point from which it is viewed 1 (c)? See the violation of this latter point in Figure 439. Presumably this inceptive axis will be a vertical center line, horizontal center line, diagonal, diameter, radius, the element of a cylinder, or a dynamic curve for a free border.

(f) *Point of Concentration.*

1. Where should the point of concentration be located upon the inceptive axis?

(g) *Unison of Enrichment and Materials.*

1. What decorative process will be adaptable to service, the material, and the contemplated design?

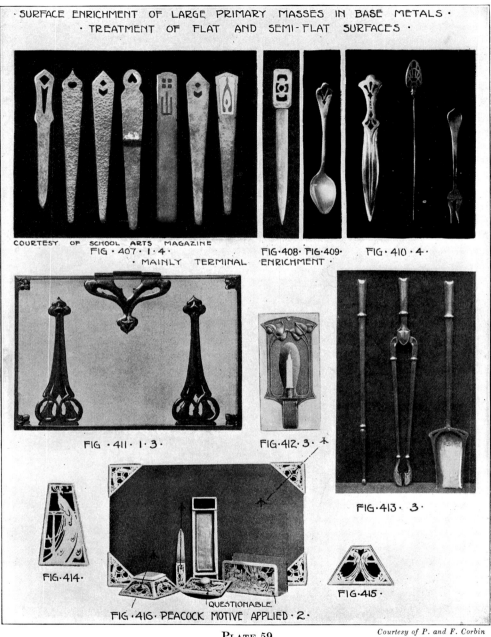

· SURFACE ENRICHMENT OF LARGE PRIMARY MASSES IN BASE METALS ·
· TREATMENT OF FLAT AND SEMI-FLAT SURFACES ·

COURTESY OF SCHOOL ARTS MAGAZINE
FIG · 407 · 1 · 4 ·

FIG · 408 · FIG · 409 ·   FIG · 410 · 4 ·

· MAINLY TERMINAL ENRICHMENT ·

FIG · 411 · 1 · 3 ·

FIG · 412 · 3 ·

FIG · 413 · 3 ·

FIG · 414 ·

QUESTIONABLE

FIG · 415 ·

FIG · 416 · PEACOCK MOTIVE APPLIED · 2 ·

PLATE 59

Courtesy of P. and F. Corbin

(h) *Type of Units.*

1. What design units are suited to the process selected in (g), appropriate to the texture and structural lines of the form to be enriched and to its ultimate service? Choice may be made from nature, geometric pattern, or historic ornament.

The above points may all be *thought out.* Now, with some assurance, the designer may take his pencil and begin to *draw* the units in their proper position upon or about the inceptive axis with the point of concentration correctly placed in position in the inceptive axis. Rules and suggestions for this execution have been previously given.

(i) *Designing of the Units.*

1. How should the units be drawn to be in harmony with the inceptive axis, the contours, and to each other?

The above points of approach to surface enrichment represent a logical reasoning process which supplies a line of sequential and developmental pictures that will reduce to a minimum the element of doubt and fog through which the average designer approaches his problem. The steps will, in time, become practically automatic and may be thought out in a surprisingly short period of time.

Rule 11c. *The type of design unit for large masses should be bolder than similar designs for small primary masses.*

As may be expected from briefly considering the illustrations for this chapter as compared with those for small primary masses, Chapter XIII, it is seen that the units for base and precious metals are larger and bolder than those used for smaller masses. The more effective designs are those whose appropriateness, simplicity, and correct structural proportions and relations appeal to our sense of fitness and beauty.

Figures 403, 404, and 406 are composed of projects designed mainly on vertical inceptive axes or center lines. The freely balanced natural units in Figure 403 have the zone of enrichment in the upper portion of the appendage (handles), and the point of concentration in the upper portion of the zone of enrichment. Formal symmetrical balance controls the placing of enrichment in Figure 404. Initial letters, through lack of consideration of design principles, are fre-

Summary o Steps in Surface Enrichment

Large Masses and Their Treatment

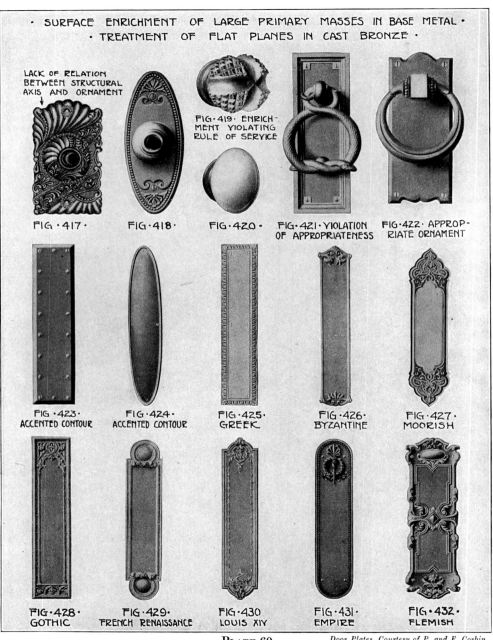

· SURFACE ENRICHMENT OF LARGE PRIMARY MASSES IN BASE METAL ·
· TREATMENT OF FLAT PLANES IN CAST BRONZE ·

LACK OF RELATION BETWEEN STRUCTURAL AXIS AND ORNAMENT

FIG·419· ENRICHMENT VIOLATING RULE OF SERVICE

FIG·417·

FIG·418·

FIG·420·

FIG·421· VIOLATION OF APPROPRIATENESS

FIG·422· APPROPRIATE ORNAMENT

FIG·423· ACCENTED CONTOUR

FIG·424· ACCENTED CONTOUR

FIG·425· GREEK

FIG·426· BYZANTINE

FIG·427· MOORISH

FIG·428· GOTHIC

FIG·429· FRENCH RENAISSANCE

FIG·430 LOUIS XIV

FIG·431· EMPIRE

FIG·432· FLEMISH

PLATE 60

Door Plates, Courtesy of P. and F. Corbin

quently misplaced on masses with little or no consideration given to their mass relations with the structural contours. As a contrast to this, notice the carefully considered relations between the letter *W* on the tea strainer in Figure 404 and its adaptation to the contours of the appendage. The stone enrichment on the handle of the paper cutter in Figure 404 in no way interferes with its use as a cutter and is therefore appropriate as surface enrichment.

The pierced enrichment of the silver box in Figure 405 contains vertical and horizontal lines which bring the decorative human figures into harmonious relation with the structural contours. Figure 406 shows both formal and free balance with center and full surface zones of enrichment. *C* and *D* could have been improved by a more strongly marked point of concentration which would have added more character to the designs.

In Chapter VIII, the contour terminal enrichment problem was described at some length. Many illustrations on Plates 58, 59, and 60 are, in a way, similar in their type of surface decoration, which is termed *surface terminal enrichment*. The "happy ending" mentioned in Chapter VIII as a suitable means of terminating the contour of a long primary mass or appendage may be similarly treated by suitable surface enrichment, particularly shown in Figures 403, 404, 407, 408, 409, and 410. The terminal is quite common as a zone of enrichment.

It is readily seen that when surface enrichment is the prevailing decorative theme it becomes necessary to subordinate contour enrichment to it, Rule 10b, otherwise the strife for dominance arising between these two forms of enrichment will lead to poor and ornate design, Figure 417. Whatever contour enrichment is used must be chosen to accord with the surface enrichment, Rule 10d, as noted in the preceding figures and in Figure 411. Here we find the closest connection, as the chased forms of the surface at many points merge into the contour. Thus surface and contour are bound together in unity with the surface enrichment, which maintains its dominance throughout.

The simple and dignified treatment of the fire set in Figure 413 is synonymous with the finest type of enrichment for service and beauty, Rule 11b. The peacock motives of Figures 414 and 415

Large Flat and Semi-flat Surfaces in Precious Metal, Plate 58

Flat and Semi-flat Surfaces in Base Metal, Plate 59

Contour *Versus* Surface Enrichment

Surface Enrichment of Hardware, Plate 60

are applied to the desk set. The motives as used in this case are generally well adapted to their respective areas and inceptive axes.

Rule 11f. *Repulsive forms should not be introduced into surface enrichment.*

Figure 417 is a typical example of over-ornamentation with the surface and contour enrichment struggling in deadly conflict for prominence. In the combat, the natural structural axis has been totally neglected for irrelevant and disconnected ornament. Figure 418 illustrates correctly related surface ornament, with a dominance of the latter form, Rule 10b. Figure 419 represents a type of decoration presumably roughened to meet the needs of service. It proves, however, to be unpleasant to the touch and unnecessary as the plain knob is preferable in every way. The naturalistic snake motive of Figure 421 is repulsive to many people; this and similar decorative motives should be avoided in preference to the more conventionalized pattern of Figure 422, Rule 11f.

Rule 11e. *Two periods of historic ornament should not be introduced into the same design.*

It is impossible to close these chapters without reference to the influence of the great schools of architectural history upon contemporary design. There is a growing tendency for manufacturers to use period patterns in house decorations which correspond to the design of the building. A Colonial building frequently calls for Colonial hardware, a Gothic church for corresponding surface enrichment of that period.

Historic Ornament Applied to Period Hardware Design Door Plates

As introductory illustrations, Figure 423 stands as a simple example of accented (beveled) contour while Figure 424 has been accented with reminiscent moulding appropriate to Colonial architecture. They might, however, be used with many simply designed articles of furniture. From this slight indication or portion of a style, we have a more pronounced beginning in Figure 425 with its clearly marked Greek egg and dart ornamental border. The acanthus leaf of the Byzantine school, Figure 426, changes to the geometric arabesques of the Moorish school in Figure 427. The Gothic arch, cusps, and quatrefoil of Figure 428 are changed to the classic acanthus foliage of the French Renaissance period. Figure 429. Figures 430 and 431 are later developments of the Renaissance. The heavily enriched Flemish pattern completes our illustrations of the use of past forms of ornamentation applied to modern designs. Only a small number from a rapidly enlarging field of period design are shown.

With circular plates and trays, the enrichment normally takes the form of a border (marginal enrichment), with the inceptive axes or center lines of the repeated units radiating from the center of the circle. Figures 433, 435, 436, 437, 438, and 439. An elliptical form frequently calls for handles and terminal enrichment as shown by Figure 434.

Shallow Circular Forms, Plate 61

Both Figures 437 and 438 have divided points of concentration and would be materially improved by the omission of the center unit *A*. The small tree used as a connecting link in the border of Figure 437 should be reversed, as it now possesses a motion or growth contrary to the larger tree units. The contour enrichment in Figure 438 could well be omitted or moved around to support the surface enrichment. The pierced enrichment *A*, Figure 439, is incorrectly used as it is not designed to be seen from above, the normal viewpoint of the tray. The design should have been based upon the horizontal axis of the project similar to Figure 439 at B.

Differing from the shallow plate, with the increased height of the low cylindrical forms of Plate 62, there now develops the possibility of enriching the sides of this class of project: a zone of enrichment not readily accessible in the shallow plate form. In addition to the sides there remain the appendages, quite capable of carrying enrichment to advantage. One should control the zone of enrichment in such a manner that the attention will not be equally drawn to both appendage and primary mass. Two points of enrichment, both calling for equal attention, divide the interest in the problem, and cause a lack of unity or oneness.

Low Cylindrical Forms, Plate 62

Rule 11d. *The eye should be attracted to one principal zone of enrichment, whether located upon the primary mass, appendage, terminals, links, or details. All other zones should be subordinate to this area.*

Enrichment upon the appendages may be found in Figures 440, 441, 442, 445, and on the upper portion of the straight sides of the primary mass in Figures 443 and 444. The decorative units com-

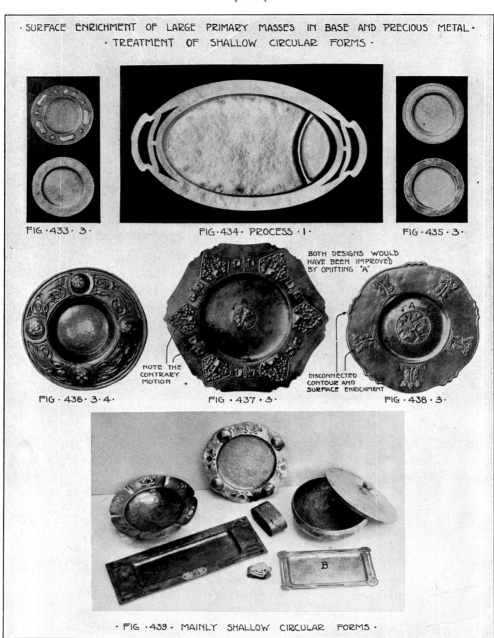

· SURFACE ENRICHMENT OF LARGE PRIMARY MASSES IN BASE AND PRECIOUS METAL ·
· TREATMENT OF SHALLOW CIRCULAR FORMS ·

FIG · 433 · 3 ·   FIG · 434 · PROCESS · 1 ·   FIG · 435 · 3 ·

BOTH DESIGNS WOULD
HAVE BEEN IMPROVED
BY OMITTING "A"

NOTE THE
CONTRARY
MOTION

DISCONNECTED
CONTOUR AND
SURFACE ENRICHMENT

FIG · 436 · 3 · 4 ·   FIG · 437 · 3 ·   FIG · 438 · 3 ·

· FIG · 439 · MAINLY SHALLOW CIRCULAR FORMS ·

PLATE 61

· SURFACE ENRICHMENT OF LARGE PRIMARY MASSES IN BASE
AND PRECIOUS METAL · TREATMENT OF LOW CIRCULAR FORMS ·

FIG · 440 · ENRICHMENT OF APPENDAGE · 6

FIG · 441 · 6 ·

FIG · 442 · 1 ·
ENRICHMENT OF APPENDAGE

FIG · 443 · 1 ·
ENRICHMENT OF PRIMARY MASS

FIG · 444 · 3 · MARGINAL ENRICHMENT

FIG · 445 · 3 ·

PLATE 62

SURFACE ENRICHMENT OF LARGE PRIMARY MASSES IN BASE AND PRECIOUS
METALS · TREATMENT OF HIGH CYLINDRICAL FORMS ·

FIG · 446 · 3 ·   FIG · 447 · 7 ·   FIG · 448 · VERTICAL CHASED ENRICHMENT · 3 ·

  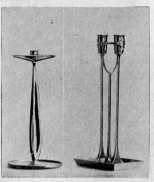

FIG · 450 · NOTE THE
FACT THAT THE ENRICH-
MENT ON BASE IS
SUBORDINATED TO THAT
OF THE SHADE ·

FIG · 449 · 3 ·   FIG · 451 · MAINLY CONTOUR
                              ENRICHMENT

FIG · 452 · ILLUSTRATING THE "ECHOING" OF A MOTIVE
· THE SYMBOL "X" SHOULD BE IN THE UPPER PORTION OF THE P·M·   FIG · 453 · 6 ·

PLATE 63

posing the border on these straight sides are designed upon the vertical element of the underlying cylindrical form as the inceptive axis. The enrichment for the appendage is well related to the contour of that member and is commonly based upon the center line of the appendage.

The principles of enriching these higher cylindrical forms in many ways closely parallel those which govern the lower cylindrical forms. The inceptive axes of the decoration on the two vases of Figures 446 and 447 may be readily analyzed as vertical elements of the cylinder. Figures 448 and 449 are quite rare exceptions of the accentuation of the *vertical* lines of the cylinder. Horizontal bands similar to Figures 444 and 447 are more common interpretations of cylinder enrichment. Figure 450 marks a successful combination of two dissimilar materials with the shade (appendage) as the dominating enriched member. Rule 10c.

High Cylindrical Forms, Plate 63

The small chased bosses used as enrichment in Figure 452 are re-echoed on the several pieces of the set which binds them into collective unity. The top portion of the primary mass seems to need some form of enrichment, as the contour adds little to the beauty of that part. The symbol X could have been better located by being moved to that place. The point of concentration should be placed in the upper portion of a large mass whenever that arrangement is possible.

It is in every way desirable that all designs should be executed full size and in full accord with the requirements of a shop working drawing. In addition the technical rendering suggested in Chapter XIII should be carefully used in each drawing.

INSTRUCTION SHEET

Plates 68 and 72 show problems suitable for class presentation. The method of development is similar to that presented on Plate 52.

SUMMARY OF DESIGN STEPS

(*a*) Draw a primary mass with reference to its proper grouping as follows:
    For flat areas draw square, rectangle, etc.
    For shallow circular forms draw a circle.
    For low cylindrical forms draw a rectangle with horizontal proportions.
    For high cylindrical forms draw a rectangle with vertical proportions.

(*b*) Locate zone of service.

(*c*) Locate zone of enrichment: appendages, terminals, margins, full surface, etc.

(*d*) Determine amount of enrichment.

(*e*) Locate inceptive axes.

(*f*) Place point of concentration in the inceptive axis where it traverses the zone of enrichment.

(*g*) Select the decorative process suited to the material and contemplated motive.

(*h*) Draw leading lines toward the point of concentration.

(*i*) Draw conventionalized design motives based upon the leading lines, converging toward the point of concentration. , Vary the contours to be sympathetically related to these design motives, provided such variation of the original primary mass is necessary to complete unity.

(*j*) Add additional views, dimension, and otherwise prepare the drawing for shop use.

SUGGESTED PROBLEM

Design a copper nut bowl and spoon. Enrich with a chased border appropriate to the subject. Enrich spoon, using fitting method of enrichment. The bowl and spoon should have a harmonious relation.

SUMMARY OF RULES

Surface Enrichment of Large Primary Masses

Rule 11a. *The preliminary steps toward surface enrichment should be thought out before they are drawn.*

Rule 11b. *Conservative application should mark the use of surface enrichment of large masses. Its use should: (1) lighten or soften necessarily heavy construction; (2) support or apparently strengthen good structure; (3) add interest to large unbroken and uninteresting surfaces.*

Rule 11c. *The type of design unit for large masses should be bolder than similar designs for small primary masses.*

Rule 11d. *The eye should be attracted to one principal zone of enrichment, whether located upon the primary mass, appendage, terminal, links, or details. All other zones should be subordinate to this area.*

Rule 11e. *Two periods of historic ornament should not be introduced into the same design.*

Rule 11f. *Repulsive forms should not be introduced into surface enrichment.*

REVIEW QUESTIONS

1. Contrast the method of enriching large and small areas of base and precious metals. Illustrate. What is the character of surface enrichment for large areas?

2. Name three essentials to good surface design for base and precious metals. Illustrate each.

3. Give nine steps necessary for the complete evolution of surface enrichment.

4. Name method of classifying the structural forms of metal into four groups. How does this compare with the classification of clay forms?

5. Between which two groups does the transition from a horizontal to a vertical primary mass occur?

6. Is there a perceptible change in the surface enrichment paralleling this change in proportions of the primary mass?

7. In which group or groups is the relation between surface and contour enrichment closest?

8. Give the characteristics of surface enrichment designed for flat or semi-flat planes.

9. State the value of the terminal as an enrichment zone.

10. Discuss common errors in the surface enrichment of hardware and their correction.

11. In what manner does historic ornament influence industrial design? Why?

12. Give characteristics of surface enrichment designed for, (a) large, shallow circular forms; (b) large, low cylindrical forms; (c) large, high cylindrical forms.

13. How does the point from which the article is to be seen affect the character of the design?

CHAPTER XV

COLOR: HUE, VALUE, AND CHROMA; STAINS

Need of Harmonious Color

In the previous chapters we have developed problems dealing with proportions, contours, and surface enrichment. The use of color, particularly in surface enrichment, is equally important inasmuch as its use is often necessary to bring the project, as for example a piece of furniture, into harmony with the surroundings which furnish its final color environment. The incorrect use of color may seriously mar a project otherwise correctly designed in line and form, and may also weaken its influence in a particular setting.

Use of Color Systems

While there are a number of excellent systems of color notation, it is well to bear in mind that a color system, however excellent, is a good servant but a poor master. It is nevertheless considered as essential to have a definite knowledge of some systematically developed color system in order that we may methodically apply color to the structural form with some degree of certainty.

Color Pigments for Design Rendering

For rendering drawings of problems involving the use of color it is suggested that the beginner use the tempera, or opaque colors now on the market. These colors readily adapt themselves to the average problem, while their rich hues are more successful than those produced from the ordinary water colors. Tubes of cobalt blue, ultramarine, light chrome yellow, vermilion, emerald green, crimson madder, black, and white will serve to solve the problems demanded by this chapter.

Application of Pigment

White is used to lighten and black to darken the pigments, which should be mixed with water to the consistency of cream, and applied to cover well the surface of the paper. One should guard against a thin, transparent wash, as the desired effect is a velvety opaque and evenly tinted surface only possible with the thick application of color. The pigment will dry out about one-quarter lighter than when first applied. The usual school color box of three pigments is useful for rendering wood stains. These pigments may be used in thin flat washes and will exhibit a transparent effect analogous to the effect of a wood stain. The natural color of wood may be first represented and, when dry, followed by a second thin wash of the hue of the wood stain.

Lacking as we are in a definite color nomenclature or standards, it now becomes necessary to describe the processes and define the terms necessary to the designer.

Hue is the technical name for color; a change of color means a change of hue. For the designer's purposes we will select twelve equally graded colors or hues from the spectrum and term them standard hues. Each hue will have twenty-seven modifications or gradations, which is a sufficient number for our purpose. These gradations are to be graphically recorded by and contained in a diagram to be known as a *hue rectangle*. There are twelve of these rectangles, one for each of the selected hues, and they are found arranged in sequence in Figure 454.

By referring to Figure 455, it is seen that the twelve selected standard hues are represented at what is termed *full chromatic intensity*, which, to the designer, means hues of the full strength of his color pigment. This is far short of the true color intensity of the spectrum, but for industrial arts purposes these hues are strong enough to serve as standards for comparison and classification. The hues should be evenly graded from red at the left to red violet at the right without noticeable unevenness in the gradations. Red violet is the link which connects the right end with the left, thus completing the circuit of the twelve hues. The following pigment table gives name and symbol of various hues.

HUES	PIGMENTS	VALUES	SYMBOLS
Red	Pure crimson madder	High dark	R-HD
Orange red	Crimson madder and vermilion	Middle	OR-M
Orange	Vermilion and light chrome yellow	Low light	O-LL
Orange yellow	Vermilion and light chrome yellow	Light	OY-L
Yellow	Pure light chrome yellow	High light	Y-HL
Yellow green	Light chrome yellow and emerald green	Light	YG-L
Green	Pure emerald green	Low light	G-LL
Green blue	Emerald green and cobalt blue	Middle	GB-M
Blue	Pure cobalt blue	High dark	B-HD
Blue violet	Ultramarine and crimson madder	Dark	BV-D
Violet	Ultramarine and crimson madder	Low dark	V-LD
Red violet	Ultramarine and crimson madder	Dark	RV-D

Locating
Standard
Hues

It now becomes imperative to locate each standard hue at its definite place in each rectangle. This invariably occurs at a predetermined point in the left vertical boundary of the rectangle of that hue. From inspection of Figure 455, it is quickly seen that violet seems to be the darkest hue; yellow the lightest, with the others between these hues. This variation of what is termed their value gives us a guide to their proper placing in the hue rectangle.

Values and
Horizontal
Value Lines

Value is that quality by which we may distinguish a dark hue from a light one. For design purposes we will imagine the hue rectangle to grade from white at the top to black at the bottom. We will draw horizontal lines or steps across the rectangle, marking nine even value steps from white to black; the top one to be termed White (W), followed by High Light (HL); Light (L); Low Light (LL); Middle (M); High Dark (HD); Dark (D); Low Dark (LD); and Black (B). These value steps may be thought of as a scale of gray or neutral values descending the *right boundary* of the hue rectangle. They have been roughly indicated in the hue rectangle at the left of Figure 454.

Relation of
the Standard
Hue to the
Hue Rec-
tangle

Each standard hue may now be located in the *left boundary* of its hue rectangle and opposite its neutral gray equivalent in the right boundary. If the standard hue is accurately determined by the designer, it will be of exactly the same value as its gray equivalent given in the "value" column of the pigment table. The small arrows leading from Figure 455 to 454 show where four standard hues are located; the remaining hues are located in the left circle of each successive row in the remaining rectangles, and upon their respective value lines. Standard hues are expressed by the symbols in the *right column* of the pigment table.

Tints

Each standard pigment or hue may be thinned with opaque white to lighten it, forming what is known as a tint of that hue. Red, in Figure 454, reaching its full chromatic intensity at the value High Dark, may be lightened four times before it ultimately arrives at white. Each step is to be considered as occurring in the left hand boundary of the rectangle above the standard hue, and is to be recorded by the symbols, R-M: R-LL : R-L : R-HL. Orange yellow has only one possible tint. Strawberry, light lavender, rose, etc., are merely nicknames for various tints.

Each standard hue may be darkened by the application of black, thus forming shades of that hue. Red is capable of producing **Shades** two shades, R-D and R-LD, which are placed in the left boundary of the hue rectangle below the standard hue. Browns, russets, and dark tans are shades of different hues.

These modifications of the standard hues into tints and shades give to the designer simple variations of his too brilliant standards. But even these modifications are not sufficiently grayed for staining or painting large wood or wall surfaces. There is a brilliancy and glare about certain tints which require modification. The shades are safer for use on large areas. The remaining space in the interior of the hue rectangle is to be devoted to the last gradation of the standard hue.

Chroma is the strength of a color. It is the quality by which we distinguish a strong color from a weak one. The standard hue is **Chroma** approximately full chromatic intensity. Likewise each tint and shade is considered to be of its full chromatic intensity, making the left-hand boundary of the rectangle the area of full chroma.

From this boundary, each tint, standard, and shade *fades out or loses chroma* until the right boundary of the rectangle is reached. In this boundary each tint, standard, and shade has faded out of its gray equivalent, but without changing its original value; in other words it has traveled along its horizontal value line to a complete grayness. The right-hand boundary of the rectangle may then be represented by a gray value scale of nine steps, including white and black.

It becomes necessary to record at regular intervals, this loss of chroma. For this purpose, we have cut the hue rectangle by three **Vertical** vertical lines. The first vertical line from the left boundary of the **Chroma** rectangle marks the position where the standard with its tints and **Lines** shades have been grayed to the point where only three-fourths of the original of hue remains. Similarly, the center and right vertical lines mark the points where one-half and one-fourth, respectively, of the color have been retained. These losses of chroma are recorded by similar fractions. With possible modifications of value and chroma each hue now has twenty-seven possible changes.

The full hue title or symbol may now be written as follows: (1) hue name, (2) amount of chroma, (3) value. Examples: GB

$\frac{3}{4}$D-V$\frac{1}{2}$HL. We are now in a position to write whatever color we may have in mind and another person will understand it, provided the other person adopts our standard. Through the teachings of Dr. D. W. Ross, Mr. A. H. Munsell, and others, the symbols and standards are now quite generally understood and have, in a slightly modified form been accepted in several standard color industries.

To familiarize oneself with the mixing of the various hues, it is excellent practice to form a vertical gray scale of the three-quarter-inch squares. There should be nine steps from white to black; an enlarged duplication of the right boundary of the hue rectangle. The warm standard hues at their full standard inten-

sities; RV-R-OR-O-OY-Y, may be formed and placed opposite their gray equivalents on the left side of the gray scale, while the remaining or cold colors may be similarly placed with relation to the gray scale but upon the right of it.

A vertical scale of tints and shades of one of the hues, duplicating the left side of the rectangle gives the character of the tints and shades. One shade and one tint should then be carried along a horizontal value line through three steps of loss of chroma to complete grayness, but without change of the original value. Yellow, by the addition of black becomes a false greenish shade which may be corrected by the addition of a small amount of vermilion.

A large percentage of natural wood hues are to be found between the hue rectangles, Red-Orange, Yellow and Green, or in the warm portion of the spectrum. As a wood stain must blend harmoniously with the natural wood color, it is reasonable to expect the best results from stains with a predominance of warm hues or warm grays in their composition.

It is possible to duplicate *nearly all* the twelve standard hues of Figure 455 with mixtures of the three so-called primary hues of red, yellow, and blue. It makes a fairly approximate scale which is, however, not sufficiently accurate for standardizing purposes. The scale is formed by mixing red and yellow in varying proportions for the intermediate hues of orange, yellow, and blue for the greens, and blue and red for the violets. This practice of mixing three primary colors together serves as an important step, governing wood stain mixing for beginners.

Developing this idea further, we may select aniline brilliant scarlet as approximating red; metanil yellow, approximating yellow; and acid green as a substitute for blue. These stains are shown in the top portion of Figure 456. By comparison with Figure 455, scarlet is found to be orange red; metanil yellow, orange, and acid green to be true standard green. These basic stains have been located in their proper positions with regard to their hue, value, and chroma. Their positions are located by the large circles in the hue diagrams of Figure 456.

These stains are modified and reduced in chroma and value by mixing them with nigrosene black, an aniline dye of blue black appearance, which fills all the needs of an ivory black in water or oil color pigment. With these four stains, almost any commercial stain may be duplicated. Aniline dye for water stains readily dissolves in water while a special aniline for oil staining is first cut with naphtha.

Dark mahogany stain in Figure 456 is orange red, $\frac{3}{4}$HD, and is indicated by the circle A in the same figure. To duplicate this stain we have as the nearest base stain, brilliant scarlet, which corresponds to orange red. This is placed at its full intensity in the circle OR on the middle horizontal value line. To duplicate dark mahogany stain it will be necessary to reduce in value a strong solution of brilliant scarlet, slightly more than one horizontal value step, by the addition of nigrosene. We shall then add a small amount of some thinning medium, oil or water, to reduce slightly the stain in chroma.

Flemish oak stain is orange $\frac{3}{4}$D. This calls for a mixture of metanil yellow and brilliant scarlet aniline to form the orange hue. We must then add nigrosene to reduce the value to D, and add a small amount of thinner to produce the necessary reduction in chroma.

This is commonly produced by fuming the wood with ammonia. The hue may however be closely duplicated by a mixture of brilliant scarlet, metanil yellow, and nigrosene. It is practically the same as Flemish oak, but possesses one-quarter more color as can be seen on the orange hue rectangle.

The circle D shows this stain to be slightly below yellow green, $\frac{3}{4}$M, in value and chroma. The hue rectangle containing it is nearer the green than the orange yellow rectangle; hence in mixing the stain we should keep the green hue dominant by adding more of it

Three Basic Aniline Wood Dyes

Wood Stain Mixing

Dark Mahogany Stain

Flemish Oak Stain

Fumed Oak Stain

Olive Green Stain

than of metanil yellow. As in other stains, nigrosene is added to reduce the full chromatic intensities of the aniline to the proper value and chroma of olive green stain.

Light Weathered Oak Stain

This stain is practically blue, $\frac{1}{4}$M, and is formed by thinning nigrosene to the proper value.

Color Changes of the Stain

Aniline dyes are apt to fade if exposed to full sunlight. There are, however, certain preventives that are beyond the scope of this book to treat in detail. The natural color of the wood is inclined to make a stain warmer than when originally mixed. This should be allowed for. Wood filler, the wood grain, porosity, qualities, and hue of the wood, all influence the final value of the stain. It frequently becomes darker in value as may be seen by comparing Figure 456 and Figures 458 to 461. It is good policy to test the stain upon different woods to observe the final effect. The tests may be kept for future reference.

It is readily seen from the few examples in Figure 456 that, with the three basic stains, almost any other stains may be produced, thus affording a broad field for harmonious selection and adaptation to the environment. The next chapters will take up the question of color harmony and its application to wood, wall surfaces, clay, and metal.

SUGGESTED PROBLEMS

See paragraph upon "Technical Practice" in this chapter, page 198.

REVIEW QUESTIONS

1. What pigments are best adapted to rendering design problems? What pigments are particularly adapted to the rendering of wood stains? How should each be applied?
2. What are standard hues? Why do we need standards of hue?
3. Define the term *values*.
4. What are tints and shades?
5. Define fully the term *chroma*.
6. Bound the hue rectangle and trace the value and chroma changes occurring on its vertical and horizontal lines.
7. Locate in its proper hue rectangle (Figure 455) the following hues: OY $\frac{3}{4}$HD; YG $\frac{1}{2}$LL; RV $\frac{3}{4}$M; YL.
8. Name the three primary hues. How may an approximate scale of twelve hues be prepared from them?
9. Name the three basic aniline wood dyes and give their relation to the three primary hues. What is the practical use of nigrosene in stain mixing?
10. Give the symbol and explain the method of mixing Flemish oak wood stain. Name and explain the method of mixing two others.
11. How does its application to wood effect the color and value of aniline stain?

Chapter XVI

COLOR AND ITS RELATION TO INDUSTRIAL ARTS DESIGN

Large Surfaces of Wood; Wall and Ceiling Areas

In the preceding chapter, the classification and standardization of color were emphasized as preliminary to the study of color harmony. **Color Harmony** Color harmony is obtained by the proper balancing of value, hue, and chroma upon a surface or surfaces to give a pleasing reaction to the eye, and through the eye to the intellect.

We are now ready to familiarize ourselves with the specific applications of these factors to practical design problems. Too many pieces of furniture are stained with no thought as to the final adaptation in the school or home. This is not wise, either from the standpoint of a complete educative process or of good taste. Figures 458, 459, 460, 461, show stains of Plate 64 applied to wood. Two new stains have been added, sage green and silver gray. These six stains are representative ones and act as a typical data for study of color harmony.

Furniture—Trim—Side Walls—Ceilings

The side walls of a room form the background for furniture; trim, wall brackets, and similarly related objects; therefore the **Backgrounds** *closest relation and harmony* should be maintained between them.

The wood stains 3, 6, 9, 12, 15, and 18, Plate 65, as they appear on various kinds of wood are, in part, duplicates of the unapplied **Value Range** stains of Plate 64, Figure 456. The effect of the wood has changed **of Wood** their values and in some instances their color as can be seen by comparing the two plates. Their *new relations* have been plotted on the hue rectangles of Figure 457, Plate 65, and the results joined by a dotted line. The circles in the diagrams contain cross reference figures in order that the stains may be traced without difficulty.

The highest value is near middle (18), and the lowest is low dark (6), showing a value range of four steps.

Value Range of Side Walls

The side walls, taken from well-known wall tint catalogs have been similarly plotted in Figure 457, and the results joined together by a heavy black line. The lightest value is light (11), and the darkest is middle value (14), an average range of three steps slightly above middle value.

Value Range of Ceilings

Ceilings are the lightest of the surfaces considered. Their range is from slightly below white (10), to light (16), a range of two values. From the results, as plotted in Figure 457, it is seen that there is a tendency to keep the ceilings within a close range of values. The results have been joined together by means of a double black line. There are exceptions to these results, but it is quite safe to keep well within the suggested range for harmonious results. We may now draw the following rules as a result of an empirical method of deduction.

Rule 12a. *An average wood stain is to be retained between the values middle and low dark.*

Rule 12b. *An average wall hue is to be retained between the values light and middle.*

Rule 12c. *An average ceiling hue is to be retained between the values white (minus) and light.*

Value Range of Side Walls and Wood Work

Averaging the value range between the wood work which includes the furniture, trim, and the side walls of Figures 458, 459, 460, 461, 462, and 463, we find that the range varies from five values in Figures 459 to slightly more than one in Figure 463. As the side walls and furniture are to be regarded as unobtrusive settings for pictures and people it is well to be very conservative with the use of values. A wide range of values will cause a lack of unity. In this respect Figure 459 may be regarded as approaching the extreme limit of contrasts of value compatible with good taste. Let us, therefore, limit the value range to four values, as, for example: low light for side walls and dark for stain.

Rule 12d. *The relation between the side walls and furniture, trim, etc., should be retained within the range of four values or less, as low light and dark.*

The ceiling and side walls in Figure 459 are four values apart and in Figure 463 this has been reduced to a one-value step. There seems to be a common average of three values as an acceptable and agreeable contrast. For dark rooms this would well be increased. For rooms with light side walls the contrast would be considerably lessened.

Rule 12e. *The relation between side walls and ceiling should be within the range of three values or less, as high light and low light.*

Value Range of Side Walls and Ceilings

HUE GROUPINGS

A wood stain should be closely related to the natural color of the wood. As this is usually a warm color we naturally find most of the wood stains included between the red and the yellow hue rectangles, inclusive of red and yellow green. Walnut then may be stained a deep shade of orange or red, but would not be adapted to a blue green stain. This arbitrary but wide range of hues of stained wood naturally affects the hue of the side walls. The plotting of the hues for the side walls, Figure 457, shows a close relation to the hues of the stain to the wall. In no instance do we find the hue rectangle of the wood work more than three hues away from that of the walls. In four instances they are within *two* hue rectangles of each other and in one instance they are both within the same rectangle. This develops the fact that *analogous* or neighboring groupings of hues prevail in relating the hues of wood work and side walls.

Hue Range for Wood Work and Walls

An *analogous* group of hues is an arrangement based upon a selection of tints and shades within three rectangles of each other, as orange and yellow. These harmonize because yellow is mixed with and becomes a hue common to both. While the analogous arrangement of hues seems to be most commonly used, and with a result that seems to justify its adoption into general practice, there are other arrangements that are pleasing to the eye.

Analogous Hues

Figure 458 illustrates what is commonly known as a *contrasted* grouping or arrangement of hues. It consists of the tints or shades of one or more hues and gray. It is the basis of color harmony between silver and semi-precious stones. If two hues are used, one of them should be reduced in chroma to nearly gray.

Contrasted Hues

Dominant
Hue

Figure 463 is typical of still another form of positive hue grouping. By consulting the yellow hue rectangle of Figure 457 it is noted
that the wood work, side walls, and ceiling of Figure 463 *are all contained in one rectangle.* This classes this color scheme as an example
of *dominant* arrangement which may be simply defined as the *tints
and shades of one hue.* The arrangement does not have the variety
supplied by analogous grouping, introducing as it does, two hues from
different rectangles, but for large surfaces dominant grouping is a
conservative and safe arrangement. Its tendency toward monotony
should be guarded against by the introduction of some object high
in chroma in the room decorative scheme. A bright colored vase
will accomplish this successfully. Rule 12o, Chapter XVII.

Rule 12f. *Color schemes for wood work and side walls should
preferably be selected from one of the following groupings: analogous,
contrasted, or dominant arrangements of hues. Analogous grouping is
preferable where variety of hue is desirable.*

Special
Arrangements

The above rule is not to be taken as arbitrary. In the hands
of competent designers attractive color schemes are developed
that differ materially from the above suggestions. But, for the
usual home setting, the above arrangement may be regarded as
satisfactory, and is given with the idea of bringing the school shop
work and the home environment into closer color harmony. A
specimen of special arrangement is given by the Circle 3A. This is
delft blue, which harmonizes with dark mahogany in a satisfactory
manner.

Hue Range
for Side
Walls and
Ceilings

In adjusting the hues for side walls and ceilings, the relations
should be of the closest. The plotting of ceiling hues in Figure 457
shows a strong tendency for the ceiling to be colored with a tint of
the side walls (dominant arrangement), or by a tint selected from the
next rectangle (analogous arrangement). Yellow or yellow-green,
very light and much reduced in chroma, seems to be the almost
universal custom. This is due to the strongly *light reflecting* qualities
of yellow.

Rule 12g. *Ceilings should be colored by a lighter tint of the side
walls or by a lighter tint of an analogous hue.*

Range of
Chroma
for Stains

Stains, as they occupy a comparatively limited area in the room
color scheme, are of their full chroma value or reduced to three-

fourths chroma. In only one instance (18), Figure 463, do we find a reduction to one-fourth chroma, demanded by the nearly gray color scheme of the walls. We find it to be an established fact that small areas are capable of enrichment by colors of greater purity and higher chroma than larger surfaces. A silver pin may be designed to contain a stone of high brilliancy, but a wall surface has to be materially reduced in chroma to possess color harmony.

Range of Chroma for Stain

Rule 12h. *Stains are usually not reduced to below three-fourths chromatic intensity. Nearly gray side walls, however, call for a reduction to one-fourth intensity.*

As the walls occupy a large proportionate area of the color scheme of the room we find it necessary to reduce them in chroma in order to soften the glare of too brilliant colors. Figure 457 shows only one instance (14) of a hue unreduced in chroma. It is retained at the full chroma for that value on account of the brightness of the sage green wood stain. The other hues represented in the diagram are grayed or reduced in chroma from three-fourths to less than one-fourth, or to nearly neutral gray.

Range of Chroma for Walls

Rule 12i. *Wall colors are usually reduced to three-fourths chroma to a minimum reduction of slightly less than one-fourth chroma.*

The same tendency toward chromatic reduction is to be seen in ceilings, although we have two examples in Figure 457 (10 and 13) of nearly white and high light ceilings that have not been reduced. To avoid crudity a reduction in chroma by the addition of gray is to be desired.

Range of Chroma for Ceilings

Rule 12j. *Ceilings should usually be reduced in chroma to three-fourths intensity with slightly less than one-fourth chroma as a minimum reduction.*

With a single exception (3A), the stains and wall tints have been selected between and including the red and green rectangles. This is customary and gives safe hue range as it insures the retention of wall and ceiling hues in unified conformity with the warm tints of the natural wood and its equally dark hued stains.

Summary

The following is a list of dry colors which may be purchased at a paint or hardware store for a few cents a pound. It is suggested for the designer or craftsman who desires to tint his own wall or ceiling. While oil paint is to be preferred, these colors are readily and quickly applied and form serviceable backgrounds.

Wall and Ceiling Pigments

Calcimine

The pigments are white, yellow ochre, chrome yellow light, chrome yellow medium, and chrome yellow dark, burnt and raw sienna, turkey and raw umber, ultramarine and ivory black. The greens are preferably mixed by adding ultramarine to one of the chromes. Shades are formed by the addition of the siennas, umbers, or black. Black and white, mixed to a gray, are useful in reducing the chroma of a hue. The stains should be mixed with hot water and a small amount of glue for a binder. White occasionally comes prepared with glue in its composition.

Opaque
Wood
Finishes

While this chapter has emphasized the transparent finish for wood treatment, as a method best fitted for woods with a distinct grain, it is realized that oil painting of wood surfaces has a distinct and important part to play in the interior decorative scheme of a room. This latter method is adapted to soft woods without a strongly marked grained surface. The warm hued rectangle of the spectrum: red, orange, and yellow with their associated hues, which are so intimately connected with the natural wood colors and their stains, no longer stand as a limiting factor in controlling the color of the wood or the side walls. The opaque nature of oil paints allows us to disregard the color of the wood, and thus select any hue of oil paint which harmonizes with the walls and decorative scheme of the room. The rules stated herein are equally applicable to opaque colors. It may be necessary to reduce oil paints in chroma beyond the point indicated in Rule 12h.

While it is not within the scope of this chapter to enter into a complete discussion of the subject of interior decoration, the following suggestions are considered as applying to our subject: viz., the surface enrichment of large areas. Complete color harmony in interior decoration generally demands the presence of the three so-called primary hues: red, yellow, and blue, in some form in the wall color scheme. While this is not always possible, two may be introduced as follows.

Northern
Exposure

The light from the north, northeast, or northwest is cold blue, supplying blue in the decorative scheme of three primary colors: blue, red, and yellow. The wall tints should then be composed of combinations of red and yellow, the remaining primaries. These may be applied to the walls by means of tints of yellow and orange reduced in chroma, or shades of orange and orange-red. No greens or blues should be used.

The light from the south, southeast, and southwest supplies plenty of yellow. It is, then, necessary to add the remaining primaries or at least one of them in the form of gray-blue, orange, or orange-yellow, reduced to one-fourth chroma and practically to neutrality or grayish-reds and greens, well reduced in chroma. Any hue strongly yellow should be avoided.

Southern
Exposure

Certain hues materially affect the apparent size of a room. If the room is small certain values and hues will make it appear much smaller. Dark values, as a rule, make the room look smaller by seemingly drawing the walls closer together. Red contracts the apparent size of a room, while yellow and blue expand it. Green and shades of yellow and red-orange, if not too dark, have little effect upon the apparent size of a room.

Effects of
Hue upon
Apparent
Size

SUMMARY OF DESIGN STEPS

(a) Determine, by its exposure, the kind of light the room receives.
(b) Choose a hue for the walls embodying one or both of the primary hues not represented by this daylight.
(c) Select a value and chroma for this hue in accordance with Rules 12b and 12i.
(d) Select a hue, value, and chroma for the ceiling in accordance with Rules 12g, 12e, and 12j.
(e) Select the correct hue, value, and chroma for paint or stain for the wood work in accordance with Rules 12f, 12a, and 12h.

SUGGESTED PROBLEMS

Develop the color scheme for the walls, ceiling, and wood work of a room with a northern exposure; southern exposure. Mix the stain for a piece of oak to harmonize with the wood work and walls of the living room of your home.

Determine the wall tints to harmonize with dark weathered oak. Mix them from dry colors.

SUMMARY OF RULES

Rule 12a. *An average wood stain is to be retained between the values middle and low dark.*

Rule 12b. *An average wall hue is to be retained between the values light and middle.*

Rule 12c. *An average ceiling hue is to be retained between the values white (minus) and light.*

Rule 12d. *The relation between the side walls and furniture, trim, etc., should be retained within the range of four values or less, as low light and dark.*

Rule 12e. *The relation between the side walls and ceiling should be within the range of three values or less, as high light and low light.*

Rule 12f. *Color schemes for wood work and side walls should preferably be selected from one of the following groupings: analogous, contrasted, or dominant arrangements of hues. Analogous grouping is preferable where variety of hue is desirable.*

Rule 12g. *Ceilings should be colored by a lighter tint of the side walls or by a lighter tint of an analogous hue.*

Rule 12h. *Stains are usually not reduced to below three-fourths chromatic intensity. Nearly gray side walls, however, call for a reduction to one-fourth intensity.*

Rule 12i. *Wall colors are usually reduced to three-fourths chroma to a minimum reduction of slightly less than one-fourth chroma.*

Rule 12j. *Ceilings should usually be reduced in chroma to three-fourths intensity, with slightly less than one-fourth chroma as a minimum reduction.*

REVIEW QUESTIONS

1. What should we have in mind when staining furniture for the home?
2. Why are the side walls important when considering the color scheme of a room?
3. Give the value range for the average wood stains, side walls, and ceiling.
4. State the value range to include wood work, furniture, trim, and side walls.
5. State the value range that includes side walls and ceilings.
6. Give the hue range for wood work and side walls.
7. Explain the analogous, contrasted, and dominant groupings of hues and name two examples of each.
8. Give the hue range for side walls and ceilings. Name several good combinations.
9. Give range of chroma for wood work, side walls, and ceiling. Explain the reasons for each change of chroma.
10. What experience have you had in mixing calcimine for wall decoration?
11. Discuss opaque finishes for wood.
12. Give the hues for rooms with northern and southern exposures. Why?
13. State the effect of hues upon the apparent size of a room.

CHAPTER XVII

COLOR AND ITS RELATION TO INDUSTRIAL ARTS DESIGN

SMALL SURFACES IN CLAY AND METAL

Before proceeding to the discussion of the application of color to clay it becomes necessary to determine what technical possibilities are presented.

Plain glazing of the entire surface is a common form of pottery enrichment. A piece of ware, thus glazed, may become a point of concentration in the color arrangement of a room, and should be definitely located in that arrangement. The ware may harmonize with the background (side wall) by analogy, dominance, or contrast or through complementary coloring. Rule 12o. A glaze from the diagram in Figure 464 should be selected as forming a part in the selected arrangement. Side wall (11), Figure 457, would harmonize with glaze C9 by virtue of its dominant relation or with M7 through analogy. The glaze selected should be higher in chroma than the side wall and will be found to form a cheerful and brilliant element in the room color scheme. The definite linking of these different factors of interior decoration into unity has been earnestly advocated in these chapters. Figures 457 and 464 show the possibilities of cross references.

Color Applied to the Surface Enrichment of Clay

It soon becomes apparent because of the coloring of clay ware that the designer must know something of the color possibilities of glazed pottery forms. The decorative processes were explained at some length in Chapter XII, wherein we described the common types of surface enrichment. As we are now primarily considering the question of color, we first regard the ware as uniformly glazed with either clear or matt glaze. The former is brilliant, of high chroma, and has a highly polished surface, while the latter is dull surfaced glaze of lower chroma.

Stains for Glazes

**Metallic
Oxides**

Metallic oxides are used to stain or color clear glazes, while under-glaze colors are ordinarily used for matts. The percentage of stains to be added to the dry glazes is stated in Figure 464 where they can be readily traced to their approximate locations in the hue rectangles by the reference letters M1, C1, etc. Certain oxides are weak coloring agents and require larger amounts of oxide to color the glaze perceptibly.

Iron and copper oxide may be mixed to produce a large variety of yellow greens; other combinations will suggest themselves. It is possible to use oxides as well as underglaze colors for staining matt glazes.

**Harmony
of Color**

We have, to this point, considered the enrichment of large surfaces whose areas were arbitrarily determined by construction, as, for example, the extent of wall surface, ceiling, or wood trim and furniture. The essential element in this type of problem is the selection of a one, two, or three-hued color arrangement that would harmoniously link ceiling, wall, and wood together. If we had introduced stencilling or figured wall paper it would have immediately called for the solution of another problem, the factor of *how much* strong color to use. In other words, it would have introduced the question of *proportionate distribution* of color upon a given area. It was thought best to limit the subject of proportionate distribution to small areas, where the designer is often forced to make decisions and to divide surfaces into proportionate color parts for his surface enrichment.

We may now repeat the definition of harmony with the accentuation placed upon a certain wording directly applicable to small surfaces. Harmony is obtained by the proper balancing and *proportionate distribution* of value, hue, and chroma upon a surface to give a unified and pleasing reaction to the eye and intellect.

**Proportionate
Distribution
of Color
for Small
Areas**

Rule 12k. *Proportionate distribution of hue, value, and chroma in surface enrichment calls for a small area, high in chroma, and contrasting in value to the rest of the surface but harmonizing with it. This is usually located in the area of concentration. The larger areas are to be sufficiently reduced in chroma and value to form a slight contrast with the background.*

Figure 465 illustrates some of the salient factors of distribution of values and hues. Hues of or near standard chromatic intensity should be used in *small quantities* and should accentuate the point of concentration. These small areas are to be regarded as giving brilliancy and life to the surface and to hold the eye at the point of concentration. Very small surfaces are capable of sustaining spots of high chroma, as is shown in the silver pin of Figure 468. The remaining portions of the surface enrichment should be kept subordinated in hue and value to the point of concentration, *but related to it.* The bands of Figure 465 are well reduced in value and make little contrast with the background, thus forming true surface enrichment or that which neither rises above or apparently falls through the surface. The point of concentration is higher in chroma than the surrounding areas.

Examples of Proportionate Distribution

Rule 12l. *One hue, or a group of analogous hues should dominate all color schemes. The point of concentration may be emphasized by one hue related to the other hues by (1) contrasted, (2) dominant, (3) analogous, (4) complementary relations. This hue should make slightly stronger value and chroma contrast than the remaining hues.*

Rule 12m. *An extreme range of five values is generally sufficient to supply contrast to a design but still retain its value unity. Restraint in the use of values is essential.*

Rule 12n. *The amount of chroma may be increased in proportion to the decrease in the decorated area. Exceptions may be made to this under Rule 12o.*

In the vase, Figure 464A, the designer selected hues from neighboring or analogous rectangles green and blue-green. The value range is restricted to four steps and the areas of concentration are placed at the top of the vase by the stronger value and hue contrasts of the foliage of the trees and dark blue rim. In both Figures, 464A and 465, the designer has used analogous hue arrangements. This is suggested to the beginner as serviceable for objects exceeding the dimensions of jewelry and includes such problems as vase forms, book stalls, and brackets. Contrasted and dominant arrangements are also good, safe, and sound arrangements, but fail to give the variety of color to small objects afforded by analogous grouping. At a later point in this chapter the subject of complementary coloring will suggest a new arrangement to the reader, but this scheme is to

Value and Hue and Chroma Range for Small Areas

be left until he has sufficiently mastered the possibilities of the arrangements just indicated.

Five values form a safe value range for small objects. It is good practice to keep the larger areas, including the background, within three steps of each other and to allow the point of concentration to form the strongest value contrast.

Over Reduction in Chroma

The chroma may range from full to three-quarters intensity. Reduction to one-half or one-fourth intensity is inclined to make a small object appear washed out or chalky. Shades, at their full intensity, are good colors to use for small surfaces in wood. Small enameled objects may be developed in full chroma, while pottery forms range from full chroma to one-half chroma in forms of slip and underglaze painting.

Color Applied to the Surface Enrichment of Metal

It is interesting to note the gradually increasing chroma percentage of the different coloring media in direct proportion to the reduction of the area of the surface to be enriched. By comparing the diagrams of Figures 464 and 457 it will be seen that there is a steady movement toward the left sides of the hue rectangles or toward stronger intensity. The wall areas are shown to be lowest in chroma, followed by the increasing intensity of wood stains, glazes, and enamels.

Enamels

Enamels, commonly used to enrich metal surfaces, are highest in chroma of the decorative materials under discussion and are to be treated with nearly as much restraint as one would use in enriching a surface with semi-precious stones, for strong hues are cheapened by excessive use. The plate in Figure 436 has small circles filled with enamel and a large field of chased or uncolored design.

Transparent Enamels

Transparent enamels are comparable to clear glazes and the coloring medium is the same. Their preparation is difficult and therefore trade names have been given in the table of Figure 464. As will be seen by consulting the diagram of Figure 464, T1, T2, T3, etc., they are all at their full value intensity. Enamels, as supplied by the trade, are much too intense for use in enrichment and consequently are applied over a coating of colorless clear enamel, technically named flux or fondant. As the thickness of coating of enamel may vary, the hue classification is to be regarded as approximate.

Opaque enamels may be compared with matt glazes, for, while the texture of the surface has a distinct gloss, the enamels themselves are not so strong in hue as the transparent enamels. By referring to the diagram of Figure 464, it may be seen that many of the opaque enamels are reduced in chroma, thus accounting for their softened hue.

Metals are capable of considerable change of color by the application of chemicals to the surface. Potassium sulphuret will lower the surface value of silver or copper to a rich velvety black associated with antiques. This may be removed in places naturally subjected to wear, thus varying the dead black appearance. Copper and brass may be coated with salt and vinegar or verdigris to give the surface a corroded and greenish appearance. Heating is a fugitive method of coloring and is, therefore, not considered.

These surface changes may be utilized to harmonize metal and its environment, as, for example, copper trimmings and a shade for a pottery lamp; or it may be used to reduce the brightness of the natural copper surface.

The surfaces of metals may be changed with actual manipulation of the surface by frosting or sanding and plating. Gold may be readily plated with gold to bring it into closer harmony with the stone. Plating, applied to base metals, merely to give the impression of a more expensive metal, is to be discouraged.

One has to consider metal as a background in much the same manner as we considered wall surfaces as a background for stained furniture. Whatever color is applied to the surface must harmonize in proportionate distribution as well as hue, value, and chroma. We have a small amount of leeway for varying the background by the different processes of oxidation and plating.

As one of the more common processes, let us consider the application of enamel to copper in the form of champleve enrichment. Our first thought would be the analysis of the natural copper color. It is found to be a shade of orange-red and will, therefore, readily harmonize with the *analogous* oranges and reds, as they both have the common hue of red. There should be a slight contrast of value between these enamels and the background. If this contrast is not present, it is well to oxidize slightly the copper to lower its value and thus produce the contrast.

The fourth harmonious hue combination, that of complementary arrangement or grouping, has been left to the last as its use is more

Complementary Arrangement

closely associated with small multi-colored projects and small areas. A hue approximately complementary to the initial hue is found by counting seven rectangles to the right or left of that hue; this will give the hue complementary to the initial hue. Thus, starting with red and moving through seven rectangles toward the right, we find the complement to be green. Any two hues so selected will be found to enhance the brilliancy of each other. The best results are secured when one hue dominates the color scheme by its increased area. Pottery may be adapted to a complementary color scheme by Rule 12i.

Rule 12o. *Small one or two-hued projects in clay, designed to be used as a part of the decorative color scheme for a room should bear a contrasted, dominant, analogous, or complementary relation to the side walls of the room. The project may be much higher in chroma than the side walls.*

The Relation of Colored Glazes to Interior Decoration of a Room

To find a glaze that will harmonize with the side walls of a room by complementary arrangement of hues, select the desired wall tint from the diagram in Figure 457. Find the similar hue rectangle in the diagram of Figure 464 and, starting with this rectangle as one, count seven hues from the side wall rectangle in either direction. In the seventh rectangle or in a neighboring one will usually be found a number of glazes answering the requirements and bearing a complementary relation to the side walls. Select a glaze from these that will make a contrast of chroma or value with the side wall. Example: background or side wall, Figure 457, No. 8, is in the orange yellow rectangle. Counting seven from this in Figure 464 we find the complement to be blue violet. As there is no glaze in this rectangle we will move to its neighbor on the left. This gives us clear glaze, C1, containing one and one-half per cent black oxide of cobalt, or a matt glaze containing seven per cent mazarine blue.

Glazes that will harmonize with side wall 8 through dominant arrangements are found in the same rectangle, O Y, and are numbered M5, M6, C7, C8. Glazes that will harmonize by analogy are C9 and M7, and are found in the left and right neighboring rectangles.

In Figure 466, the copper fob, R O, is combined with its complementary blue-green. Let us look at Figure 464. Counting seven intervals or hue rectangles to the right of the orange red rectangle we find T4 which is transparent blue green enamel. We may associate with this an analogous enamel from the green rectangle; this proves to be T5 medium green transparent enamel.

The point of concentration may now be emphasized by an enamel complementary to the blue green hue. Counting seven rectangles to the *left* we again encounter the red orange rectangle. Here there are no enamels but in the red hue rectangle we find T7 which is slightly orange-red. A small portion of this, Rule 12k, is applied and is found to center the design at the point of concentration in a satis-factory manner. Slight oxidation brings out the colors of the enamels.

Development
of Design
for Enamel
on Metal

Upon attempting to develop the same figure in opaque enamels it is soon seen that there are no pleasing complementary enamels of this type, but many analogous combinations. Autumn brown with the point of concentration developed in orange (O5) would be an excellent compromise.

Rule 12p. *Correct color for surface enrichment should neither apparently rise above nor drop below the surface to which it is applied, but should stay upon the plane of that surface. Correct value and chroma range will accomplish this.*

The gray-blue color of silver lends itself to a great number of gem stones, forming examples of contrasted arrangements. Care should be taken to form contrasts of *value*. Figure 467 is an example of a weak and insipid combination, lacking in value and hue contrast. The amethyst of Figure 468 corrects this error, while the oxidation of Figure 469 has partially corrected the lack of contrast shown in Figure 467. These illustrations tend to show that even stronger contrasts may be attempted with small gems and semi-precious stones than with enamels. This again proves the rule that the smaller areas are capable of sustaining stronger contrasts of hue, value, and chroma than are large ones.

Color for
Silver
Enrichment

SUMMARY OF DESIGN STEPS

The outline of the surface enrichment is considered as complete.

(a) METAL OR WOOD. Analyze the background into its hue, value, and chroma.
CLAY. Select a background that will harmonize with the controlling hue or hues of the proposed color scheme. Rule 12o. If this is a one hued

color scheme without gradation or surface enrichment the design steps may terminate at this point.

(*b*) METAL, WOOD, AND CLAY. Select the extreme value range of the color scheme, considering, if possible, the background as a balancing or pivotal value point upon which the values may balance above and below. As the side walls formed a balancing point for the ceiling and furniture or wood work, so may the background of metal, wood, or colored clay become a similar balancing factor for small surfaces. Rule 12m.

(*c*) METAL, WOOD, AND CLAY. Select a hue or hues which will harmonize with the background through dominant, contrasting, or analogous relations. Rule 12l. In selecting the hues consider the final placing of the object.

(*d*) METAL, WOOD, AND CLAY. Select a chroma range. Allow the point or area of concentration to have a slightly higher chromatic relation than the other hues. The point of concentration may be one of the hues already selected or it may bear a *complementary* relation to them. The hues may be averaged and a complementary to the average selected. Rule 12n.

(*e*) METAL, WOOD, AND CLAY. Apply the rule of proportionate distribution, Rule 12k.

(*f*) METAL AND WOOD. Using the pigments suggested in Chapter XV, design the problem. Test the result by applying Rule 12p.

(*g*) CLAY. If the design has been developed in slip or underglaze painting, select a glaze for an overglaze coating that will harmonize with the prevailing hues by *dominance or analogy*. Other arrangements may destroy the hues of the original color scheme.

(*h*) Develop the problem in its material.

SUGGESTED PROBLEMS

Design a bowl for nasturtiums; make the color arrangement harmonize through analogy with the hues of the flowers.

Design a vase for chrysanthemums; make the surface enrichment and the color arrangement harmonize through dominance with the hues of the flowers.

Design a hat pin for a blue hat; materials, copper, and transparent enamels.

Design a brooch to be worn with a gray dress.

Design a pottery and copper lamp with amber art glass in the shade. Through oxidation and glazing, bring the lamp into color unity.

SUMMARY OF RULES

Rule 12k. *Proportionate distribution of hue, value, and chroma in surface enrichment calls for a small area high in chroma and contrasting in value to the rest of the surface, but harmonizing with it. This is usually located in the area of concentration. The larger areas are to be sufficiently reduced in chroma and value to form a slight contrast with the background.*

HUES FOR SMALL OBJECTS

Rule 12l. *One hue, or a group of analogous hues should dominate all color schemes. The point of concentration may be emphasized by one hue related to the other hues by (1) contrasted, (2) dominant, (3) analogous, or (4) complementary relations. This hue should make slightly stronger value and chroma contrast than the remaining hues.*

Values for Small Objects

Rule 12m. *An extreme range of five values is generally sufficient to supply contrast to a design but still retain its value unity. Restraint in the use of values is essential.*

Chroma for Small Objects

Rule 12n. *The amount of chroma may be increased in proportion to the decrease in the decorated area. Exceptions may be made to this under Rule 12o.*

Rule 12o. *Small one or two-hued projects in clay, designed to be used as a part of the decorative color scheme for a room should bear a contrasted, dominant, analogous, or complementary relation to the side walls of the room. The project may be much higher in chroma than the side walls.*

Rule 12p. *Correct color for surface enrichment should neither apparently rise above nor drop below the surface to which it is applied, but should stay upon the plane of that surface. Correct value and chroma range will accomplish this.*

REVIEW QUESTIONS

1. State the value of mono-hued pottery in the decorative scheme of a room.
2. What are generally used as stains for clear glazes; matt glazes?
3. What is highest in chroma—matt, or clear glaze?
4. Make a table of metallic oxides and the hues produced by them.
5. Why will iron and copper oxides produce a yellow green stain? What stains will be produced by cobalt and copper oxides; cobalt and manganese oxides; cobalt and nickel oxides?
6. Describe the type of room which you regard as best fitted for clear glazed pottery forms; matt glazed pottery forms.
7. Define harmony of color.
8. What is meant by proportionate distribution? Describe proportionate distribution.
9. Give the value, hue, and chroma range for small areas. See Rules 12l, 12m, and 12n.
10. How does the size of the area to be enriched by color affect the color medium, *i.e.*, stains, glazes, enamels, etc.?
11. Describe enamels, their types, characteristics, and range of hues. Consult catalogs for fuller possibilities.
12. What is the effect of oxidation; what is its value?
13. Describe fully complementary arrangements and give illustrations for enamel on silver or copper.
14. State the color scheme for a fob to be worn with a blue-green dress; with a gray suit for a man.
15. Select a stone for a silver brooch that would harmonize with a light blue dress; for a dress of orange dark hue and value. See catalogs of dealers in semi-precious stones for color of stones.
16. What problems of hue, value, and chroma would arise in Question 15?

SUMMARY OF THE GENERAL AND SPECIAL RULES IN THE PRECEEDING CHAPTERS

HORIZONTAL AND VERTICAL PRIMARY MASSES

Rule 1a. *A primary mass must be either vertical or horizontal according to the intended service, unless prohibited by technical requirements.*

PROPORTIONS OF THE PRIMARY MASS

Rule 1b. *The primary mass should have the ratio of one to three, three to four, three to five, five to eight, seven to ten, or some similar proportion difficult for the eye to detect readily and analyze.*

HORIZONTAL SPACE DIVISIONS

Rule 2a. *If the primary mass is divided into two horizontal divisions, the dominance should be either in the upper or the lower section.*

Rule 2b. *If the primary mass is divided into three horizontal divisions or sections, the dominance should be placed in the center section with varying widths in the upper and lower thirds.*

SEQUENTIAL PROGRESSION OF MINOR HORIZONTAL SPACE DIVISIONS

Rule 2c. *A primary mass may be divided into three or more smaller horizontal masses or sections by placing the larger mass or masses at the bottom and by sequentially reducing the height measure of each mass toward the smaller division or divisions to be located at the top of the mass.*

VERTICAL SPACE DIVISIONS

Rule 3a. *If the primary mass is divided into two vertical divisions, the divisions should be equal in area and similar in form.*

Rule 3b. *If the primary mass is divided into three vertical divisions, the center division should be the larger, with the remaining divisions of equal size.*

Rule 3c. *In elementary problems, if more than three vertical divisions are required, they should be so grouped as to analyze into Rules 3a, and 3b, or be exactly similar.*

APPENDAGES

Rule 4a. *The appendage should be designed in unity with, and proportionately related to, the vertical or horizontal character of the primary mass, but subordinated to it.*

Rule 4b. *The appendage should have the appearance of flowing smoothly and, if possible, tangentially from the primary mass.*

Rule 4c. *The appendage should, if possible, echo or repeat some lines similar in character and direction to those of the primary mass.*

Outline or Contour Enrichment

Rule 5a. *Outline enrichment should be subordinated to and support the structure.*

Rule 5b. *Outline enrichment should add grace, lightness, and variety to the design.*

Rule 5c. *Outline enrichment, by its similarity, should give a sense of oneness or unity to the design, binding divergent members together.*

Rule 5d. *Parts of one design differing in function should differ in appearance but be co-ordinated with the entire design.*

Rule 5e. *In cylindrical forms outline curves with a vertical tendency should have their turning points or units of measurement in accordance with the horizontal divisions of Rules 2a and 2b.*

Rule 5f. *Dependent outline enrichment should be related to essential parts of a design and influenced by their forms and functions; it must be consistent with the idea of the subject.*

Rule 5g. *A curve should join a straight line with either a tangential or right angle junction.*

Surface Enrichment

Postulate. *The design should conform to the limitations and requirements of tools, processes, and materials, and should be durable and suitable for service.*

Rule 6a. *Surfaces to be enriched must admit of enrichment.*

Rule 6b. *Surface enrichment must be related to the structural contours but must nor obscure the actual structure.*

Rule 6c. *The treatment must be appropriate to the material.*

Continuous Bands and Borders for Partly Enriched Surfaces

Rule 6d. *Bands and borders should have a consistent lateral, that is, onward movement.*

Rule 6e. *Bands and borders should never have a prominent contrary motion, opposed to the main forward movement.*

Rule 6f. *All component parts of a border should move in unison with the main movement of the border.*

Rule 6g. *Each component part of a border should be strongly dynamic and, if possible, partake of the main movements of the border.*

Rule 6h. *Borders intended for vertical surfaces may have a strongly upward movement in addition to the lateral movement, provided the lateral movement dominates.*

Rule 6i. *Inlayed enrichment should never form strong or glaring contrasts with the parent surface.*

Rule 6j. *Carved surface enrichment should have the appearance of belonging to the parent mass.*

Enclosed Enrichment — Partly Enriched Panels for Surface Enrichment

Rule 7a. *Marginal panel enrichment should parallel or be related to the outlines of the primary mass and to the panel it is to enrich.*

Rule 7b. *Marginal points of concentration in panels should be placed (1) preferably at the corners or (2) in the center of each margin.*

Rule 7c. *To insure unity of design in panels, the elements composing the point of concentration and links connecting them must be related to the panel contour and to each other.*

Enclosed Enrichment — Fully Enriched Panels for Surface Enrichment

Rule 7d. *The contours of fully enriched panels should parallel the outlines of the primary mass and repeat its proportions.*

Rule 7e. *The points of concentration for a fully enriched square panel may be in its center or in its outer margin.*

Rule 7f. *The points of concentration for a fully enriched vertical panel should be in the upper portion of the panel.*

Rule 7g. *The fully enriched panel and its contents should be designed in unified relation to the structural outlines, with the center line of the panel coinciding with the inceptive axis of the structure.*

Free Ornament for Partly Enriched Surfaces

Rule 8a. *Free ornament for partly or fully enriched surfaces should be based and centered upon an inceptive axis of the structure.*

Rule 8b. *Free ornament should be related and subordinated to the structural surfaces.*

Rule 8c. *Points of concentration in free enrichment of vertically placed masses are usually located in and around the inceptive axis and above or below the geometric center of the design.*

Surface Enrichment of Clay

Rule 9a. *Surface enrichment of clay must be so designed as to be able to withstand the action of heat to which all ware must be submitted.*

Rule 9b. *Incised, pierced, and modeled decoration in clay should be simple and bold and thus adapted to the character of the material.*

Rule 9c. *A border should not be located at the point of greatest curvature in the contour of a cylindrical form. The contour curve is of sufficient interest in itself at that point.*

Surface Enrichment of Base and Precious Metals for Small Masses

Rule 10a. *Designs in precious metals should call for the minimum amount of metal necessary to express the idea of the designer for two reasons: (1) good taste; (2) economy of material.*

Rule 10b. *Contour and surface enrichment should never appear to compete for attention in the same design.*

Rule 10c. *Parts of a design differing in function should differ in appearance but be co-ordinated with the entire design.*

Rule 10d. *Surface enrichment should at some point parallel the contours of both primary mass and point of concentration especially whenever the latter is a stone or enamel.*

Rule 10e. *In the presence of either stone or enamel as a point of concentration, surface enrichment should be regarded as an unobtrusive setting, or background.*

Rule 10f. *Stone or enamel used as a point of concentration should form contrast with the metal, either in color, brilliancy, or value, or all three combined.*

Rule 10g. *The inceptive axis should pass through and coincide with one axis of a stone and at the same time be sympathetically related to the structure.*

Rule 10h. *The position of the inceptive axis should be determined by: (1) use of the project as ring, pendant, or bar pin, (2) character of the primary mass as either vertical or horizontal in proportion.*

Rule 10i. *Caution should be exercised with regard to the use of enamel. Over-decoration by this material tends to cheapen both process and design.*

Rule 10j. *All surface enrichment should have an appearance of compactness or unity. Pierced spots or areas should be so used as to avoid the appearance of having been scattered on the surface without thought to their coherence.*

Rule 10k. *Built, carved, and chased enrichment should have the higher planes near the point of concentration. It is well to have the stone as the highest point above the primary mass. When using this form of enrichment, the stone should never appear to rise abruptly from the primary mass, but should be approached by a series of rising planes.*

Rule 10l. *The lanes or margins between enameled spots should be narrower than the lane or margin between the enamel and the contour of the primary mass.*

Rule 10m. *Transparent and opaque stones or enamel should not be used in the same design.*

SURFACE ENRICHMENT OF BASE AND PRECIOUS METALS
FOR LARGE PRIMARY MASSES

Rule 11a. *The preliminary steps toward surface enrichment should be thought out before they are drawn.*

Rule 11b. *Conservative application should mark the use of surface enrichment of large masses. Its use should: (1) lighten or soften necessarily heavy construction; (2) support or apparently strengthen good structure; (3) add interest to large unbroken and uninteresting surfaces.*

Rule 11c. *The type of design unit for large masses should be bolder than similar designs for small primary masses.*

Rule 11d. *The eye should be attracted to one principal zone of enrichment, whether located upon the primary mass, appendage, terminal, links, or details. All other zones should be subordinate to this area.*

Rule 11e. *Two periods of historic ornament should not be introduced into the same design.*

Rule 11f. *Repulsive forms should not be introduced into surface enrichment.*

APPLICATION OF COLOR TO LARGE AREAS
VALUES

Rule 12a. *An average wood stain is to be retained between the values middle and low dark.*

Rule 12b. *An average wall hue is to be retained between the values light and middle.*

Rule 12c. *An average ceiling hue is to be retained between the values white (minus) and light.*

Rule 12d. *The relation between the side walls and furniture, trim, etc., should be retained within the range of four values or less, as low light and dark.*

Rule 12e. *The relation between the side walls and ceiling should be within the range of three values or less, as high light and low light.*

HUES

Rule 12f. *Color schemes for wood work and side walls should preferably be selected from one of the following groupings: analogous, contrasted, or dominant arrangements of hues. Analogous grouping is preferable where variety of hue is desirable.*

Rule 12g. *Ceilings should be colored by a lighter tint of the side walls or by a lighter tint of an analogous hue.*

CHROMA

Rule 12h. *Stains are usually not reduced to below three-fourths chromatic intensity. Nearly gray side walls, however, call for a reduction to one-fourth intensity.*

Rule 12i. *Wall colors are usually reduced to three-fourths chroma to a minimum reduction of slightly less than one-fourth chroma.*

Rule 12j. *Ceilings should usually be reduced in chroma to three-fourths intensity, with slightly less than one-fourth chroma as a minimum reduction.*

DISTRIBUTION

Rule 12k. *Proportionate distribution of hue, value, and chroma in surface enrichment calls for a small area, high in chroma, and contrasting in value to the rest of the surface, but harmonizing with it. This is usually located in the area of concentration. The larger areas are to be sufficiently reduced in chroma and value to form slight contrast with the background.*

HUES FOR SMALL OBJECTS

Rule 12l. *One hue, or a group of analogous hues should dominate all color schemes. The point of concentration may be emphasized by one hue related to the other hues by (1) contrasted, (2) dominant, (3) analogous, (4) complementary relations. This hue should make slightly stronger value and chroma contrast than the remaining hues.*

VALUES FOR SMALL OBJECTS

Rule 12m. *An extreme range of five values is generally sufficient to supply contrast to a design but still retain its value unity. Restraint in the use of values is essential.*

CHROMA FOR SMALL OBJECTS

Rule 12n. *The amount of chroma may be increased in proportion to the decrease in the decorated area. Exceptions may be made to this under Rule 12o.*

Rule 12o. *Small one or two-hued projects in clay, designed to be used as a part of the decorative color scheme for a room should bear a contrasted, dominant, analogous, or complementary relation to the side walls of the room. The project may be much higher in chroma than the side walls.*

Rule 12p. *Correct color for surface enrichment should neither apparently rise above nor drop below the surface to which it is applied, but should stay upon the plane of that surface. Correct value and chroma range will accomplish this.*

APPENDIX

The following plates comprise complete courses for applied art problems in thin metal (copper and silver), and clay. The problems are based upon what is known as the "group system." The process forms the basis for each group in each course. The stated problem in each group is merely one of many that might be selected which involves the process of the group.

The design rule that should be applied to each problem has been indicated by its proper figure and letter on each plate, as 10a, etc. The plates are sequentially arranged in order of the difficulty of the process and may be summarized as follows.

THIN METAL

Plate 67: Bending. Sawing. Riveting.
Plate 68: Bending. Soft Soldering.
Plate 69: Raising. Piercing. Etching.
Plate 70: Raising and Planishing.
Plate 71: Bending. Piercing. Etching. Hard Soldering.
Plate 72: Hinge Construction.
Plate 73: Raising. Planishing. Hard Soldering.
Plate 74: Raising. Planishing.
Plate 75: Champleve Enamelling.
Plate 76: Precious Stone Mounting; Pins.
Plate 77: Precious Stone Mounting; Rings.
Plate 78: Precious Stone Mounting; Pendants.

POTTERY

Plate 79: Hand Built Tile.
Plate 80: Hand Built Bowl, Coil and Strip Method.
Plate 81: Same with Appendage Added.
Plate 82: Hand Building; Spouts, Lids, Handles.
Plate 83: Poured Forms and Mould Making.
Plate 84: Slip Painting.
Plate 85: Glaze Testing.

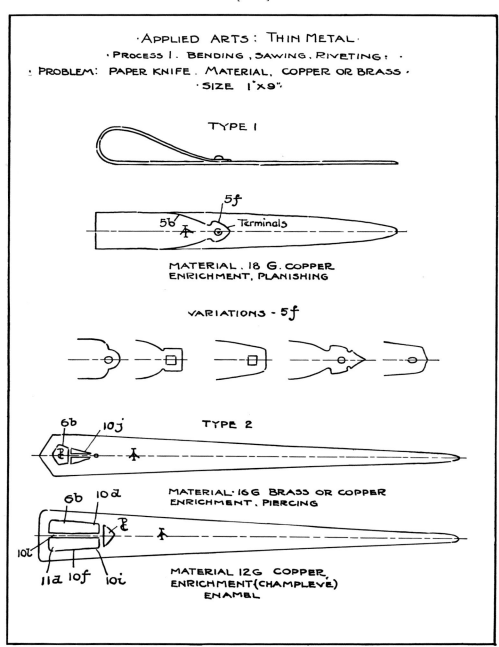

·APPLIED ARTS : THIN METAL·

·PROCESS 1. BENDING , SAWING , RIVETING: ·

: PROBLEM: PAPER KNIFE . MATERIAL, COPPER OR BRASS ·

·SIZE 1˝ x 9˝·

TYPE 1

5ƒ

5b   Terminals

MATERIAL . 18 G. COPPER
ENRICHMENT, PLANISHING

VARIATIONS - 5ƒ

6b   10j   TYPE 2

MATERIAL·16G BRASS OR COPPER
ENRICHMENT, PIERCING

6b   10a

10l

11a 10ƒ 10i

MATERIAL 12G COPPER,
ENRICHMENT(CHAMPLEVÉ)
ENAMEL

PLATE 67

· APPLIED ARTS THIN METAL·

· PROCESS 2: BENDING AND SOFT SOLDERING

· PROBLEM: CARD TRAY – MATERIAL 18 G COPPER OR BRASS ·

SIZE: 1 P 4½˝ SQ.

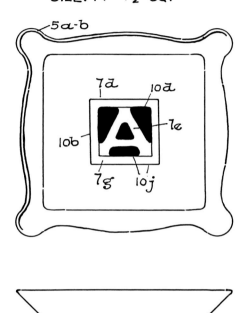

ENRICHMENT: PIERCED PLATE

VARIATIONS

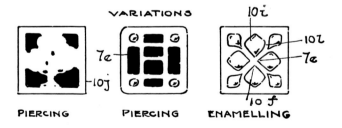

PIERCING   PIERCING   ENAMELLING

PLATE 68

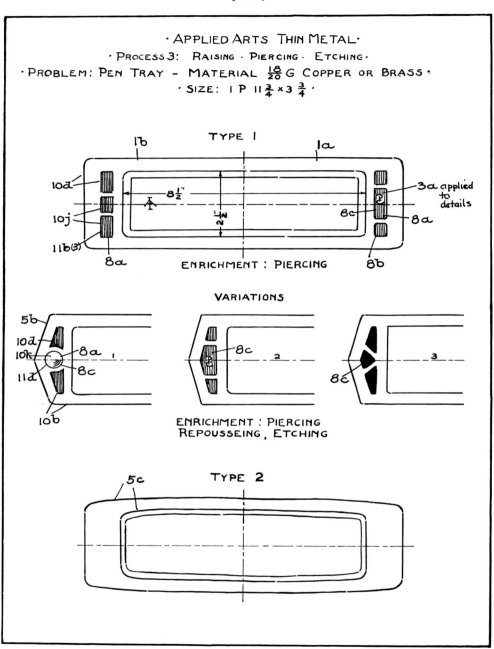

PLATE 69

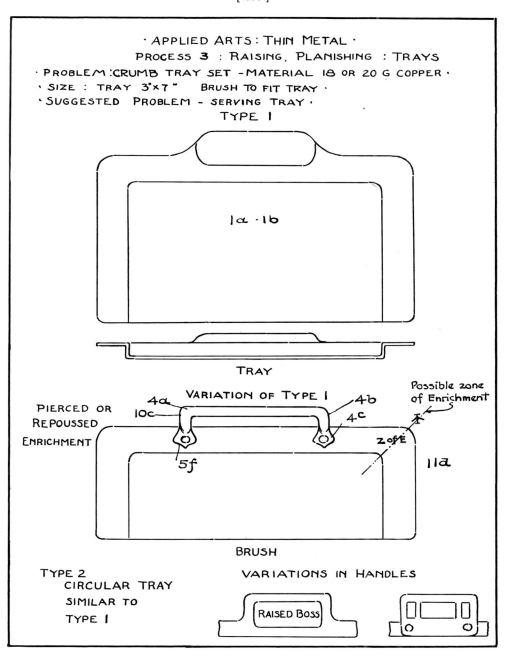

· APPLIED ARTS : THIN METAL ·

PROCESS **3** : RAISING, PLANISHING : TRAYS

· PROBLEM : CRUMB TRAY SET - MATERIAL 18 OR 20 G COPPER ·

· SIZE : TRAY 3"×7"   BRUSH TO FIT TRAY ·

· SUGGESTED PROBLEM - SERVING TRAY ·

TYPE 1

1a · 1b

TRAY

VARIATION OF TYPE 1

4a   4b

PIERCED OR   10c   4c

REPOUSSED

ENRICHMENT

5f   Z of E   11a

Possible zone
of Enrichment

BRUSH

TYPE 2   VARIATIONS IN HANDLES

CIRCULAR TRAY

SIMILAR TO

TYPE 1   RAISED BOSS

PLATE 70

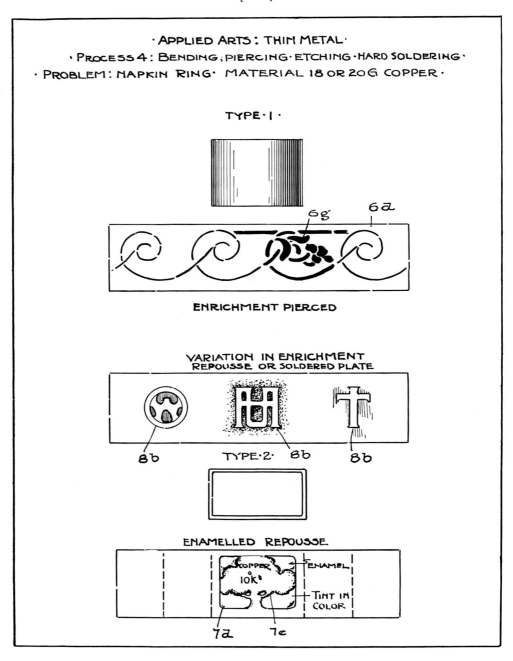

· APPLIED ARTS : THIN METAL ·
· PROCESS 4 : BENDING; PIERCING · ETCHING · HARD SOLDERING ·
· PROBLEM : NAPKIN RING · MATERIAL 18 OR 20 G COPPER ·

TYPE · 1 ·

6g   6a

ENRICHMENT PIERCED

VARIATION IN ENRICHMENT
REPOUSSE OR SOLDERED PLATE

8b   TYPE · 2 ·   8b   8b

ENAMELLED REPOUSSE

COPPER
10K   ENAMEL

TINT IN
COLOR

7a   7c

PLATE 71

·APPLIED ARTS : THIN METAL·
·PROCESS 5. HINGE CONSTRUCTION·
· PROBLEM: STAMP OR JEWEL BOX · HINGED·CATCH OPTIONAL ·
· MATERIAL· 18 OR 20 G COPPER · BOX $2\frac{5}{8}$"x$2\frac{5}{8}$"x$1\frac{1}{4}$" $1\frac{3}{4}$"x 3"x 5"·

TYPE·1·

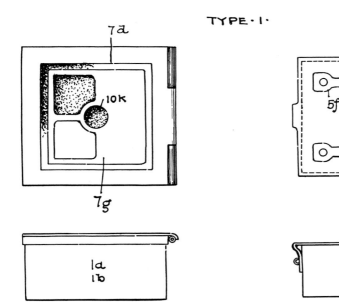

SOLDERS

SOFT SOLDER: VARYING PARTS OF LEAD AND TIN
   "   "   FOR PEWTER·THE SAME WITH BISMUTH

BRAZING SOLDER : EQUAL PARTS COPPER AND ZINC
   "   "   :(SOFTER) LARGER AMOUNT OF ZN WITH SB AND SN

HARD OR SILVER·SOLDER: SEVEN PARTS OF SILVER – 1 OF BRASS
   "   "   "   5   "   "   1   "
   "   "   "   3   "   "   1   "
   "   "   "   2   "   "   1   "

SOLDER FOR ENAMELLED PARTS: 1 OZ. SILVER · 5 DWT · COPPER ALLOY

PLATE 72

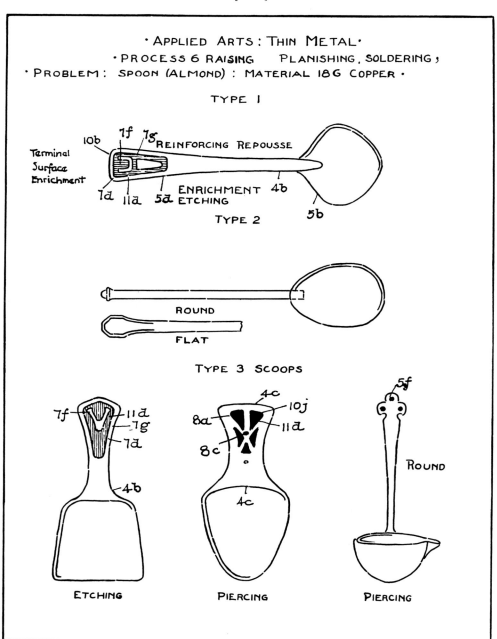

· APPLIED ARTS : THIN METAL ·

· PROCESS 6 RAISING   PLANISHING, SOLDERING ;

· PROBLEM : SPOON (ALMOND) : MATERIAL 18 G COPPER ·

TYPE 1

10b · 7f 7g REINFORCING REPOUSSE

Terminal Surface Enrichment

7d 11d 5d ENRICHMENT ETCHING   4b   5b

TYPE 2

ROUND

FLAT

TYPE 3 SCOOPS

7f · 11d · 7g · 7d · 4b

4c · 10j · 8a · 11d · 8c · 4c

5f · ROUND

ETCHING   PIERCING   PIERCING

PLATE 73

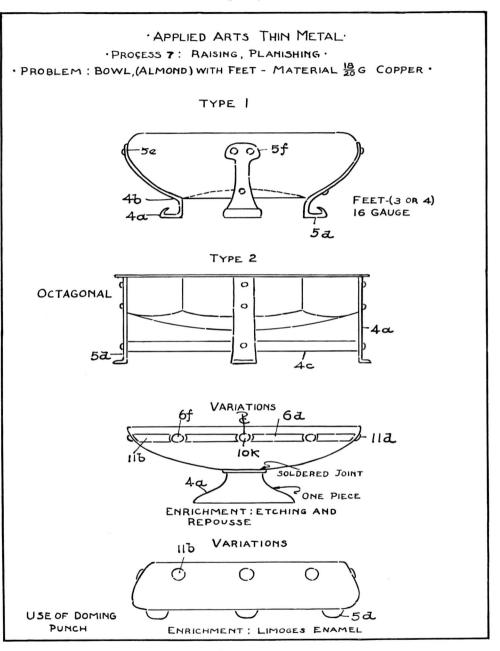

·APPLIED ARTS THIN METAL·

·PROCESS 7 : RAISING, PLANISHING·

· PROBLEM : BOWL, (ALMOND) WITH FEET – MATERIAL $\frac{18}{20}$ G COPPER ·

TYPE 1

5e   5f

4b
4a

FEET-(3 OR 4)
16 GAUGE

5a

TYPE 2

OCTAGONAL

4a

5a

4c

VARIATIONS

6f   6a

11a

11b

10k

SOLDERED JOINT

4a

ONE PIECE

ENRICHMENT: ETCHING AND
REPOUSSE

VARIATIONS

11b

USE OF DOMING
PUNCH

5a

ENRICHMENT : LIMOGES ENAMEL

PLATE 74

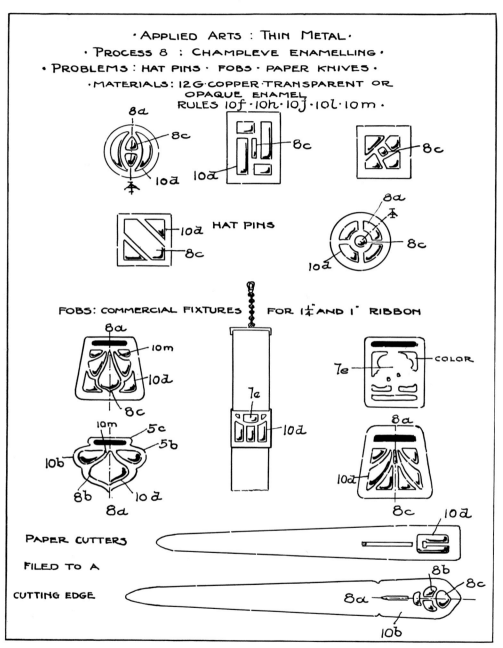

·APPLIED ARTS : THIN METAL·

· PROCESS 8 : CHAMPLEVE ENAMELLING ·

· PROBLEMS : HAT PINS · FOBS · PAPER KNIVES ·

·MATERIALS: 12G·COPPER·TRANSPARENT OR OPAQUE ENAMEL
RULES 10f·10h·10j·10l·10m ·

HAT PINS

FOBS: COMMERCIAL FIXTURES FOR 1¼" AND 1" RIBBON

COLOR

PAPER CUTTERS

FILED TO A

CUTTING EDGE

PLATE 75

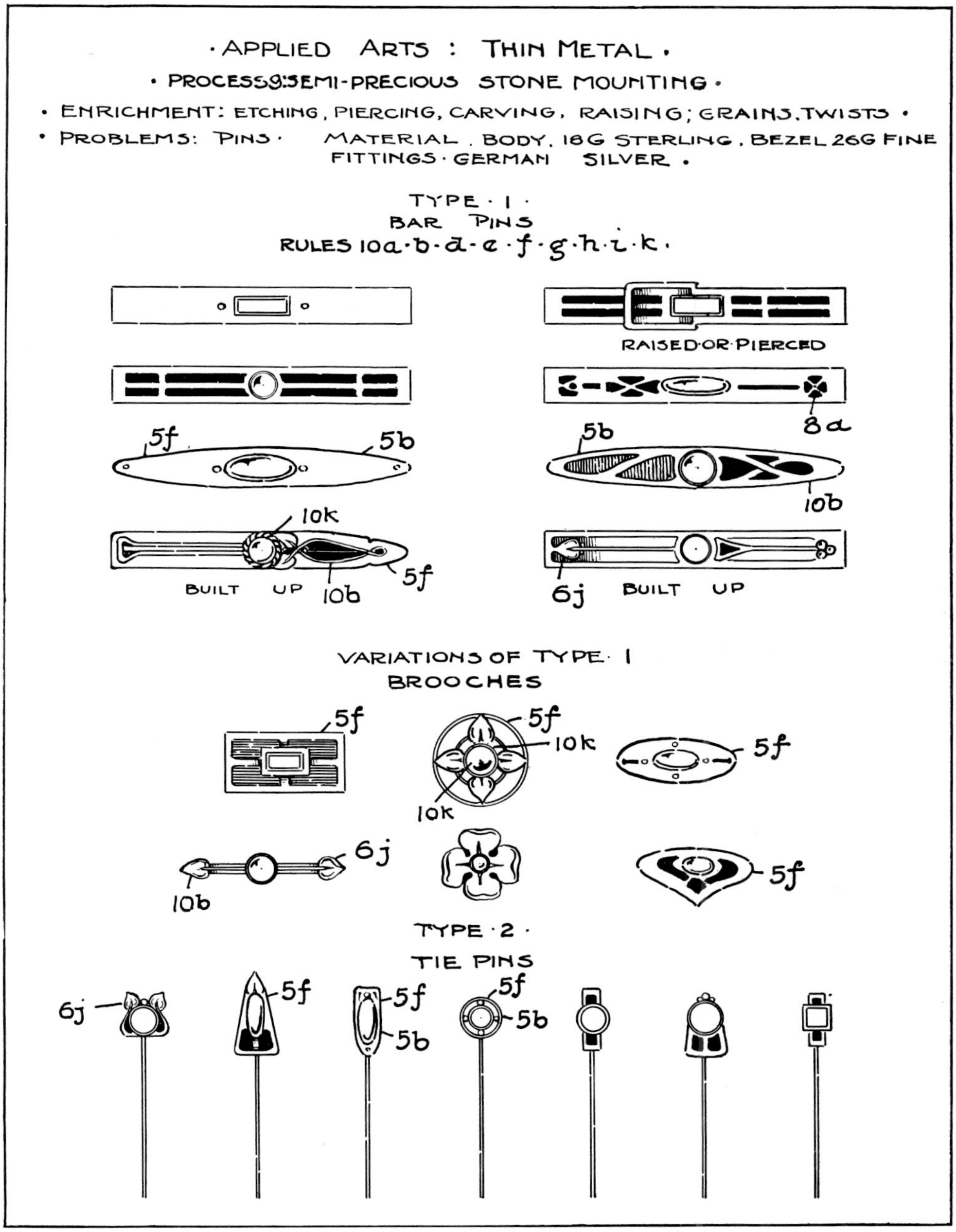
· APPLIED ARTS : THIN METAL ·
· PROCESS 9: SEMI-PRECIOUS STONE MOUNTING ·
· ENRICHMENT: ETCHING, PIERCING, CARVING, RAISING; GRAINS, TWISTS ·
· PROBLEMS: PINS · MATERIAL. BODY, 18 G STERLING, BEZEL 26 G FINE
FITTINGS · GERMAN SILVER ·
TYPE · 1 ·
BAR PINS
RULES 10 a · b · d · e · f · g · h · i · k ·
RAISED · OR · PIERCED
8 a
5 f
5 b
5 b
10 b
10 k
BUILT UP
10 b
5 f
6 j
BUILT UP
VARIATIONS OF TYPE · 1
BROOCHES
5 f
5 f
10 k
5 f
10 k
6 j
10 b
5 f
TYPE · 2 ·
TIE PINS
6 j
5 f
5 f
5 b
5 f
5 b

PLATE 76

· Applied Arts : Thin Metal ·

· Process: 10 Soldering, Carving, Stone Mounting ·
· Problem: Ring Construction ·
· Material: 18 G Sterling · Bezel 26 G Fine Silver ·

Rules 10 a · b-d · e-f · g · h · j · k ·

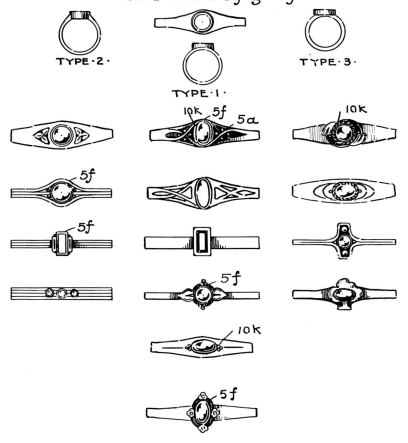

TYPE · 2 ·

TYPE · 1 ·

TYPE · 3 ·

Note: Rings Designed to Be Worn by Women Should Be Lighter Than Type · 1 ·

PLATE 77

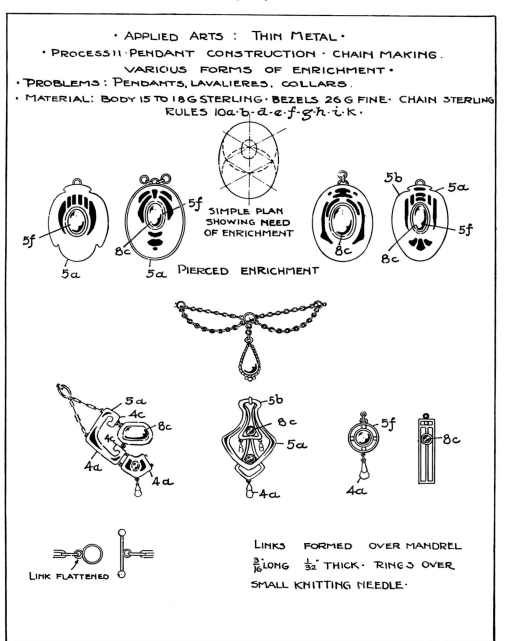

· APPLIED ARTS : THIN METAL ·

· PROCESS II · PENDANT CONSTRUCTION · CHAIN MAKING.

VARIOUS FORMS OF ENRICHMENT ·

· PROBLEMS : PENDANTS, LAVALIERES, COLLARS.

· MATERIAL: BODY 15 TO 18 G STERLING · BEZELS 26 G FINE · CHAIN STERLING

RULES 10 a · b · d · e · f · g · h · i · k ·

SIMPLE PLAN SHOWING NEED OF ENRICHMENT

PIERCED ENRICHMENT

LINK FLATTENED

LINKS FORMED OVER MANDREL $\frac{3}{16}$ LONG $\frac{1}{32}$ THICK · RINGS OVER SMALL KNITTING NEEDLE ·

PLATE 78

FIGURE 470.— Inceptive Axes.   Partial Illustration of the Metal Course

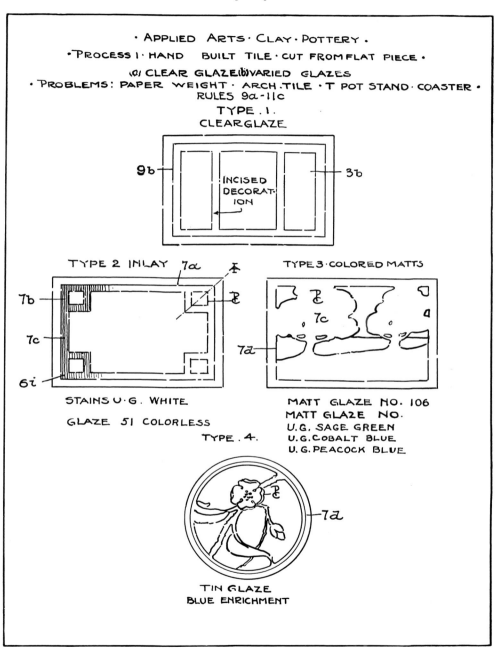

· APPLIED ARTS · CLAY · POTTERY ·

·PROCESS I· HAND BUILT TILE· CUT FROM FLAT PIECE ·

(a) CLEAR GLAZE(b)VARIED GLAZES

· PROBLEMS: PAPER WEIGHT · ARCH .TILE · T POT STAND · COASTER ·
RULES 9a-11c

TYPE .1.

CLEAR GLAZE

9b   INCISED DECORAT-ION   3b

TYPE 2 INLAY   7a

7b

7c

6i

STAINS U·G. WHITE

GLAZE 51 COLORLESS

TYPE 3 · COLORED MATTS

7c

7a

MATT GLAZE NO. 106
MATT GLAZE NO.
U.G. SAGE GREEN
U.G.COBALT BLUE
U.G.PEACOCK BLUE

TYPE .4.

7a

TIN GLAZE
BLUE ENRICHMENT

PLATE 79

·APPLIED ARTS : CLAY· POTTERY ·

·PROCESS 2:   HAND BUILDING ·COIL AND STRIP

MATT GLAZE – STAIN No 603 ·

· SUBJECT : CONTAINER – FLOWER BOWL – ENRICHMENT RAISED LEAF

RULES 9a – 11c ·

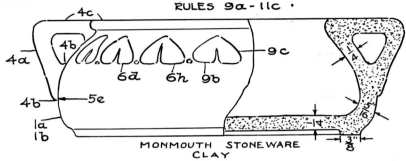

MONMOUTH STONEWARE
CLAY

VARIATIONS

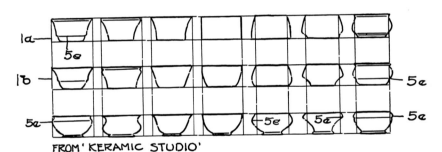

FROM 'KERAMIC STUDIO'

GLAZE 106

BASE	ALUMINA	ACID
PbO .77	AL_2O_3 .14	SiO_2 .8
K_2O .11		
BaO .12		
1.00		

SUB-SILICIOUS MATT GLAZE MATURING AT

1070°C (1958°F) OR CONE .04

R O 1:1

PLATE 80

· APPLIED ARTS : POTTERY ·
· PROCESS 3 : HAND BUILDING, SPOUT, HANDLE, LID.
PROBLEMS : POURER (CREAMER) CONTAINER (SUGAR)
ENRICHMENT : INCISED BORDER ·
RULES 9a - 11c

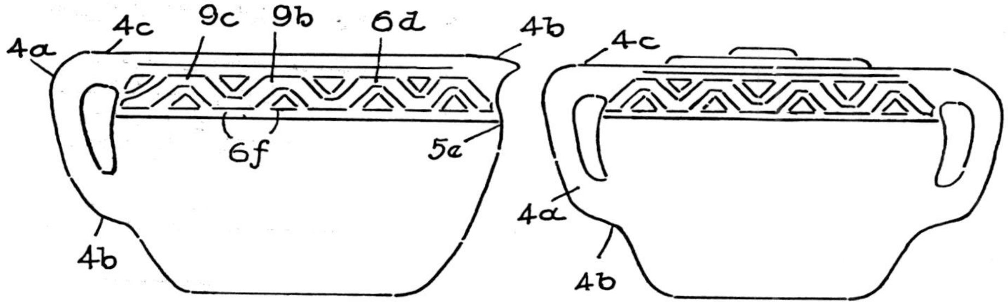

GLAZE 51
STAIN 640

BASE			ALUMINA	ACID
Pb O	.52		Al_2O_3 .38	SiO_2 1.68
Ca O	.2	1.00		
Zn O	.12			
K_2 O	.16			

SESQUI SILICIOUS CLEAR GLAZE MATURING AT 1070°C (1958°F)
CONE .04
TIN ENAMEL
GLAZE 304

BASE			ALUMINA	ACID
PB O	.48		Al_2O_3 .136	SiO_2 1.69
CA O	.29	1.00		SnO $\underline{.48}$
K_2 O	.09			2.17
ZN O	.13			

BI-SILICIOUS OPAQUE GLAZE MATURING AT 1070°C (1958°F)

PLATE 81

· APPLIED ARTS : CLAY POTTERY ·
· PROCESS 3 : HAND BUILDING ; SPOUT, HANDLE, LID
CLEAR GLAZE ·
· SUBJECT : POURER : TEA POT : RATTAN OR REED HANDLE ·

RULE 9α

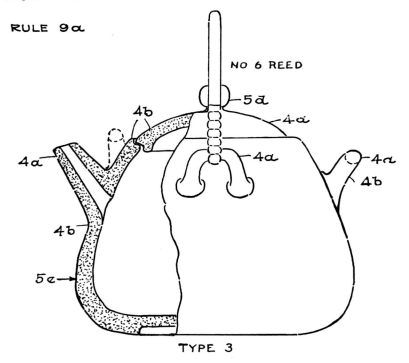

NO 6 REED

TYPE 3

GLAZE·51·
STAIN 640·
ALUMINA

BASE		ACID
PbO .52		
CaO .2	Al_2O_3 .38	SiO_2 1.72
ZnO .12		
K_2O .16		

MONOSILICIOUS CLEAR GLAZE MATURING AT
1070°C (1958°F) OR CONE .04
RO 1:1

PLATE 82

·APPLIED ARTS: POTTERY·
· PROCESS 4 · POURED FORMS · TWO AND THREE PIECE MOULDS
CLEAR GLAZE ·
·SUBJECT: CONTAINER · CUP (CHINESE) ENRICHMENT· INITIAL ·
TYPE I

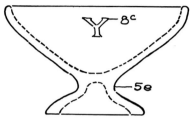

MATRIX DRAWING
ONE -EIGHTH ADDED FOR

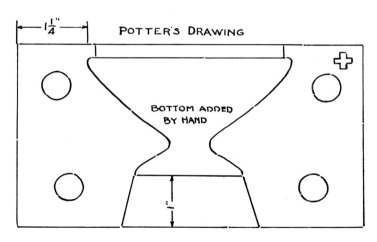

POTTER'S DRAWING

GLAZE 51

BASE	ALUMINA	ACID
Pb O .52		
Co O .2		
Zn O .12	$Al_2 O_3$ .38	$Si O_2$ 1.72
K_2 O .16		

SESQUI SILICIOUS CLEAR GLAZE MATURING AT
1070°C (1958°F) OR CONE .04
R O 2:3

PLATE 83

· APPLIED ARTS : POTTERY ·
· PROCESS 5 : SLIP PAINTING (UNDER GLAZE DECORATION) ·
· PROBLEM : TILE OR OTHER FLAT OR ROUND FORM ·
· MATERIAL: CLAY, U.G. COLORS, CLEAR GLAZE ·

TYPE I.

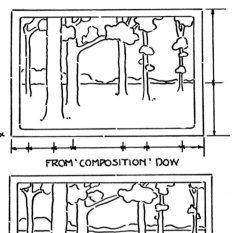

FROM 'COMPOSITION' DOW

NOTE :
THICKNESS OF ALL
TILES $\frac{1}{2}$" FOOT $\frac{1}{4}$" WIDE
approximately $\frac{3}{32}$" deep.

GLAZE 51 (CLEAR)   GLAZE 51   STAIN 603

| PALETTE FOR WHITE GLAZE | | | | | | | | | | | | |
COLORS	Dark Blue	Lt. Blue	Dk. Green	Lt. Green	Dk. Brown	Lt. Brown	Orange	Yellow	Crimson	Purple	Lilac	Grey
White Slip	96	90	90	94	90	90	90	90	90	90	90	90
Cobalt	4									1		
U.G. MattBlue		5		2								
Peacock			5	2								
Chrome Green			6	2								
French Green			2	2								
Choc. Brown					10							
Golden Brown						10						
Orange							10					
Yellow								10				
Crimson									10	9		
Lilac											10	
Pearl Gray												10

| PALETTE FOR GREEN GLAZE | | | | | | | | | | | |
COLORS	Black	Dk. Blue	Lt. Blue	Orange	Yellow	Claret Br.	Dk. Green	Olive Green	Lt. Green	Blue Green	Turquoise
White Slip	90	90	94	90	90	90	90	90	95	94	95
Peacock Blue	6	5								2	4
Claret Brown	4					10					
Matt Blue		5	6						2		
Orange				10							
Yellow					10						
French Green								10		3	2
Oxide Chrome									10	4	

* FREE BALANCE · CF
'COMPOSITION' BY DOW ·

PLATE 84

· APPLIED ARTS : POTTERY ·

· PROCESS 6 : GLAZE TESTING ·

· PROBLEMS : VARIOUS POURED FORMS : TESTS TO BE MARKED IN U.G. BLACK AS FOLLOWS — CLEAR 1-99, MATT 100-199, FRITTS 200-299, TIN ENAMEL 300-399, REDUCTION 400-499, CRYSTALLINE 500-599, STAINS 600-699 STUDENTS' INITIALS UNDER GLAZE NUMBER. ·

201-633
C · E · J ·

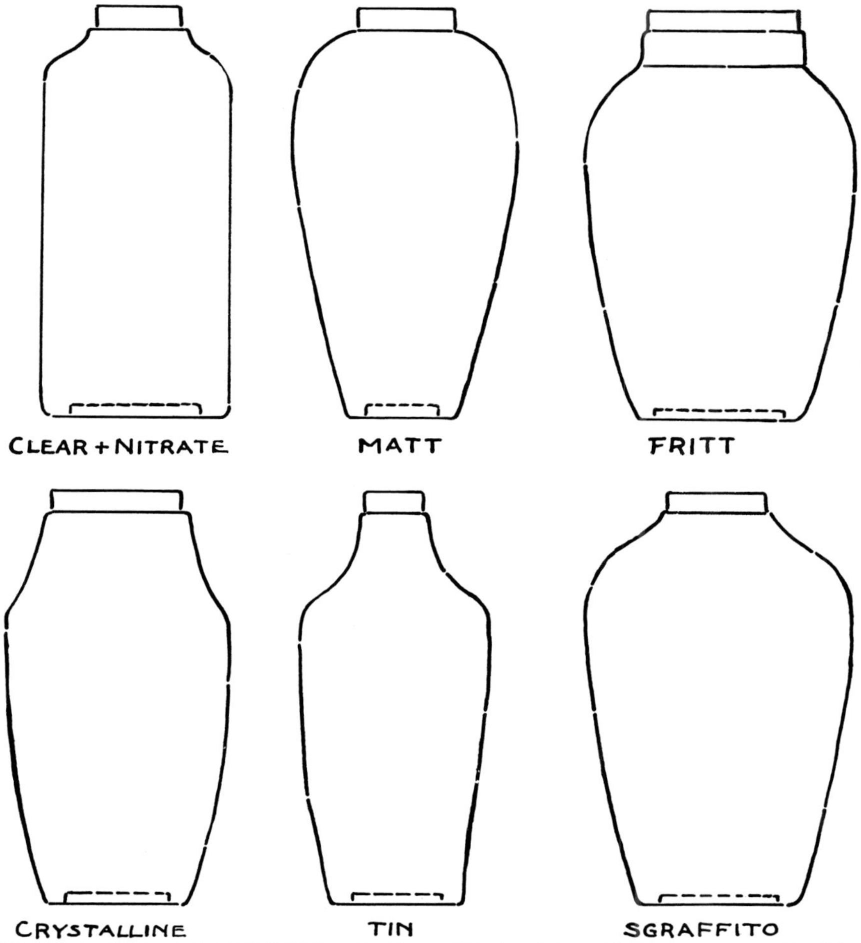

CLEAR + NITRATE   MATT   FRITT

CRYSTALLINE   TIN   SGRAFFITO

PLATE 85

FIGURE 471.— Results of the Pottery Course

Figure 471 shows the actual results produced by the preceding course. The process to which the individual pieces belong is indicated by the small figure placed on the table and in front of the ware. The preceding sheets should be regarded in the light of suggestions for original thinking on the part of the student. They merely suggest technical guidance, in order that his progress may be sequential and fitted to his increasing skill.

The glazes are stated in the terms of the ceramist with the proportions of base, alumina, and acid content of each glaze clearly stated. By referring to the textbooks mentioned in the preface, these glazes may be developed into the potter's formulae.

In both metal and pottery courses, two or more types are frequently represented upon one plate. These types will allow the teacher to assign a more difficult problem to the student with some previous experience.

INDEX

[245]